Program Management

Program Management

MICHEL THIRY

Published by
Gower Publishing Limited
Wey Court East
Union Road
Farnham
Surrey, GU9 7PT
England

Gower Publishing Company
110 Cherry Street
Suite 3-1
Burlington
VT 05401-3818
USA

www.gowerpublishing.com

Michel Thiry has asserted his right under the Copyright, Designs and Patents Act, 1988, to be identified as the author of this work.

British Library Cataloguing in Publication Data
A catalogue record for this book is available from the British Library.

Library of Congress Cataloging-in-Publication Data
Thiry, Michel.
  Program management / by Michel Thiry. -- [Second edition].
    pages cm. -- (Fundamentals of project management)
  Includes bibliographical references and index.
  ISBN 978-1-4724-7427-8 (paperback) -- ISBN 978-1-4724-7428-5 (ebook) --
  ISBN 978-1-4724-7429-2 (epub) 1. Project management. 2. Strategic
planning. 3. Organizational change. I. Title.
  HD69.P75T467 2015
  658.4'04--dc23
                              2015022232

ISBN 9781472474278 (pbk)
ISBN 9781472474285 (ebk – PDF)
ISBN 9781472474292 (ebk – ePUB)

MIX
Paper from
responsible sources
FSC
www.fsc.org   FSC® C013985

Printed in the United Kingdom by Henry Ling Limited,
at the Dorset Press, Dorchester, DT1 1HD

Contents

List of Figures

List of Tables

Preface

I was brought up in Canada where I started my professional life as an architect; as such, I worked within a project environment from the beginning. Architects traditionally represent their clients and are expected to act "in lieu" of the client in their relationship with the authorities (planning department, construction permit department, etc.) other professionals (engineers, urban planners, landscape architects, interior designers, etc.) and contractors (suppliers, building trades). So, as an architect, I have traditionally aimed to understand the needs and expectations of my clients and translate them as best as I could to achieve their dream home, corporate head office, marketable housing or office development, historical building restoration or landmark city-regeneration.

Very early in my career, I realized that there was little integration between the different players in the field and that mostly, the client's needs were not well understood, either because they were not able or willing to clarify them or because those that were supposed to fulfil them did not make the effort to work them out. After having worked in most areas of my profession, from urban planning to architectural programming, design, specifications writing and site supervising, I decided that it was time to integrate all this knowledge. So I opened my own practice and started developing turnkey projects for my clients. This meant that I needed to understand the clients' needs and expectations very well and be able to express them, not only in a drawing, but into and actual building. It also meant that I needed to work in harmony with all the actors of the project.

After a few years, I joined a larger firm that shared this philosophy and became their Director of Development. That is when I started calling myself a *Project Manager*. It was during that time that we developed some techniques and methodologies that enabled us to be recognized for our expertise in fast-track construction. Many of these techniques were concurrently developed in IT/IS and are today known as "agile management". As our expertise became recognized, we got to work on large multi-phased construction projects and, by still focusing on clients' needs and expectations, started to develop a reputation for pragmatic and effective long-term planning and development. Today, this type of expertise would be called *Program Management*.

Since then, I have moved to the UK where I have worked as a trainer and consultant in program management and related disciplines for the last 20 years of which 15 as the founder and managing partner of Valense Ltd. an international network of consultants and trainers. As such, I have been traveling extensively and worked with organizations in Asia Pacific, the Gulf Region, North Africa, Turkey, Europe as well as North and South America.

I have endeavoured to bring this worldwide expertise of program management at senior level into this book and hope it will appeal to a wide-ranging audience.

Acknowledgements

This second edition of *Program Management* would not have been achievable without the people who have trusted me to apply my expertise to their programs. In the last 20 years, many of them have helped shape the methodology that forms the backbone of this book. Let me acknowledge among these, Malcolm Davis and Peter Czarnomski from Pfizer UK; Eric Miart from Eurocontrol, Brussels; Rod Gozzard from NAB, Melbourne; Anna Massot from Bayer, Germany; Sulaiman Mohammad Al Marzougi from Kuwait National Petroleum and Bader Salman Alsalman and Saud Hamed Alsharari from ELM, Riyadh.

Following the publication of the first edition, I was privileged to be asked by the Project Management Institute to be a contributor to the Third Edition (2013) of their *Standard for Program Management* as well as being sought by the Project Management Association of Japan to review the English version of the Third Edition (2015) of *P2M: A Guidebook of Program & Project Management for Enterprise Innovation*. This has enabled me to gain a broader perspective of the discipline and of its evolution.

More specifically, I want to thank Alberto Brito from Brazil, Anne Boundford from the UK, Mustafa Dülgerler from Abu Dhabi, Rick Heaslip from the US, Bader Salman Alsalman from Saudi, Chris Stevens from Australia, who are all extremely busy but took the time to read the final draft of this second edition to provide their endorsement.

Finally, I would particularly like to recognise the contribution of Motoh Shimitzu and Eric Norman. Motoh shared his thoughts in multiple face-to-face and virtual discussions about the difference of program management approaches in Japan and the Western world and enabled me to use some of his ideas and concepts in this book. Eric and I have had numerous challenging conversations on the purpose, philosophy and approach of program management; he took the time to review the whole final draft and almost all his comments made it into the final print.

Reviews for
Program Management

Thiry's revised landmark work embraces many important changes. He takes a broad and in-depth view of multiple professional standards, explaining pragmatically the essence of key focus areas, for executives, managers, and students alike, on how to lead, step-by-step, successful program outcomes. This is essential reading for those moving from narrow technical to broader leadership skills, critical to value-driven organisations under pressure to deliver better strategies through program management.

Chris Stevens, Principal, Project Standards and Practice, NBN Co, Australia; member of PMI's Standards Members Advisory Group

Already a cornerstone in the library of important industry publications, the first edition of Program Management *by Dr Michel Thiry broke new ground in 2010 by providing a clearly understandable and practical context for sifting through an assortment of conflicting and sometimes competing views about the application of program management in organizations. In many ways, the first edition was a catalyst for many of the advances in program management practice we recognize and enjoy today. This second edition reflects the deep understanding Dr Thiry has gained since the first publication through careful observation, critical thinking, and the art and science of hard-won experience. This latest update by one of the industry's foremost thought leaders reveals an awareness of the critically important role program management now plays in organizations large and small for the delivery of key strategic benefits and real, measurable value in an increasingly complex, fast-paced, unpredictable and continually evolving (shall we say ... "agile") business environment. The second edition is destined to take its place as a frequently referenced, often quoted, dog-eared and battle-worn guide for the serious program manager. On my bookshelf, it stands next to its heavily marked-up and Post-It-littered brother, the first edition. If the second edition of* Program Management *by Dr Michel Thiry isn't part of your library, it should be.*

Eric S. Norman, practising program manager; Chair of PMI's 'The Standard for Program Management Third Edition' Core Committee

Programs are characterized by complexities, ambiguities and consequently significant uncertainties. Each program management standard of North America, Europe and Japan has a different approach to overcome such difficulties based on each business cultural background. The author has made a thorough analysis of these diverse standards and presents common and essential perspectives thanks to his long experience and deep insights on the subject. The book gives a big picture of program management rather than details of processes to provide a guiding principle for both researchers and expert practitioners.

Motoh Shimizu, member, The Engineering Academy of Japan;
Nippon Institute of Technology, Japan

Michel's book has created an important resource for researchers and practitioners in the program management domain. It brings up a clear and rational alignment between program components within an organizational context, which will help in executing the strategies and realizing real value. Anyone involved in program management will treasure this book!

Bader Alsalman, PMO Manager, ELM company, Saudi Arabia

Program Management *provides new insights about the program manager's critical role in managing organizational decision making and change. Michel Thiry's perspectives on integrating the principles and practices of established program management standards and guides provide a valuable contribution to the fields of both program and project management. I found it to be full of valuable perspectives and contributions to the field, and have very much enjoyed reading it.*

Richard Heaslip, author of Managing Complex Projects and Programs;
Adviser to executives sponsoring complex programs

As a practitioner of programme management I live and breathe this world every day and Michel does a great job at structuring and bringing programme management to life in a constructive way. The book is very useful for me because it spans and links multiple standards. I work with people who come from a PRINCE2 background and it can relate to what they do. When in doubt or simply in need of inspiration this book provides you with ideas on how to move forward. Overall, a great book.

Anne Boundford, PMP Programme Manager at Rolls Royce

We all know the decision making process; but most of us are not familiar with decision management within the context of program management. This is one of the numerous gaps in the practical application of program management that Michel has addressed in his book, making it a must-read for program and project managers undertaking complex initiatives.

Mustafa Dülgerler, Senior Enterprise Architect at National Bank of Abu Dhabi

This is a must read book! For strategy management scholars interested in the theme of strategy execution, as it brings state-of-the-art discussion on the importance and use of program management as a vehicle for implementing strategic changes; for senior executives, as it provides the guidelines to establish the organization and governance structure to achieve strategic goals; for program managers and program team members, as it provides a roadmap to manage programs, through a concise program life cycle and a set of management tools for each stage of the proposed life cycle. Finally, it is not a book based on current standards, but a book that the review of program management standards will be based on.

Alberto S. Brito, Founder and Managing Partner at CDA Tecnologia

Reviews of previous edition

Well organized with the ending of one chapter leading into the next. Very informative on the subject matter, supported by references and tables ...

Prize: 'Award of Merit' 2010, Canadian Project Management Book Awards, run by the Project Management Association of Canada

I believe Program Management *addresses a significant gap in program management literature. Thiry ties many years of research and findings from Value Management to Project Based Organization and relates it to Program Management. He explores utilization of Program management in a multi-faceted approach, from organizational aspects to benefit management, from program lifecycle to deployment of a strategy as a program, from measurement to dissolution of the program.*

Program Management *provides an excellent bridge between PM theory and practical ways to reach organizational goals using program management. This is truly brilliant!*

Deniz A. Johnson, PMP, Vice President, Program Management, Acadian Asset Management LLC, Boston

If you are interested in improving your delivery capability and effectiveness then Program Management *should be on your must read list. In my 15 years of project and program management experience I have yet to find a book which has addressed the subject from such a global perspective.*

Chris Richards, PMP, Assistant Director Business Operations, US-Based Technology Services Company

Program Management describes the practical considerations often overlooked when translating ideas into real, value generating programs. The model marrying Programs to Strategic Decision Management (Chapter 3) is alone worth the book.

Ron Sklaver, Enterprise Program Manager, Tate & Lyle, US-UK

Thiry provides an excellent example of his Benefit Breakdown Structure (BBS), showing benefits at Level 1, followed by critical success factors, specific actions, and deliverables. It is further detailed...with actions describing the current state and the proposed future state, plus capabilities and dates required to achieve them. He presents an achievability matrix for projects within the program and a discussion of risk packages. A program manager could take the BBS plus these concepts and relate it to the program work breakdown structure and have a powerful technique to apply.

Project Management Journal

I would recommend that program managers who want a simple and useful guide to get hold of a copy of the book and keep it handy. Organizations should place a copy of the book in their library along with books on strategy and strategy implementation. For academics teaching a course in program management it would be a good as a textbook or as a reference book from which relevant readings can be suggested to students.

Associate Professor Shankar Sankaran University of Technology, Sydney for PPPM eJournal

I would recommend this book and have in fact used it at work to help clarify governance issues and solutions with colleagues. Definitely a book to add to your library.

ProjectManager.com, Australia

This is an informative book full of useful illustrations providing visual interpretations of the text ... The book is well structured into three parts: the programme content, the programme components and the programme lifecycle, with a very useful conclusions section at the end. This structure made it easy to go forward and backwards without losing the thread. Although aimed at larger organisations, this book will prove valuable for any project of programme manager.

Quality World Magazine, September 2012

I consult and teach in this area and welcome this book as a very useful contribution on the topic ... It is certainly the best book I have read on the specific subject of Program Management, and represents considerable research, reflections on experience and new thinking on a current prominent subject.

Harold Ainsworth on Amazon.com

Introduction

Purpose of this Book

According to a number of recent surveys, executing strategies to realize value is one of the failures of today's management and optimizing the use of resources to achieve this is even more of an issue. Programs, by definition, constitute the missing link between the executive level strategy and the projects and operations that will enable it to deliver value. Program management concerns the harmonized management of a number of projects and other actions that will generate competitive advantage. The purpose of this book is to make executives, managers, students or academics understand the issues that arise from the practice of Program Management and be able to, not only perform it, but also implement it sustainably in their organizations.

Strategic managers often lack the time, specific expertise, technical skills and/or means to make their strategies concrete to deliver the expected benefits. Project managers lack the proficiency and/or capability to understand or question strategic language and are often not aware of expected benefits. Operational managers understand the benefits they need, but often find it difficult to express them in strategic terms or understand the implications of their implementation.

After more than 40 years of working for organizations of all sizes and more than 20 years of worldwide management consultancy practice in a wide range of industries, I have come to realize that many organizations still don't understand how to integrate their business practices. This is especially true of the end-to-end process necessary to implement strategic decisions, realize benefits and, ultimately, create value; especially in a turbulent environment that requires constant realignment and agility. The program management methodology described in this book will provide executives with the means to achieve their objectives and increase their organization's competitive edge, it will provide sponsors with a clear method for defining outcomes and benefits and mastering their delivery and finally users will have the assurance that their needs will be fulfilled, as much as is possible within the stated parameters.

This book is meant to represent a wide view of program management practice and not be tied to any particular standard. Although I favour techniques that I am familiar with, some of which I developed over years of practice, I will aim to refer to a range of applicable techniques and methods at each stage of the process.

Changes in the New Edition

In recent years, I have had multiple opportunities to implement program management methodologies and coach program teams in large corporate organizations worldwide and have from these experiences compiled data about maturity and the implementation of program management in organizations. In parallel, the Project Management Institute, the Office of Government Commerce in the UK, and the Project Management Association of Japan have published new standards. These facts have led me, in true program management fashion, to make important changes in this new edition.

In Part I the main changes concern the discussion on the latest versions of program management guides and standards, which are today much more integrated. As the situation has evolved I have reviewed my vision of program classification and added a new section on agile management in programs. I have also added a measure of maturity based on a tool that I have developed in recent years.

In Part II I have relabelled program components into program functions to avoid confusion with the PMI term for component projects I have added a new section on change management as this is more and more becoming an integral part of the management of programs. My recent experience has also enabled me to clarify further the roles and responsibilities of the different program actors and, in particular, that of the business integrator.

The integration of program management in the organizations I have worked with in the last five years have inspired me to write Part III of the book in a much more hands-on fashion so that practitioners and sponsors alike will be able to follow clear steps in the management of their programs. It has also allowed me to consolidate my confidence that the methods I have been promoting for the last 10–15 years are effective. Finally, the better harmonization of practice and of program management guides and standards has led me to review the program life cycle that I had proposed in the first edition to align better with a more unified view of program management that has emerged in the last few years.

Executive Summary

I have provided this executive summary for readers who are not practitioners or students and who will want to focus their available time on the sections that matter most to them. Each section outlines one part or chapter of the book and highlights sections that are of particular interest for specific group of readers.

Part I: The Program Context

Part I aims to set the scene for program management and how it fits within the greater organizational and business context. Chapter 1 explains the emergence of program management and compares views from different professional bodies. Chapter 2 compares and sets programs within the greater organizational context, in particular other similar strategy delivery methods. Finally, Chapter 3 outlines what constitutes program maturity for an organization and how to set up a program culture.

CHAPTER 1: BACKGROUND AND DEFINITIONS

Program Management has emerged as a distinct discipline in the late twentieth century. As project management was applied to more and more complex projects, it has progressively been aimed at the management of strategic objectives or the management of multiple interrelated endeavours to produce strategic benefits. It is now generally agreed that programs are a significant undertaking consisting of multiple actions spanning multiple business areas and that they are generally complex. Program management deals in both high ambiguity and uncertainty and requires a high degree of organizational maturity. There are currently three main program management guides, or standards, published by distinct professional bodies in America, Europe and Asia. Whereas past editions were more discordant, the last editions of the standards are more harmonized than ever before. Today, Program Management is universally perceived as a strategy execution method and a means to deliver sustainable change.

This chapter will interest both *managers* and *practitioners* since it defines what a program is in relation to other similar methods and explains why program management is ideally suited to realize strategic decisions.

CHAPTER 2: ORGANIZATIONAL CONTEXT

There are boundaries, overlaps and differences between programs, projects, portfolio, operations and strategy. In order to be competitive, a project organization – one that conducts the majority of its activities as projects and/or privileges project over functional approaches – will use programs to link a number of business processes and create synergy between its different components. Traditional organizational structures are well adapted to stable well-defined environments; they are hierarchical and the portfolio is typically divided into sub-portfolios, programs and projects. Recently promoted organizational models are more adapted to today's turbulent and fast-moving environment. These organizational models are similar to a supply or value chain and the program methodology is at the centre of the strategic decision management process. In this type of organization, Program Management could be labelled as:

> *The governance and harmonized management of a number of projects and other actions to achieve targeted benefits and create value for the program sponsors in the short-term, change recipients in the medium-term and the organization in the long-term.*

This chapter will particularly interest *executives*, *strategists* and *program sponsors* as program management is used more and more to manage organizational change. In particular they will be interested in the new section on Program and Agile Management. As such, the program becomes a vehicle for interaction between stakeholders to generate creative ideas and innovative products that increase the organization's competitiveness.

CHAPTER 3: MATURITY AND CULTURE

Traditionally most organizations undertake projects as part of their work. Mostly these projects are treated as separate entities, independent from one another. They are often generated within a business unit and managed with that unit's resources. Larger projects undertaken either for external clients or for strategic purposes are usually managed on an ad hoc basis by a dedicated team. Programs can either be "deliberate", driven by the strategy, or "ad hoc", a convenient grouping of existing projects. More mature organizations will favour deliberate programs as they are more integrated and favour agility because of their strong vision; they are more likely to realize business benefits. The second section of the chapter will clarify why simply transferring project management tools and techniques to the program level does not work and describe a program maturity framework. It will be completed by the presentation of a tried and tested maturity measure. Finally, developing a program culture involves a shared understanding of a number of objectives and a wide stakeholder approach. Experienced managers understand that changing culture takes time and requires a lot of sensemaking before it is made acceptable and accepted.

This chapter will interest *executives* and *managers* who want to implement program management in their organization, specifically the maturity measure and practical advice to support culture shift.

Part II: The Program Constituents

Part II examines the various constituents that make program management what it is. Chapter 4 covers five key program functions: decision management, program governance, stakeholder engagement, change management and benefits management. Chapter 5 outlines the responsibilities of the different actors of the program in each of these areas and details the role of the program manager along the life cycle of a program.

CHAPTER 4: KEY PROGRAM FUNCTIONS

Five "functions" can be identified as essential to the practice of program management, they are: decision management, governance, stakeholder engagement, change management and benefits management. These five functions are intimately linked to one another: stakeholders' needs drive benefits, key stakeholders make decisions based on expected benefits; governance provides the structures necessary to achieve them and change management enables the successful transition of benefits into the business. The main program guides and standards already recognize governance, stakeholder and benefits management as key program functions or "Performance Domains".

Decision management is a new area of development that requires both a learning cycle, the actual decision-making process, and a performance cycle, the decision realization process. Managers will understand that decision-making is not just about tools, but about making the right choices, based on objectives that have been agreed and can be measured. Change management has developed in the last three years as an essential element of any project or program effort and three guides have been issued on the topic by professional associations in 2013 and 2014. I will discuss the application of change management methods to program management. This chapter also outlines some new ideas for each of these functions. Whereas most organizations focus on the control aspect of governance, it will consider the broader view of *leading*: defining the vision; *structuring*: providing the structures and resources necessary to achieve the vision; and *conforming*: making sure the vision and value are achieved. The stakeholders' management section goes beyond roles and responsibilities of the different program stakeholders to include the steps necessary to manage and engage stakeholders. Finally, the benefits management section is a detailed discussion on the development of a sound benefits management system, from the definition of meaningful expected benefits to their actual measurable realization.

This whole chapter should be of interest for *executives* and *sponsors*.

CHAPTER 5: PROGRAM ACTORS

This chapter compares different terms used to define different program roles; in particular, it compares the PMI®1 Standard with the MSP™2 Standard. Understanding these roles is an essential element of good program management because both boundaries and relationships between the responsibilities of the different program actors should be clearly identified to enable a smooth transition process between the strategy, the program and operations. Roles and responsibilities of different actors, regarding specific elements of the program, are compared in both traditional and integrated organizational structures. The responsibility of the different actors for governance, change management, benefits realization and stakeholder engagement in different settings is also discussed. This first part of the chapter can be a particularly interesting section for *managers* and *Program Board* members and those

---

1   PMI is a Registered Trade Mark of the project management Institute.
2   MSP is a Trade Mark of the Office of Government Commerce, UK.

who work in multicultural and multinational environments since it compares program roles and responsibilities in different standards and organizational cultures.

The second part of the chapter examines specific competencies required from the program manager at each stage of the life cycle, which can be useful for *human resource managers* and line managers who want to hire and/or develop competent program managers. Both *managers* and *practitioners* will find their role described in detail, both in terms of the responsibility to lead and manage the key components and their role in each stage of the program's life cycle.

Part III: The Program Life Cycle

Part III describes the process necessary to realize business strategies from the development of the vision to the realization of value and the transfer and utilization of the program knowledge. Chapter 6 outlines the program life cycle, and Chapters 7 to 11 detail each program stage: Definition, Deployment and Closure. These last five chapters detail the actual process and methods required to lead and manage programs. The process described concerns mostly deliberate programs. Ad hoc programs will typically go through similar processes, but some of these may be applied retroactively or in a different order than the one described in Chapters 6 to 11.

CHAPTER 6: PROGRAM LIFE CYCLE OUTLINE

For many years, books and guides on program management have suggested that program management is just an extension of project management, larger and more complex. In this perspective they have simply duplicated the project life cycle into programs. In Parts I and II, we have seen that program management is different from project management. It is complex, subjected to high ambiguity and uncertainty, cyclic in nature and has an important learning aspect. This chapter presents a comparative view of the program life cycles from different guides and standards and a model based on a combination of agreed concepts and tested practice. The program life-cycle model presented is divided into three main program stages: Definition, Deployment and Closure, each of them is then further subdivided into specific steps which form each of the following chapters. It explains how the project and program life cycle differ and why the program life cycle needs to be related to strategic management.

This chapter will be particularly useful to *program sponsors, Program Board* members and *practitioners,* especially if they work in a multinational environment, because it compares existing standards. It also provides new ideas to build upon in different contexts.

CHAPTER 7: DEFINITION (FORMULATION)

The formulation process enables the program team, its sponsors and other key stakeholders to achieve agreement on the benefits that the program must realize and how they will be assessed. The formulation stage of the program is typically a learning cycle consisting of a strategic level decision-making process during which all the key stakeholders are able to agree the objectives of the program and set its critical success factors, as well as the measures that will ensure its success. Strategic objectives are typically the starting point of deliberate programs. If the program is ad hoc, existing projects are the starting point of the program and the first step is to define what underlying strategic objective(s) drives the effort. The roles of the *Program Board* and *Program Team* in the development of the program and the preparation of the preliminary business case are a key aspect of the formulation stage. This stage is a cyclic process that is revisited regularly, following development of the preparation stage and assessment of the tangible results achieved by the program.

Executives will be particularly interested in the transition from strategy to program and the development of a strategic decision into program objectives, including the structuring of the business case for the program. *Program sponsors* and *Program Board* members will also find that this whole chapter is of interest to ensure their objectives are understood and met.

CHAPTER 8: DEFINITION (PREPARATION)

Once the program purpose and objectives have been agreed, the program team develops the strategy and plan for the realization of the program's benefits. Many organizations fund the program preparation as a separate cycle, which includes the program assessment and full definition. This process leads to the release of a detailed program business case which includes the program roadmap, budget and resources requirements. At the end of this stage, the program is re-evaluated and full funding is agreed for deployment.

During the preparation stage, the core program team defines the projects that will be part of the program's first, or next, cycle. It is also at this stage that the team aligns the program structures with the organizational governance approach; develops the means to engage all the key stakeholders, considers transition and sustainment activities, and finalizes a realization plan for the program. This realization plan is an integrated effort and combines a range of activities: projects, transition and interdependencies, as well as defined milestones: key deliverables and benefits. All these elements are combined in the program roadmap and the detailed business case.

This chapter is central to the role of *Program sponsors* and *Program Board* members because it is the basis for governance and appraisal of the program.

CHAPTER 9: DEPLOYMENT (DELIVERY AND TRANSITION)

The deployment stage involves the transition of the business from the current state to an improved state, including transfer activities and integration of new capabilities. I have divided this stage into two chapters: *capabilities delivery and transition* and *capabilities integration and benefits appraisal.*

The main objective is to realize the benefits by initiating, planning and executing component projects, carrying out interfacing and transition actions, and committing resources to them. This is the essence of capabilities delivery, which concerns the management of the program components. The deployment stage also comprises the monitoring and control of component project results and project level change management. The whole process is driven by the pacing defined in the Benefits Realization Plan. This chapter is divided in two segments: *Capabilities Delivery*, which consists of the activities required to oversee and direct the delivery of projects and other supporting actions and *Capabilities Transition*, which includes the activities required to manage the program organizational resources and systems.

Chapter 9 is especially valuable for *program practitioners* who lead transition and interfacing activities during deployment and *project managers* who are expected to manage individual projects.

CHAPTER 10: DEPLOYMENT (INTEGRATION AND APPRAISAL)

Chapter 10 is divided into three sections: *Capabilities Integration*, which consists of the activities required to prepare the organization for change and implement the new capabilities that will deliver the benefits to the organization, including adaptive changes. *Benefits Appraisal* is the process of assessing benefits realization and embedding in the business. And finally *Transition to Next Cycle* concerns the activities necessary for the preparation for the next deployment cycle.

An important part of the capabilities integration process is the support that the program team will provide to the business; the main focus of this process is the management of change. The capabilities integration and benefits appraisal are run in parallel. As soon as the first project results, operational capabilities and business benefits are delivered, the program team can start to appraise benefits realization on a regular basis and determine if changes need to be undertaken. Integration and appraisal results are used to market the program benefits and therefore, demonstrating quick wins is important. During the integration and appraisal process, any changes to the critical success factors are identified and examined to understand how they might modify the expected benefits of the program. Based on this evaluation, the program team and board evaluate the need for adaptive changes and authorize changes that add value.

Although integration and appraisal are continuous, the periods of stability, which mark the end of each cycle, are the ideal time to reassess the program as a whole. This is the period when the program board reviews the program's purpose and benefits and decides to continue to the next deployment cycle as planned, continue with a realigned plan, or stop the program. The data produced through the integration and appraisal processes is used to support effective knowledge management.

All the *key stakeholders*, particularly those that are interested in realizing and measuring benefits, will find this chapter useful for its focus on organizational and operational level assessment, change management and knowledge management.

Chapter 10 describes the integration of the new capabilities into the organization, which is mostly significant for *business integrators* and *operational managers*.

CHAPTER 11: CLOSURE

The decision to enter program closure is based on the fact that the investment in the program resources and structure cannot be justified anymore and that the rationale for its existence is no longer defensible. This can be for positive reasons: all the objectives have been achieved; or negative reasons: the team will not be able to achieve them. When, following appraisal, this is established, the team enters the closure stage. Definition and deployment are intimately linked and based on an iterative process where the program is progressively developed while continually verifying benefits and value realization. Closure is decided on the basis of significant and measurable data defined at the formulation and preparation stages. This chapter covers the closure of the program, including transfer of residual work, discusses the reasoning behind it and the steps to be taken to realize full value. It also explains how knowledge can be transferred and utilized by the organization.

The first part, which concerns the basis on which the decision to stop the program is taken, should attract the interest of *executives* and *program sponsors*, who are often the key decision-makers in this process. The latter part of this chapter, which concerns the mechanics of dissolution, is destined mostly to *program practitioners* and the members of the *program management office* who will implement the closure process and knowledge transfer.

Conclusion

Whether you are an executive, a sponsor, manager of the PMO, a program or project manager this book will help you understand what your role in a program is and how program management can help your organization achieve its objectives.

Program management is the link between the business strategy and the value it will generate when implemented. It is the process through which *executives* will be able to express their needs and make sure they are fulfilled. *Sponsors* will be able to define the improvements they are expecting and clearly link them to the strategy to ensure they are realized and aligned with the business objectives. *Program managers* will understand how to support both executives and sponsors in a tangible way and how to deliver measurable results to the business. *Project managers* will understand how their role is essential to the program's success and finally, *operational* and *technical actors* will be able to make sure the expected improvements are well integrated and produce the expected results.

PART I
THE PROGRAM CONTEXT

Part I concerns the program context. Chapter 1 explains why program management is an essential tool for achieving strategic decisions, how programs are viewed differently by different people and how program management became what it is today; it also examines and compares the latest program standards. Chapter 2 outlines the relationship between programs and other components of the business and explains how developing project, portfolio and program management concepts can create synergy in the business and increase agility and competitiveness. Finally, Chapter 3 describes how a program culture can be developed and how organizations can increase their program maturity. It outlines what constitutes program maturity for an organization and how to set up a program culture.

CHAPTER 1
Background and Definitions

The purpose of Chapter 1 is to give a historical perspective of the development of program management as a distinct discipline and to explain how programs are viewed differently by different communities. It explains how it can fill a gap in current management practice by helping realize strategic decisions and complement other project-based practices. It also takes a critical look at the current program standards.

1.1   The Emergence of Program Management

As practitioners started applying project management concepts to more complex projects, to the management of strategic objectives or to the management of multiple interrelated projects to produce strategic benefits, they recognized the limitations of traditional project management techniques. Well-publicized large-scale studies (Standish Group, 1996; KPMG, 1997) have demonstrated that up to 30 per cent of projects are cancelled before the end and that large-scale long-term projects are "significantly less predictable" in terms of time and scope. These studies exposed the failure of traditional project management methods to respond to emergent situations and to ambiguity, as well as the lack of integration between strategic intent and the results generated by projects. Program Management has emerged as a distinct discipline from the maturing of the project management discipline at about the same time as these studies were published. This could be seen as a result of the maturing of project management and the development of what the PMI has called "Organizational Project Management" (OPM).

1.2   Visions of Program

In project management practice and the associated literature, program management (PgM) is defined in many ways. Etymologically, the word program derives from the Greek *prographein*, meaning: to write before. It has evolved in Latin and French to mean a "notice or list of a series of events". One of the definitions of the *Merriam Webster Collegiate Dictionary 2000* is: "a plan or system under which action may be taken toward a goal". In architecture a program is the written functional description of the needs of the customer, which becomes the mandate of the architect. The concept of program used in the project management community probably originates from a number of sources. Today, typical uses of the word program are quite varied. A search on the Internet (www.google.co.uk) using the word "programme" (British spelling) yielded the following:

- UN and Governmental Programmes (United Nations Development Programme and National Toxicology Programme).
- Computer programmes (Windows XP and Adobe Acrobat Programmes).
- Space Exploration Programmes (Mars Exploration Program).
- Non-Governmental Non Profit Programmes (Fullbright Programme, International Baccalaureate Programme).
- Television programmes (BBC Programme).
- Large publicly funded undertakings (Chesapeake Bay Programme, Endangered Species Programme).

This search shows the diversity of the uses of the word in the public, but also points towards defining a program as a larger undertaking consisting of multiple actions of smaller scale with a higher-level objective.

Some authors also draw a difference between governmental and non-profit organizations and commercial or for-profit organizations:

> *Nonprofits usually refer to programs as ongoing, major services to clients, for example, a Transportation Program, Housing Program, etc. For-profits often use the term for very large business efforts that have limited duration and a defined set of deliverables. Nonprofits and for-profits might refer to programs as a one-time or ongoing set of activities internal to the organization, for example, a Total Quality Management Program, Workplace Safety Program, the Space Program, etc. (McNamara, 1999)*

1.2.1   A DEFINITION FOR THE TWENTY-FIRST CENTURY

In the late 1990s and early 2000s many different definitions of program and program management coexisted and were often contradictory, going anywhere from: a collection of similar projects, mega-projects, the combination of projects and operations, a top-down realization of strategic process to the bottom-up tactical grouping of actions. Typical definitions were still wide-ranging and included:

> *The co-ordinated management of a portfolio of projects that change organizations to achieve benefits that are of strategic importance. (CCTA, 1999)*

> *A collection of projects related to some extent to a common objective. (APM, 2000)*

> *A collection of change actions (projects and operational activities) purposefully grouped together to realize strategic and/or tactical benefits. (Murray-Webster and Thiry, 2000)*

> *A group of related projects managed in a coordinated way to obtain benefits and control not available from managing them individually. (PMI, 2006)*

Since then, the project and program management community have generally agreed on a view of what program management is. In its 3rd Edition, the PMI Standard defines a program as:

> *a group of related projects, subprograms and program activities that are managed in a coordinated way to obtain benefits not available from managing them individually. (PMI, 2013a, p. 9)*

MSP defines a program as:

> *a temporary flexible organization created to coordinate, direct and oversee the implementation of a set of related projects and activities in order to deliver outcomes and benefits related to the organization's strategic objectives. (OGC, 2011, p. 5)*

P2M states that:

> *A program is established to carry out the business strategy. (PMAJ, 2015, p. 30)*

The PMI definition insists on the grouping of interrelated projects and other related activities for strategic and tactical reasons; the MSP definition focuses on the organization required to deliver strategic benefits and outcomes. The PMI also identifies the need to deliver benefits over and above those that could be achieved by managing the projects independently. For P2M the program consists of the integration of all the activities necessary to successfully create value for the organization on the basis of a strategic mission.

I would suggest that the following definition is relevant in today's context: "A program is a collection of change actions purposefully grouped together to realize value for a number of stakeholders" (adapted from Thiry, 2007, p. 118). This definition underlines the fact that the grouping of actions within a program has to be purposeful, identifying important interdependencies and synergy both between actions and stakeholders. It recognizes that programs comprise projects and other transition and integration activities that need to be managed together to create sustainable change, either strategic or incremental, and that they aim to realize targeted benefits, either strategic or tactical. As shown in Figure 1.1, programs comprise a number of projects, and other operations that, once integrated, deliver benefits to the business in a consistent, harmonized way.

For example, an organization might aim to improve its competitiveness. In order to do so it may require preparing a marketing campaign, standardizing its processes, training some its employees, improving its production methods and

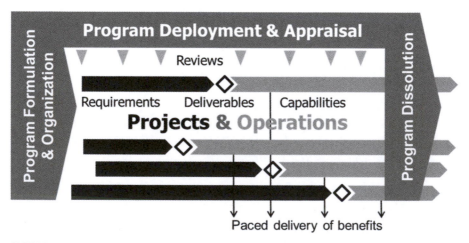

FIGURE 1.1   THE PROGRAM AND ITS ELEMENTS

logistics and finally updating its IT systems. If all these projects are undertaken without a centralized vision and clear strategic objectives it is very possible that the results will not achieve the stated objectives and that many projects will overlap or even work against each other. For example, HR may prepare training that is not in line with the new standards that will be put in place or IT may put in place new systems that do not align with production and logistics' improved methods.

The program management team needs to align the program with both the corporate strategic objectives and the objectives of each of the business units and make sure the projects within the program are aligned and synchronized. These issues are probably better addressed by the following definition of program management: The governance and harmonized management of a number of projects and other actions to achieve targeted benefits and create value for the stakeholders.

As explained further (Chapter 4, p. 81), governance is the process of defining and maintaining direction, putting in place the structures necessary to ensure success and making sure the stated objectives and benefits are achieved. Harmonization is necessary to create synergy between different interrelated actions and their outputs to deliver an integrated outcome. Expected benefits should be stated from the beginning; this is an essential element of both good governance and good management. The ultimate purpose of a program is to deliver value to its multiple stakeholders through the use of new products and services that enhance the organization's capabilities and increase its competitiveness. This concept is also promoted in P2M (PMAJ, 2015), the Japanese Standard for project and program management that outlines the dual role of the program manager in defining the program's mission and proactively creating value for the business.

Finally it is worth mentioning that agile management and program management are both based on the concept of an integrated, mutually reinforcing set of decisions that form a coherent whole aimed at creating stakeholder value. And that, as such, they share a number of common concepts, among which:

1. an *evolutionary and adaptive development,* which translates into gradual and measured release of benefits;
2. the *team as an integrated evolving system* where all stakeholders are actively involved; and finally
3. an *approach based on simplicity* to improve response to changing demands and turbulent environments.

In both programs and agile development, *responsiveness is the measure of value* whereas in project and traditional management, efficiency and reliability are the keys to success (Thiry, 2010). This is exemplified by the nature of programs that are intrinsically ambiguous, as well as uncertain.

1.3   The Issue of Uncertainty and Ambiguity

Over the years researchers and practitioners have tried to understand the reasons why program management is needed and why it has emerged as distinct from project management. These reasons can probably be best understood through the concepts of uncertainty and ambiguity and how they affect decision-making, strategy development and management practices. Early research by Earl and Hopwood (1980) on the factors that determine the choice of a decision-making approach and later by Mintzberg (1990) and Weick (1995) on management methods in uncertain environments has identified how uncertainty and ambiguity influence both decision-making and management methods in different contexts. Today's organisational context is recognized as being both highly complex and turbulent; it is also generally accepted that complexity breeds ambiguity and that turbulence, or fast pace, increases uncertainty.

A few authors have made attempts at program classification. Most of those classifications use two scales, from "known to emergent" vs "impact on organization" (Pellegrinelli, 1997), "pre-existence of projects" vs "business impact" (Vereecke, Pandelaere and Deschoolmeester, 2003), "predictability of outcomes" vs "focus of change" (MSP, 2011), and "Uncertainty" vs "Ambiguity" (Thiry, 2010). In all these statements the first element is related to uncertainty; the second element is linked to ambiguity. They could be defined as:

> *Uncertainty* can be mostly linked to the lack of verifiable information and the difficulty predicting a cause-effect relationship. It hinders the ability to predict the outcome of even clearly identified objectives. It can be expressed as a continuum from likely, to unlikely and unknowable.

> *Ambiguity* is characterized by a number of possible solutions and stakeholders without a clear agreement on objectives. It is related to the likelihood of objectives to change over time. It can be expressed as a continuum from agreed to negotiated and emergent.

As shown in Figure 1.2, low uncertainty is the domain of ongoing actions and traditional management methods, and high uncertainty is the domain of change management and entrepreneurial methods. The bottom left-hand corner is the domain of routine: the process of organizing people and resources efficiently; typical of these activities are: keeping IT systems running, issuing pay checks to all employees, maintaining offices. The top left-hand corner is characterized by power-based methods. Typical of these activities is the annual budget allocation or portfolio management where data is generally available and outcomes are fairly predictable but power struggles arise concerning the allocation of resources to activities. Project management is typical of performance-based methods. It is a change process but, when using traditional single project methodology, it is best limited to low-ambiguity situations where clear deliverables and parameters have been identified.

In cases of high ambiguity, outcomes cannot be clearly defined and decisions are still to be made; it is an area where learning and understanding of the situation are crucial. Typical of actions situated in this quadrant are the development of business strategies in fast-moving environments, business transformation leadership or the preparation of mergers and acquisitions. This area is typically the domain of Business Analysis (when transformation

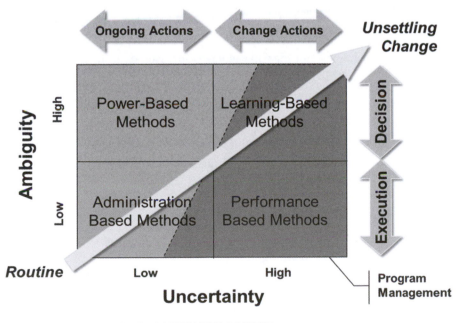

FIGURE 1.2   THE AMBIGUITY-UNCERTAINTY CONTEXT

can rely on hard data) and Value Management (when there is a need for soft data analysis). In the last 20 years, program management has emerged as a methodology that integrates many disciplines, from strategic development to project management and operational transition to enable organizations to deal with increased ambiguity and complexity (represented by dark grey zone in Figure 1.2). It is well suited to reduce ambiguity, an essential procedure for project management to be effective, and to transition change enabling the business to realize benefits (see also Section 4.2).

In this second edition of *Program Management*, I will suggest that projects and programs can be classified according to the *Convergence of Objectives*: the degree to which the different actors agree on the objectives of the project or program, linked to ambiguity, and the *Predictability of the Outcome* the degree to which the final outputs or outcomes can be accurately predicted at initiation, linked to uncertainty (see Figure 1.3). Lack of convergence of objectives is directly linked to ambiguity because the different actors will have a number of different and often divergent views of the same situation and will require frequent decisions along the way, therefore increasing complexity; lack of predictability of outcomes is directly linked to uncertainty because, even when objectives are agreed, a lack of verifiable information can be caused by a high degree of turbulence, volatility or increased pace of change.

For example, a program with an *system or operational focus* like the development of the 4G mobile technology would have high convergence of objectives (low ambiguity) and low predictability of outcomes (high uncertainty), whereas a program which addresses a *transformational or strategic change* within known boundaries, like a change in immigration law or an urban development program, would initially have divergent objectives (high ambiguity) but relatively good predictability (low uncertainty). These types of programs are well covered in the current program management standards and guides.

On the other hand, the recent Affordable Care Act (ACA) program launched in March 2010 in the USA, the transformation programme to modernize the Royal Mail in the UK, or the launch of Debit Cards and the installation of one-quarter million point-of-sale terminals for debit/credit cards at merchant establishments by HDFC Bank in India, would be considered to have both high uncertainty and high ambiguity because they require, not only technical changes to current systems which are difficult to predict accurately, but also people and cultural transformation that are characterized by divergence of opinions and objectives. These types of programs, which I have called complex, agile, or even chaotic, are currently not well covered in standards and guides and their success (or failure) is often due to individuals and teams (or lack of) that have exceptional qualities of leadership and vision.

In order for organizations to respond to a more and more complex and turbulent environment, there is an urgent need to develop these areas of program management by codifying the methods and techniques used by the most progressive, innovative and agile organizations like Cirque du Soleil, Google, Amazon, Gore-Tex, Netflix, The Virgin Group, and others.

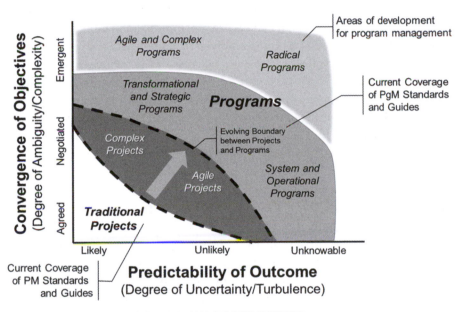

FIGURE 1.3   CURRENT PROGRAM MANAGEMENT CONTEXT

TABLE 1.1   CLASSIFICATION OF PROGRAMS AND PROJECTS: LEGEND

Convergence of Objectives	Predictability of Outcomes
Agreed: Alignment of stakeholders; typically few stakeholders and predictable interactions	*Likely:* Data/knowledge available enables to establish direct cause-effect relationship
Negotiated: Multiple internal stakeholders; likelihood or alignment; predictable interactions	*Unlikely:* Data/knowledge not readily available; indirect cause-effect relationship
Emergent: Multiple internal and external stakeholders; unpredictable interactions	*Unknowable:* Unavailability of data, lack of knowledge does not enable cause-effect relationship

1.3.1   RELATIONSHIP WITH PROJECT MANAGEMENT

Projects cover an area that requires fairly high predictability. The whole concept of project management is based on the capability to predict the outputs of the project and ensure that the project will be realized within set parameters. This requires a fair confidence in the available historical data and an accurate baseline (project plan). As witnessed through the recent improvement of IT projects' predictability, accuracy has become better as historical data has become more available. Another example is construction, which has had historical data available for more than a century and is therefore quite predictable and reliable. Business and social endeavours are notably more ambiguous and complex than engineering and technology endeavours because of the influence of multiple stakeholders that increase their rate of change and turbulence. Therefore, current project tools and techniques can be used with a fairly high rate of success for predictable engineering or technology projects and highly predictable social or business projects, like setting up a new accounting system in a company or building a new social housing development. When the situation becomes less predictable or involves greater ambiguity, traditional project management cannot be used to manage the process because the outputs cannot be clearly defined from the start. This is the domain of program management.

As outlined in Figure 1.3, the boundary between projects and programs is shifting as project management is being used to deal with more and more complex and turbulent situations; this has given rise to new "project" disciplines like agile project management and complex project management, covering areas previously associated with program management and blurring the boundary between projects and programs. Complex projects are generally characterized by their large scale, whereas agile projects are usually relatively small but highly complex and turbulent. Both these new areas of development have been documented in guides and standards and use a mix of traditional project and program management methods and techniques.

As a consequence, program management is more and more associated with strategic initiatives. Although both agile and complex projects share a lot of techniques and concepts with program management; contrarily to program managers, their project managers are usually not accountable for delivering benefits.

A number of governmental and defence agencies have published Complex project management guides that overlap ideas and concepts promoted in program management, such as: the Australian Department of Defence International Centre for Complex Project Management (ICCPM) which published a "Complex Project Management Competency Standard" in 2012. The Transportation Research Board's (TRB) Strategic Highway Research Program, which published "Guide to Project Management Strategies for Complex Projects" in 2015. The Chartered Institute of Building (CIOB) in the UK and others.

Too often though, undertakings labelled as "Complex Projects" are simply large complicated projects subjected to high uncertainty where project managers consider their work packages as sub-projects. If ambiguity is high because large projects are not well defined and have a high degree of complexity, they are in fact programs in the formulation phase and should be called and managed as such.

1.3.2   RELATIONSHIP WITH PORTFOLIO MANAGEMENT

Portfolio management is a decision management process (high ambiguity) which is ongoing and based on verified data (low-uncertainty). It sits in the top left-hand corner of the diagram in Figure 1.2 and relies on power-based methods. It is in many ways similar to the organizational budget allocation process where the available resources, the different organizational departments and their needs are well known, but choices ought to be negotiated and made. Whereas many maturity models acknowledge portfolio management as the more mature OPM state and although it sits higher in the hierarchy of the organization, it may be argued that program management is subjected to both high ambiguity and uncertainty and that, therefore, its practice requires more maturity than that of portfolio management. In the next chapter, I will explore the maturity required to manage programs, both at organizational and personal level. The main difference lies in the fact that, in a portfolio, the level of uncertainty is much lower and, although ambiguity can be high, data is more reliable and a linear cause-effect relationship can be better established, assuming accurate data is available to make decisions.

1.4   Comparison of Leading PgM Standards

Currently there are three widely recognized program(me) management "standards": The "MSP-Managing Successful Programmes" in the UK (OGC, 2011); "The Standard for Program Management" published by the Project Management Institute (PMI, 2013b); and "P2M Project & and Program

Management for Enterprise Innovation" promoted by the Project Management Association of Japan (PMAJ, 2015). Each of these standards covers a slightly different area of the whole range of endeavours that businesses undertake to realise strategic change.

Aside from these standards, two recent publications are worth mentioning. In 2012, the PMI published a book by Dr Motoh Shimizu, "Fundamentals of Program Management", which, although not a standard, is very interesting in comparing the impact of Western and Japanese culture on the practice of strategy execution and program management. In 2013, the PMI published "Managing Change in Organizations: A Practice Guide". This guide has a whole chapter on program management and is aligned both with the PMI Standard Third Edition and with this book's content.

The UK government (CCTA, 1999) was first to issue a guide (professional standard) for Program(me) Management, "Managing Successful Programmes", commonly referred to as MSPTM. This guide has always taken the view that program management's objective was "... to achieve benefits that are of strategic importance" (CCTA, 1999). The PMI was first to acknowledge the fact that "programs also include elements of ongoing operations" (PMI, 1996). The PMAJ's viewpoint saw program management as an evolution, a shift from second-generation to third-generation project management (PMAJ, 2004).

Today, most professional organizations and writers agree that programs are more complex than projects and are a means to execute the organization's strategic objectives; they are aimed at delivering social or business benefits, not solely a "unique product, service, or result" (PMI, 2013, p. 2), which is the purpose of projects.

The PMAJ sees program management as an extension of the strategy where: "After the program mission is gained from the business strategy as a concept, a program is created to carry out the program strategy" (PMAJ, 2015, p. 32). For P2M, programs are an intrinsic part of organizations that have to deal with a globally competitive environment and need to deliver year to year in pursuit of innovation. PMAJ divide programs into two main categories: *creative or transformation-type programs* that are ambiguous and destined to create something entirely new and/or dramatically transform the current state and *operation-type programs* that have agreed-upon objectives and create values such as increased profit, new knowledge, etc.

MSP authors claim that MSP (Managing Successful Programmes) can deal with all these types of programs but is better suited for business transformation (OGC, 2011). It may be used in a "scaled down" form for technical or low unpredictability projects/programs and may become "less appropriate" for high unpredictability societal programs (OGC, 2011). This insight is particularly valuable because it recognizes that there are a range of programs and that each of them needs to be managed in different ways.

Finally, the PMI has taken a drastically different approach for the development of its third edition. Following criticism that claimed the second edition did not truly represent program management practice, but was more an extension of project management practice, they used a group of expert practitioners to review and develop the third edition of the PMI Standard.

This third edition defines programs as: "a means of executing corporate strategies and achieving business or organizational goals and objectives" (PMI, 2013b, p. 4). To support this view, the Standard defines five interrelated "performance domains": Strategy Alignment, Benefits Management; Stakeholder Engagement; Governance and Life Cycle Management. Its Life Cycle is now truly representative of program management, in particular in the concept of adaptive change, which promotes the idea that a program's strategy and plan can and will change over the course of the program in order to deliver its intended benefits.

This view has further been reinforced by the new *Managing Change in Organizations: A Practice Guide* (PMI, 2013c) which devotes a whole chapter to the relationship between change management and program management and focuses particularly on the transition and integration aspects of the program.

In summary, MSP provides methodologies aimed at delivering business benefits, covering issues like governance, leadership and stakeholder engagement, benefits realization, transformational change and capability improvement. The PMI provides a strong framework for the management of programs in a real-life context and emphasizes the relationship between program management and change management. P2M focuses on integration and relationships, thus representing the Japanese "ba" culture where enterprises are communities aimed at creating value through innovation. As such, it fosters creativity and close teamwork.

1.5   From Program to Organization

Chapter 1 has outlined the essence of program management: how it became what it is, how different professional communities interpret it and what the standards that describe it cover. In Chapter 2, I will describe the organizational context in which programs are undertaken, their relationship with other project-based methods and its relation to strategy.

CHAPTER 2

Organizational Context

Chapter 1 outlined how different people and organizations view programs in different ways; It also reviewed existing PgM standards and analysed them in regards of their suitability in different situations. Chapter 2 completes this review of the usefulness and appropriateness of programs by examining the context of program management, more specifically, in the first section, it discusses different types of project-based organizations and how programs fit in. The relationship between programs and other project organization components like portfolios and projects are examined, as well as the relation between programs and the organization's strategies and value.

2.1 Projects, Programs and Portfolios

In order to understand the objectives and characteristics of program management, it is essential to clarify the different views that exist concerning other project-based components of the organization.

2.1.1 COMPARISON BETWEEN PROJECT, PROGRAM AND PORTFOLIO

In order to clearly distinguish programs from projects, we need to understand the distinction between the European and the American approach to the term project management.

Traditionally, the European view of Project Management has been wider ranging than the North American view. For European practitioners and project associations, project management is more than the management of projects. It starts with an initiating idea and business justification and ends with the "operationalization" of its deliverables, often covering multiple discrete projects. This links and often overlaps the concepts of project management with change management. For example, the UK's Association of Project

Management's Body of Knowledge 6th Edition (APM, 2012) has 53 knowledge areas, as compared with the 10 of the Project Management Institute's (PMI®) *PMBOK® Guide* (PMI, 2013a). Europeans, to some extent, describe a discipline rather than a process (IPMA, 2006; APM, 2006); in contrast, North Americans have mostly taken the view that project management is a process to manage single projects: the management of a project. The different views of what a program is have definitely been influenced by each project perspective. In North America, the term program has traditionally been associated with large complex projects, and more recently with delivering strategies through projects, whereas in Europe, and especially the UK, it has been associated with the management of change. In the last few years, the difference between these two approaches has dwindled as the PMI has promoted the concepts of OPM (organizational project management) and Managing Change in Organizations.

When project management is limited to the processes between the attribution of a mandate to the project manager and the project closing, it is assumed that the project deliverables can be accurately described and that any required handover or transfer period is outside the scope of the project (PMI, 1996, 2000, 2004; CMAA, 2002; DSMC, 1999; NASA, 1998). This view allows for a clearer distribution of responsibilities and distinction between project and program. Theories aside, practice has shown, even in Europe (OGC, 2005), that, more often than not, the role of project manager is limited to the management of the activities taking place between initiation and closure. The "directing" and operational integration roles are usually taken on by distinct people who often have authority over the project manager. Most practitioners and writers now agree that the discipline that oversees the role of the project manager and connects projects to the business and strategy is program management and that the program manager should be the sponsor of the project when the project is part of a program.

Until recently, the boundary between programs and portfolios was often blurred; there was confusion and often divergence about what distinguished them. Elonen and Aarto (2002) stated:

> Terms closely related or in some contexts almost synonymous to project portfolio management include program management and multi-project management. (p. 2)

For example, Dye and Pennypacker (1999) were giving the following definition of portfolio:

A project portfolio is a collection of projects to be managed concurrently under a single management umbrella. Each project may be related or independent of each other. The projects share the same strategic objectives and the same scarce resources.

At the same time, the PMI (2000) was defining programs as:

a group of projects managed in a coordinated way to obtain benefits not available from managing them individually.

And the CCTA (1999) as:

The co-ordinated management of a portfolio of projects that change organizations to achieve benefits that are of strategic importance.

Additionally, as stated earlier, many endeavours called "programs" are in fact ongoing operations, which Sergio Pellegrinelli (1997) called "portfolio programmes" and "heartbeat programmes" and Murray-Webster and Thiry (2000) called "portfolio programmes" and "incremental programmes". A good example of these are large governmental programs like housing programs, crime prevention programs or others that often start as a strategic program, but typically become almost operational in essence after the initial impetus decreases and the initial program becomes a series of relatively limited initiatives within an overarching strategy.

The 2000 version of the *PMBOK® Guide*,[1] states:

This diversity of meaning makes it imperative that any discussion of program management versus project management be preceded by agreement on a clear and consistent definition of each term … (p. 10)

At this point in time, there is relative agreement on the focus and purpose of projects, programs and portfolios. The current views can be summarized as:

Projects generally deliver outputs: a single product or service. They are reasonably well defined and although they can be complicated, they are generally not complex. Their focus is tactical or operational.

---

1   *PMBOK® Guide: A Guide to the Project Management Body of Knowledge* (PMI, 2004). *PMBOK® Guide* is a Registered Trademark of the Project Management Institute.

Programs deliver outcomes: sets of capabilities which, together, produce benefits. They are generally complex with frequent realignments required during their life cycle. They are aligned with strategic objectives and are business focused.

Portfolios can cover two areas: the organization's projects or its whole investment portfolio. They have an overall corporate deliverable and are ongoing and recurrent. They are fairly predictable in terms of their outcomes, but require constant adjustments. They have a mission focus and are aligned with the corporate strategy.

Table 2.1 compares these three components of the organization on a series of elements.

TABLE 2.1   DETAILED COMPARISON BETWEEN PROJECTS, PROGRAMS AND PORTFOLIOS

Area	Project	Program	Portfolios
Scope	Set, limited scope with clearly defined deliverables.	Broad scope with flexible boundaries to meet medium-term expected business benefits.	Organizational scope adapted to corporate goals.
Change	Change should be avoided; baseline is key.	Change is first seen as an opportunity.	Monitor environmental changes that affect the corporate strategy.
Success	Measured through respect of cost, time, quality preset parameters: the PM triangle.	Measured in financial terms, value creation and benefits realization.	Measured in terms of overall portfolio performance: maximum results, minimal resources.
Leadership	Transactional leadership, authority-based directive style, management of subalterns, conflict resolution. Rational decision-making.	Facilitating style, management of powerful stakeholders, conflict resolution. Intuitive decision-making.	Administrative style focused on adding value, power results from allocation of resources. Rational decision-making.
Role	Task and parameters management; product (project output) delivery.	Pacing and interfacing of projects; benefits delivery.	Resource management across portfolio; deliver value to corporate stakeholders.

TABLE 2.1   CONTINUED

Area	Project	Program	Portfolios
Responsibility	Project output delivery to parameters; reporting, performance-based focus.	Strategic decision implementation, develop opportunistic emergent strategies.	Align portfolio with corporate strategy, adjust portfolio in regards of changes in organizational environment.
Main Tasks	Negotiate scope, define WBS, minimize adverse risks, manage delivery of the product of the project. Maintain project team stamina and motivation, monitor and control external team.	Coordinate component project resources and key deliverables; market program and build business case on a regular basis; develop and maintain project managers' team spirit and contribution to program.	Allocate resources to portfolio components reassess portfolio on an ongoing basis; collect and use program and project data to make decisions.
Control	Monitor and control tasks and project parameters retrospectively against the baseline; report to project sponsor.	Appraise component project deliverables and resource usage prospectively against expected benefits; report to business stakeholders.	Measure aggregate value of portfolio retrospectively against preset corporate performance indicators; report to corporate stakeholders.

Source: Michel Thiry, 2008, chapters 3 and 4.

2.1.2   RELATIONSHIP BETWEEN PROGRAMS AND THE ORGANIZATION

Program management fits in the larger context of the organization; it is therefore important to appreciate how it interacts with the other components of a project organization as well as how they relate to each other to form an effective organizational system that delivers the organization's strategy.

In a project-based environment, the corporate strategy defines the high-level vison and mission of the organization and identifies corporate goals; the integration of business activities with the corporate strategy is supported by *portfolio management*. The business strategy defines the business benefits and the adjustments required to achieve the corporate goals; delivery of the business strategy is ensured by *program management*. At functional level the strategy clarifies capability requirements and describes tangible deliverables;

it is supported by project management. Finally at the operations and/or sales level the strategy consolidates the offer by surveying and assessing product or service implementation and integration issues; this is operations management. Typically, strategy writers describe corporate strategy as defining the organization's purpose through the vision and mission which guides multiple business units. Corporate strategies define the medium- or long-term forecasts of the organization's future position. Business strategy, on the other hand, coordinates different operating units within a business unit. Currently, there are two approaches to the development of business strategies:

1.   each unit competes with each other for the same resources, which is the case in most organizations that privilege a resource optimization and control-based approach; or
2.   effective relationships are created between units to realize value, which is the case in organizations that privilege a stakeholder and empowerment approach.

An organization that has not integrated the program approach will reveal a focus on single discrete projects and a multi-project management approach that focuses on resource allocation and data gathering. Project managers would be expected to play a predominantly product-delivery role and "program managers" a coordination and monitoring role. This view is currently supported by many of the "program" IT tools sold on the market. They focus on resource allocation and basic project data gathering, reinforcing the focus of project management on product delivery. They typically advertise: "Improvements in Business Performance", "Streamline Operations and Execution", "Time and Expense Management", "Robust Project Scheduling and Management" as the features of their tools.

An organization that has mature program integration processes will display strong interrelationships between projects and both its business and corporate strategies; in such an organization managers are expected to view program management as an integrative process to deliver value to the business. This level of maturity displays integrated, mutually reinforcing business processes that form a coherent end-to-end (E2E) process from the expression of a business strategy to value realization. This approach is considered a strategic decision management process (Thiry, 2004), which includes the decision-making, the

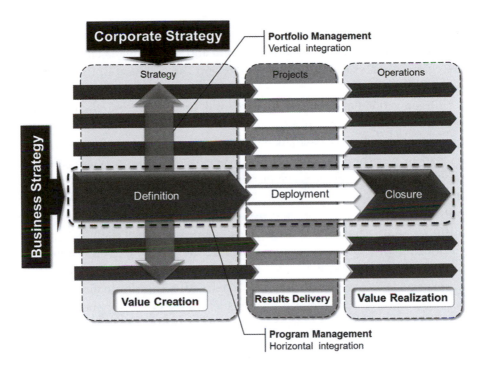

FIGURE 2.1   VERTICAL AND HORIZONTAL INTEGRATION OF STRATEGIES

decision-execution and the realization of the objectives. Figure 2.1 graphically represents this organizational integration.

Program management takes into account the fact that multiple stakeholders may have differing needs and that complexity is an integral part of its practice. Its objective is not to deliver a single product or service, but the benefits that will lead to value realization. In the example of the organization described in Chapter 1, HR has an objective to train a number of employees before a certain date and will hire a training consultant that has developed their own methodology, the quality department, on the other hand, may focus on a standard that is recognized worldwide; IT's objective is to integrate any new systems with the existing organizational standards, whereas production and logistics may obtain a very good deal from a vendor that fits right into their budget. If the objectives of these different business units are not aligned, the program will fail. As seen earlier, the realization of the corporate strategy is the domain of portfolio management, which is an ongoing management approach. On the other hand, the realization of the business strategy is the domain of program and project management, which are change processes. Both the corporate and the business strategy need to be coordinated.

Organizations are continually subjected to pressures to change. These pressures can be external, like the arrival of a new competitor, the availability of a new technology, a new law or regulation, a change in the market or a change in government. They can also be internal, like new processes or procedures, a change of director, the development of new capabilities, the development of a new product, or even a merger or acquisition. These pressures define corporate objectives and business needs that drive the formulation of a business strategy. This business strategy then leads to the clarification of strategic objectives which define programs. The formulation of the program involves defining measurable benefits and the outcomes that are expected to deliver them. The key benefits that contribute directly to the strategic objectives are labelled critical success factors (CSF) and measured using quantitative key performance indicators (KPI). Often, outcomes are used as performance indicators. Outcomes are a tangible output of a capability improvement and benefits are a qualitative output of the outcome. As part of the program definition process, a number of actions are proposed to realize these outcomes; they are projects and other actions that are meant to deliver the products or services (deliverables) that will create new capabilities (outputs) for the organization. When these enhanced capabilities are implemented in the organization, they generate improvements that enable the realization of the expected outcomes and benefits. These in turn should ease the pressure that was the trigger for the initial strategy. It is also possible that the strategy may need to be reformulated to address issues created by the realization of these objectives or new developments on the context of the organization. This formulation-reformulation process is called "strategy formation" (De Wit and Meyer, 2004). This relationship between the strategy, the contribution of program and project management to its realization through operational improvements are illustrated in Figure 2.2 opposite.

This diagram is based on the concept that organizations aim to realize value and that expected value is expressed through a value proposition stemming from a sound strategy formation process. It is then realized through the process described above. The process is cyclic to enable learning and knowledge management from the actual realization of results, which are essential aspects of highly competitive organizations.

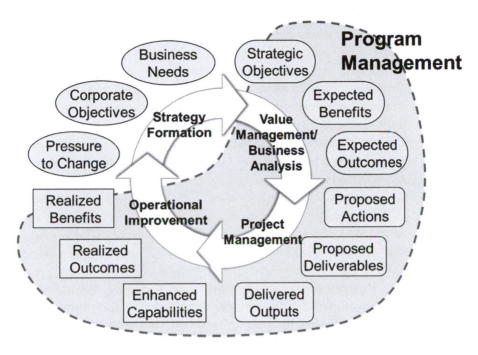

FIGURE 2.2   REALIZING BUSINESS VALUE

2.2   Project-Based Organizations

It is not the purpose in this section to go into the detail of project organizations, but there are some important points to be made about the different program approaches in different types of project organizations. First, let's define project organization.

Project Organizations (PO) can refer to a number of different organizational structures. The entire firm can be a PO (construction, consultancy and professional services), the PO could refer to multi-firm consortia or networks, as well as temporary organizations (movie or event industry). In some cases project focused subsidiaries or divisions of larger mainly functional corporations can also be considered a PO (IT or Facilities Management Department of large manufacturing organization). The key feature of POs is that they conduct the majority of their activities as projects and/or privilege project over functional approaches. In project terms, POs cover a variety of organizational forms from weak matrix to fully "projectized". In management terms, they can display most types of structures on the continuum from mechanistic to organic as defined by Burns and Stalker (1961). The two key points that deserve emphasis in this section are:

1. the issue of *compartmentalization*, typical of traditionally structured organizations, versus *integration*, typical of networked organizations; and
2. the use of program management to run temporary organizations, either in the transition stage of organizational change or to deliver a time-limited event.

2.2.1 PROGRAM APPROACHES IN DIFFERENT ORGANIZATIONAL CONTEXTS

The current organizational management context is still dominated by mechanistic, control-based organizational models set in the industrial era (Hatch and Cunliffe, 2006; Hamel, 2011;). Traditional organizational structures typically emphasize hierarchy, vertical communication, specialization and control; they are well adapted to stable well-defined environments. Post-industrial era models like networks, strategic alliances and virtual organizations, although they have become more and more common, are still not accepted as mainstream. Recently a number of organizational models have been developed to adapt to more turbulent and fast-moving environments; they foster flatter hierarchies, horizontal communication and interfaces, empowerment, outsourcing, informal relationships and innovation. The emergence of program management could be considered part of this adaptation process.

Traditional organizational structures are hierarchical in nature and typically separate project work from operations. In a PO set in this type of structure, the portfolio of projects is typically divided into sub-portfolios, programs and large projects; each sub-portfolio and program is then broken down into smaller projects, which are broken down in work packages and deliverables. As shown in Figure 2.3 opposite, this type of structure is very top-down and focused on resource allocation and vertical control.

Innovative organizational models have been influenced by developments in systems thinking, learning organizations, agile management and stakeholder governance theories. Organizations that favour this type of structure foster active communication between all involved parties and comprehensive integration of processes and systems; they are more fluid and most stakeholders are involved in requirements definition and the delivery of business benefits.

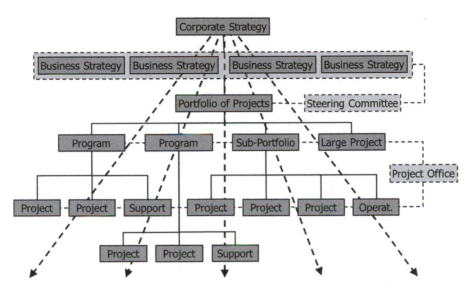

FIGURE 2.3   TRADITIONAL COMPARTMENTALIZED PROJECT ORGANIZATION

There is a strong emphasis on the continual measurement of results and the iterative nature of the process, the organizational model resembles more a supply or value chain, as illustrated in Figure 2.4.

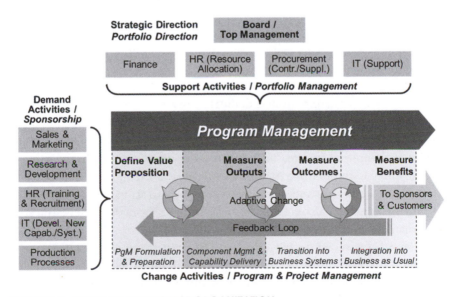

FIGURE 2.4   VALUE CHAIN PROJECT ORGANIZATION

In this case, the program methodology is at the centre of the strategic decision management process and guides the flow of all the change actions of the organization, integrating demand and support activities, projects and operations, benefits delivery with business as usual and customer service.

2.2.2   THE PROGRAM AS A TEMPORARY ORGANIZATION

More and more, program management is used to manage organizational change. Today, the PMI Standard (PMI, 2013b), MSP (OGC, 2011) and P2M (PMAJ, 2010) promote the use of programs for changing organizations, the community and even society. As such, a program becomes more than "an efficient grouping of projects to enhance or develop organizational capabilities to achieve measurable organizational goals and objectives" (PMI, 2006), which are characteristics of the traditional model of organizational change. As a temporary organization, the program becomes a "Complex Adaptive Model of Organization Change" (Olson and Eoyang, 2001). This model of change emphasizes the need to adapt to "unknowable, unpredictable and uncontrollable" behaviours, to accept the fact that cause and effect are not necessarily related in a linear way and that people need to be empowered and organizations responsive. In this model, the program becomes the transition stage towards a transformation state that is yet to be detailed. These are cases where the program is used as a vehicle for social interaction between stakeholders to generate new patterns of behaviour, creative ideas and innovative products that increase the organization's competitiveness.

Within that perspective, programs can also be used to test new ways of doing business, develop new business models or prototype emergent organizational structures. By committing limited dedicated resources for a set timescale to the program, while maintaining a strong structure for the core business, the organization limits its corporate risk and increases its responsiveness to both external and internal inputs. This ensures the organization always stays at the edge of their competitive market without jeopardizing their capability to run day-to-day business and putting the core organization at risk. The use of program management also creates a strong strategic focus that will help secure senior management's support.

To be most successful, this approach requires strong collaboration and a knowledge-sharing culture where multiple stakeholders will work together to define the blueprint of the future business and be ready to commit to a vision that may not yet be fully formed.

2.2.3   PROGRAM AND AGILE MANAGEMENT

Program management has evolved from the complexity created by a number of interrelated projects and multiple involved stakeholders, from the need to span from strategy to operations and from the ambiguity involved in constantly emergent decision-making. Agile methods were developed to deal with projects that could not be dealt with using traditional project management methodology. Projects that are complex, involving many unknowns in terms of design and the effect that results have on expected benefits cannot be managed using traditional project management methods. In 2001 a group of thinkers of what was then called "lightweight methods" issued the "Agile Manifesto" to tackle complex, fast-moving IT programming projects. This Manifesto states four basic ideas:

- responding to change over following a plan;
- working software over comprehensive documentation;
- individuals and interactions over processes and tools;
- customer collaboration over contract negotiation.

The principles stated in the Agile Manifesto are shared by program management. Agile management and program management are based on the concept of an integrated, mutually reinforcing set of decisions that form a coherent whole aimed at creating stakeholder value. Agile management is a development method, not a project method. In fact agile management is very similar to fast-track project management, a method where design occurs in parallel with construction. Having worked on a number of large construction fast-track projects in the late 1980s and early 1990s, the company I was working for developed new project management methods very similar to agile and relied on the same basic concepts (see also Section 1.3 and Figure 1.2).

As can be seen through these clarifications, both program and agile management develop in an iterative way and are constantly realigned, based on measured results, to ensure they deliver stakeholder value. Both put a great focus on prioritization of effort and requirements, this is definitely a value management approach. They share a number of common concepts, among which:

1.   The need to be responsive to evolving stakeholder/user demands during benefits delivery.
2.   The requirement for evolutionary and adaptive development supported by a robust decision management system.

3.   The team as an integrated evolving system where all stakeholders are actively engaged.

4.   A governance approach based on simplicity to improve response to changing demands and turbulent environments.

2.2.3.1   Responsiveness as the measure of value (Benefits Management – see Section 4.6)

The PMI Standard for Program Management states:

> Programs and projects deliver benefits to organizations by generating business value, enhancing current capabilities ... or developing new capabilities for the organization to use. A benefit is an outcome of actions, behaviors, products or services that provide utility to the organization as well as to the program's intended beneficiaries or stakeholders. (PMI, 2013b, p. 5)

Managing Successful Programmes, the UK Standard, defines a benefit as:

> the measurable improvement resulting from an outcome perceived as an advantage by one or more stakeholders and which contributes to one or more organizational objective(s). (OGC, 2011, p. 283)

In layperson's terms, a benefit is a positive outcome that stems out of the use of a product or capability; it is an outcome of the execution of the strategy. In both program and agile management, benefits are measured at operational level.

As demonstrated in Figure 7.3, the goal is to balance required capabilities with available capabilities and offered benefits with expected benefits. So, responsiveness to evolving stakeholder/user demands and stakeholder involvement is the key to success. But how can one respond to continually changing demands and still stay in control? This is where the concept of decision management comes into play.

2.2.3.2   Evolutionary and adaptive development (Decision Management – see Section 4.2)

As discussed in Section 4.2, decision management consists of setting up a system whereby key stakeholders take the time to discuss issues, to agree a shared strategic vision and to make series of small decisions on an ongoing basis in alignment with this vision. This is basically the concept of iterative development, which forms the basis of agile methods. In agile projects and programs the overall benefits realization plan is refined in the first few iterations or cycles; this is what Larman (2004) has called *adaptive planning* in contrast to *predictive planning*. As the situation evolves, results are evaluated and new decisions are made that continually reinforce or realign the vision to reality, this aspect corresponds to the evolutionary and adaptive development concept as is the case for complex programs and new product development.

Both program and agile management are driven by a clear vision that can be broad at the start and needs to be refined as the program/project evolves. It is driven by the delivery of a series of prioritized capabilities/benefits that, through continual feedback, influence the next stage. Evolutionary methods assume that the solution can evolve and be refined during implementation rather than be "set" in an early plan. One of the key aspects of good iterative development is user involvement; one of the key aspects of good program management is stakeholder engagement. Without the involvement of decision-makers during the process, lots of time and effort will be lost redesigning solutions that are not satisfactory.

2.2.3.3   Team as an integrated evolving system (Stakeholder Engagement – see Section 4.4)

In agile management, as well as in program management, the team is seen as a complex adaptive system, in contrast to the traditional "command and control" style favoured by many organizations. Agile teams are built on the principles of self-organization and self-management; this goes against the traditional project culture of most organizations and requires a culture change. But it enables team to be much more creative and flexible. Program management uses a stakeholder value chain approach to create a flow of learning and performance that enables ongoing delivery of benefits and re-evaluation of requirements and expectation, based on the analysis of results (see Figures 2.4 and 3.2).

Collaboration between all the actors in the process is essential to ensure that the program and its component projects deliver the strategic objectives. In programs, if the strategic objective and expected benefits have not been defined accurately and prioritized, the result will not deliver value. In a turbulent environment, agile management, through its user involvement, ensures that an ongoing stream of working deliverables are produced and well integrated into a whole.

2.2.3.4   Approach based on simplicity (Governance – see Section 4.3)

Governance is one of the most misused terms in business, governance is currently associated with disaster prevention, risk mitigation and consequently, tighter controls. Most current organizational structures and projects are based on tight controls; this approach complicates the management system and removes a lot of the innovativeness and flexibility within the organization; it favours prevention over empowerment. Many governance related tasks, like requiring sign-off on a full requirements document before development can start, interfere with the agility of the solutions.

In a well-integrated governance context, programs would sustain a value creation perspective, supported by innovativeness and empowerment; they would focus on maximizing opportunities rather than reducing threats. Program sponsors would also seek a wider set of success criteria, a drive towards sustainability over short-term results and, overall, an increased focus on the link between expected benefits and results. This system does not prevent frequent measurement, on the contrary, it encourages regular measurement of results based on the realization of expected benefits. But measurement is made at significant gateways and based on results rather than on a pre-set schedule and mere respect of the baseline.

Simple governance systems based on clear objectives and significant requirements will help program and agile teams to deliver benefits regularly and with a high degree of success.

FIGURE 2.5   AGILITY IN PROJECT ORGANIZATIONS

2.2.3.5   The Big Picture

Programs are the link between the business strategy and the projects whilst agile methods are the link between the project and the technical and operational aspect of the delivery. In today's context, there is a need to manage ambiguity. Program management and agile methods can help achieve this because: projects are predictive, agile methods are adaptive and program management, which harmonizes them, is both predictive and adaptive.

2.3   Program Offices

The acronym PMO is now widely used and accepted, but can have such different meanings from an "Enterprise Program Management Office" (EPMO), that is responsible for the management of the whole portfolio of programs and projects in an organization to a project support office, which provides expertise to one single project. It is not the purpose of this book to discuss PMOs; however, I wanted to clarify some of the definitions that directly affect program management.

Currently there is agreement between the main program management guides and standards on the following definitions, which will be used in this book.

> *Program Management Office* (PMO): the structure responsible for defining and managing the program-related governance, procedures, templates, and so on across multiple programs and projects. The program management office should be independent from individual programs. Sometimes the program management office also has a portfolio management responsibility, at least in the ongoing gathering and analysis of program and project data though reporting and review. It often has responsibility for managing resource allocation (personnel, schedule and budget) at the program level.

> *Program Office*: the function providing central administrative support to program managers and teams within a program. This function is mostly used in large programs where information, data, communication, reporting, monitoring and control from different projects and the program needs to be coordinated centrally. It is also at the program office level that procedures and templates used by projects are coordinated and monitored.

2.4   From Managing Programs to Program Maturity

In this chapter, we have seen how programs relate to projects and portfolios and how different organizational approaches affect the management of programs. We also looked at the program process and how good program integration helps achieve the organization's strategic objectives. Chapter 3 examines how mature organizations configure and structure the program itself and how they can develop a sound program culture.

CHAPTER 3

Program Context

As explained in Chapters 1 and 2, program management is a means to realize strategies and, as such, it has to be clearly linked to the strategy and thoroughly integrated in the organizational processes. In mature organizations, the program process involves a number of stakeholders from different departments and different levels of the organization working as a cross-functional team, regardless of their hierarchical affiliation.

A few professional bodies and many writers still promote the view that programs are extensions of project management and can be managed in a similar way. The reality is different and the knowledge required to manage a program is fundamentally distinct, although somewhat linked, to that of project management. This chapter outlines the differences between a traditional single project approach and a mature program approach, the characteristics of a program culture, the reasons why groups of projects should be managed as programs and, finally, how to develop a mature program culture.

3.1   Program Culture

Program culture is intrinsically linked to the maturity of organizations in terms of the integration of the different actors involved in realising strategic initiatives. Mature program organizations will favour a wide stakeholder approach over a narrow shareholder-only approach and empowerment and accountability will be privileged over hierarchy and control. In fact, program is more akin to a leadership approach, where opportunity seeking, agreement building and decision-making dominate, than to a management approach focused on baselining, execution and control, which are features of project management.

In this first section, I will touch upon many aspects of the program culture: program maturity and its development; how roles and responsibilities change in a strong program culture as compared to a project or traditional culture; and finally, what kind of leadership and competencies are expected from mature program managers.

3.1.1   ISSUES WITH SINGLE PROJECT CULTURE

One of the most difficult aspects in the development of a program culture is for project managers to move from an individual to a team accountability perspective. Project managers are typically focused on the success of "their" project; it is already difficult for them to refocus on "our" program, and control-focused organizations do not provide project or program managers with opportunities to experiment with team accountability. Most of the work is divided and scoped into discrete projects or organizational departments and performance evaluation is based on individual measures. Introducing program management in these circumstances creates mixed messages between the organization's implicit expectations and the environment's explicit limits. Many of our recent consultancy assignments consist in establishing a clear and strong link between projects of a same program and promote the need for project managers to contribute to the program rather than focus on control-based performance goals.

Sadly, most projects are still evaluated solely on financial factors and control is exercised on cost, time and quality. This not only limits the contribution of the projects to strategic objectives, it also prevents project managers from taking a broader view of their project's purpose and its contribution to organizational value. In a program environment, projects should be evaluated on program-specific critical success factors; this creates a common ground for all projects within the program. Typically, project planning will be focused on specific tasks and deliverables; program management requires that project managers take a holistic, systemic view of planning and reporting and clearly link project deliverables to expected benefits, as well as on links between projects and with key stakeholders. The project managers' reporting process can then be focused around meaningful key deliverables and milestones; those that directly contribute to target benefits through the critical success factors.

Traditional project communication processes focus on the project management information system; meetings and reports are usually based on the assessment of the project's conformity to a set baseline. In a program culture, this short-sighted focus negates the capability for the program to adapt to changing circumstances and to deliver on target benefits. Programs have a longer life cycle than projects; there is a need to regularly motivate sponsors concerning the value of the program and to demonstrate the added benefits and control obtained through the program. In this context, marketing is emerging as a key element of program management, aimed at developing an interactive communication system which, if it is well planned, will help the program team secure ongoing support and funding by marketing realized benefits and added value of the program.

In most project environments the project management information system and the documents that support it are developed to enhance control; they do not really serve the project manager's needs and definitely not the program's need for flexibility. Organizations would gain from developing processes and documents that are meaningful to the project managers and useful to the organization rather than develop control processes that increase the sense of command and control. When the documents that support control processes are seen to achieve strategic objectives and ease the management job of both the project managers and the program manager their intake is usually positive.

Another key issue with the project perspective is that of risk management. Traditionally risks are considered independently for each project and program risks are identified separately as higher-level risks. Project risks that could affect more than one project are better managed at program level where higher perspective and authority will increase the quality of their response. The traditional quality-cost-time triangle evaluation of risk impact is too limited at program level as it does not allow for a true program view of the impact of risks. Because program managers are concerned mainly with the delivery of target benefits, risk impact assessment must take into account a much wider range of factors. Finally, although most standards now agree that project risks include both threats and opportunities, project risk culture still focuses mainly on threat reduction; this is inappropriate for programs where the management of opportunities is an essential success factor.

In a traditional project environment, competence-based trust – the trust that someone can do the job, based on past performance and competence – is easily recognized; this is readily exported to a program environment where team members will respect the program manager, based on their project competence. It is more difficult when the program manager's project knowledge is secondary to their strategic management competence. Integrity-based trust – the trust that someone will vouch for you in difficult situations – seems more complicated to achieve in a context where program and project managers are subjected to rigid top-down performance requirements. An empowerment culture is best suited to support the development of that type of trust, which is very important in the team accountability context of programs.

The project managers within a program are often a very diverse, albeit competent, group of people. They are usually asked to approach this new environment in a conventional manner, and to focus on performance rather than understanding and learning, whereas our experience shows that project managers are more productive when they are empowered. In a research conducted with some of my partners, project managers working in a program management environment have expressed the need to "develop lateral, more creative thought processes and encourage a bit less conformity" in order to foster a new work environment that encourages potential and growth (Thiry and Deguire, 2004).

Finally, whereas in projects practice tends to be standardized, which is good in a controlled environment, program management creates conditions that allow – rather than force – solutions to evolve and encourage – rather than stifle – diversity between project teams. Working in this way, the program manager enhances the program team's creativity and potential.

3.1.2   CHARACTERISTICS OF PROGRAM CULTURE

Program management is a systemic approach to the management of change. Because of the current dominant organizational culture, its foundations lie in the traditional mechanistic organizational paradigm, thus facing an increasing challenge to adopt newer management models that embrace change and complexity. Recent experience shows that these newer, more agile models correspond to new organizational paradigms as well as to the needs of managers and team members when several projects are integrated to support strategic decisions at the program level. It is more effective for program management to take a holistic, systemic view of planning and reporting, concentrating on expected business benefits and the links between projects, as well as with and between key stakeholders, rather than on specific tasks.

3.1.3   PROGRAM DEFINITION PROCESS

In mature organizations the program is an extension of the strategic decision-making process, program management being the method of choice to implement strategies. Obviously, the scope and extent of program management services will vary depending on the maturity of the organization or its cultural paradigms. When offering program management services, whether internally, or as an external expert, one needs to understand these issues thoroughly.

The first measure of program maturity related to organizational culture lies in the way the program is initially defined. MSP (OGC, 2011) has identified three distinct types of programs, based on their definition process:

1. *Vision-led programs*: which are driven from a clearly defined strategy.
2. *Emergent programs*: which evolve from a number of disparate projects and activities that are grouped after realizing they all lead to a common objective and could generate synergy and higher benefits if managed together.
3. *Compliance programs*: which are forced upon the organization by law or regulations or compelling market forces.

In this book, I will just consider the first two, since the third can be regarded as a subset of either of these. I will relabel Vision-Led programs as "Deliberate Programs" to underline a purposeful decision process and emergent programs as "Ad Hoc Programs" so as not to mistake the term with the concept of emergent strategies and to underline the unplanned and informal nature of their definition.

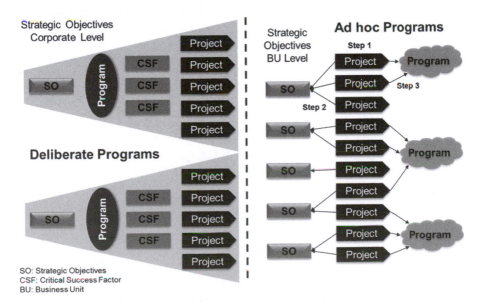

FIGURE 3.1   DELIBERATE VS AD HOC PROGRAMS

3.1.3.1   Deliberate programs

This is the most mature type of program where a strategy is defined, a number of objectives are identified and programs are shaped out of these strategic objectives. Most organizations have not achieved the level of maturity necessary to regularly generate deliberate programs. This is often due to the excessive focus that organizations put on control. Deliberate programs are difficult to define early on, and therefore to control in a traditional way. The program process which I called "formulation" is meant to clarify the vision and define the program purpose. The company needs to invest in the program before they define what projects are going to be part of it. The PMI's PgM Standard 3rd Edition, for example, although it stated that the purpose of program initiation is to define the scope and benefit expectations of the program, indicated that this process also entails configuring or grouping proposed projects and existing projects into a program. This view, which is still shared by a large proportion of project organizations, implicitly assumes that projects, either proposed or existing, precede the program and that a fairly precise scope can be defined early on, which is not true of deliberate programs.

For example, Southern Bank is a large conservative bank; it has dominated the Australian market for a number of years, but has recently been strongly challenged by new consumer demands and its competitors. It has lost enough ground to trigger a number of major reorganization initiatives. Under pressure from the board, the CEO is driving the changes very hard. The CEO hires a new manager to head the technology operations department which employs over 500 people. They are tasked with leading a major organizational restructuring of the department with the clear objectives of supporting corporate strategy by improving delivery and increasing efficiency, while preparing the department to face future challenges.

A departmental strategy is formulated though a set of objectives that each of the heads had identified for their section. It is quickly agreed that program management is required to organize the objectives and drive the change. The first objective of the program manager is to deliver a business plan for the transformation which will clarify the vision of the leadership team and subsequently organize and plan the change. The flexibility of the program approach has enabled a diverse team of organizational development, business management, business development, solutions and projects, technical services, service management and technology strategy and innovation, to maintain the department's overall vision while taking into account changes in their specific environment. Although the change impacts different areas of the business and requires coordination with other business areas, the stakeholder engagement capabilities of the program approach enables the department managers to achieve their objectives as well the organization's.

The complexity of a program and the early ambiguity it displays require a lot of flexibility at the beginning. The formulation of the program can be linked to the development of a strategy where high ambiguity requires the vision to be clarified before undertaking any planning. The deliberate program is based on a clear, often led from the top, purpose, but the formulation stage can bring the sponsor or sponsoring group to decide not to pursue the program or to change it significantly. When making these decisions and developing the program's business case, the program's contribution cannot simply be assessed in economic terms, but must be on a wide-ranging set of organizational benefits. As it progresses and the benefits start impacting the customer organization (external or internal) the program process should allow for emergent strategies.

To evolve constructively, deliberate programs require an organic approach where empowerment and creativity are privileged over a mechanistic control-based approach. However, this can be difficult to implement because the current paradigm in organizations still tends to focus on minimizing risks rather than maximizing opportunities.

3.1.3.2 Ad hoc programs

An ad hoc program evolves from existing business initiatives when a potential sponsor realizes after the fact that these initiatives can be better managed in a coordinated way. This type of situation can lead either to the set-up of a sub-portfolio or a program. In the portfolio set-up, the projects and other initiatives are not necessarily interdependent, although they can be related. A good example of this is projects grouped by client or by category (IT, Engineering, etc.) and labelled program. By contrast, in the program set-up, there is a deliberate purpose that can be identified for the whole and all the component initiatives contribute to it.

For example, due to significant business growth in the last year, WorldPharma planned to bring their research division's workforce in the UK to 1,700 people, most of which will be relocated in new buildings. This growth has triggered a number of major projects in every department; these are currently not coordinated at the corporate level. They include:

- four new buildings with all the necessary infrastructures (parking, roads, utilities, etc.), including a new head office (Facilities Management);

- the recruitment of 500 new employees (HR);
- job redesign and business process re-engineering (Operations with External Consultant);
- introduction of new Information and networking systems (IT);
- number of smaller corollary projects (Health and safety, Security, Social Services, etc.).

A few members of the board identified the need to group all these projects under a single management stream, but are not sure how to proceed. The head of facilities management decides to take the lead and call a meeting of the senior management level sponsors of all these projects to suggest a program approach. Following are some of the critical drivers that were identified for this program:

- Coordinate several construction projects' phasing and physical constraints.
- Implement business process reengineering whilst maintaining corporate culture.
- Integrate all aspects of relocation process (soft and hard).
- Ensure high-quality standards for facilities.
- Effectively relocate 1,700 staff in new buildings within two years.
- Maintain quality compliance and ensure critical areas continuity.
- Integrate all processes between departments.

This is the vision statement that the facilities manager, who became the sponsor, made for the program:

> It is a strategy that looks at the completion of several projects and their planned occupation, each separately phased if necessary, in order to ensure the minimum disruption at the same time as ensuring a continuous level of productivity. It also takes into account the timing of required services that must be in place to support the staff that will relocate to these new facilities.

The grouping of a number of diverse projects under the program banner and a common strategy enabled minimum disruption to the business and maximum effectiveness of the projects' outputs. The benefits of the program were achieved through the managed interdependencies of the different projects that had not been identified before the program was instated. Projects were retrospectively linked to strategic objectives, which enabled their review and to focus them on business benefits rather than simple outputs.

My practice, as well as that of many colleagues, has shown that a fair proportion of programs are currently ad hoc, although the tendency has evolved in the last few years. Projects are typically initiated in business units or departments, based on each unit's own needs. At budget approval time the projects are assessed against the available funds and retroactively linked to strategic objectives to justify budget demands. Very little consideration is given to programs. As executives realize the need to gain a corporate view of all these initiatives, they will first implement a portfolio approach and group projects together by business unit, department, client, specialty or other. Ad hoc programs are usually initially managed as sub-portfolios.

When true program management is finally introduced, as in the above case, the projects are all linked to the strategic objectives and, based on that analysis, projects that do not contribute to the program objectives are culled or reassigned to other sub-portfolios or programs. It may also be acknowledged that some aspects of the strategy are not covered and require new projects to be launched as part of the program. Once such steps are taken, the program can be considered deliberate and managed as such. This is also the view shared by MSP (OGC, 2011, p. 9).

The key for ad hoc programs is to clearly identify the vision and the mandate of the program as soon as possible, in order to be able to quickly identify the projects and other activities that are required to ensure its success and eliminate those that do not contribute to it. It is only when this is achieved that one can talk about program management rather than multi-project management.

3.1.3.3   Program outcome

One could ask the question: Why bother classifying programs into different types? The main reason researchers and practitioners try to categorize programs, or projects, is to understand their level of impact on the organization and choose the methods they will use to manage them, based on the type of activities the program needs to coordinate and the goal it pursues. P2M (PMAJ, 2010, p. 52) uses three labels for programs, based on a typical product development process of creativity, transformation and operation. In this second edition, I have decided to use a similar approach based on the typical strategic development decision process. I have relabelled program types as Strategic, Tactical and Operational (see also Figure 1.3).

Strategic programs can be developed either as a deliberate or ad hoc program, they aim to deliver medium-to-long-term benefits in support strategic initiatives that transform the organization or the way it does business. Their outcome is strategic or contextual and their focus is structural or cultural; they transform the way the organization does business or the way a community functions. They form part of the strategy implementation portfolio. Examples of such programs can include: from a business point of view: market repositioning, innovative product development, internal restructuring, regulatory compliance, organizational change, mergers or acquisitions or, from a social point of view: housing, health, change of measures system (imperial to metric), infrastructure and other governmental programs, or from a non-governmental organization point of view: disaster relief, pandemic disease control and human rights initiatives.

Tactical programs can often be managed as sub-portfolios and would usually be developed as an *Ad Hoc Program*. This type of programs is also labelled "large-scale system programs" (Shimizu, 2012, p. 11). They typically have a strategic outcome and structural focus, but are essentially of managerial, operational or technical nature; their level of uncertainty is typically high and ambiguity medium to low. The decision input for these programs is generally strategic, coming from a desire to improve business performance through organizational efficiency. These programs comprise projects managed together to increase tactical benefits, improve performance or deliver new business capabilities; they are part of the organization's project portfolio. Typically, they are medium-to long-term and limited in time, are reasonably predictable and focus on organizational efficiency. Examples include account management, developing and implementing a new ERP (Enterprise Resource Planning) system, marketing, or real estate development. Tactical programs are sometimes associated to complex projects, but generally comprise a number of different initiatives like technical development, conformity, training, that are all discrete projects and their objective is not to deliver a product, but tactical level organizational benefits. If the discrete projects within the program are strongly related, like the ERP example, they would be managed as a program or as a complex project, if the projects are not truly interdependent, as in the case of account management, they would be managed as a sub-portfolio.

Operational programs are not true programs. They are concerned with incremental improvement: the maintenance of the organization's performance through a mix of operations and small short-term projects. The main decision input to this type of program comes from operations and performance measurement; its main objective is to consistently improve performance.

This type of program would typically be part of the organization's operations portfolio. It would be considered a sub-portfolio of the organization's portfolio and managed as such. Examples include; a career development program, induction training, IT upgrading or facilities management. These programs are ongoing, generally highly predictable and focus on continuous improvement; their objective is the maintenance of the organization's performance through a mix of operations and small short-term projects.

Finally, some programs will evolve from strategic to operational over time. They go through more than one development stage during their full life cycle. Many strategic programs, whether they started as ad hoc or deliberate, end up in a state where most of the initial benefits have been achieved, but there are still many projects that need to be undertaken in order to fulfil their initial purpose. They can go through a tactical state before becoming decisively operational. This is often the case with large governmental programs, like Eurocontrol's Airport Capacity Improvement programme; the UK's Youth crime prevention programmes; Drought Prevention Schemes in Australia, the water management program for the State of São Paulo in Brazil or NASA's Space Shuttle Program.

In fact many of these programs have become ongoing over the years and have no foreseeable end in sight. They could be compared to continuous innovation of operational improvement initiatives. The risk in these large programs is either to lose sight of the mission and to invest program and project resources in activities that are essentially operational. After the initial delivery of strategic benefits, these programs should be managed as sub-portfolios, where a number of projects need to be coordinated to align with high-level requirements, but not as programs.

Let's just conclude by saying that operational programs are better managed as sub-portfolios. Tactical programs, depending on the degree of agreement on objectives, can be managed as sub-portfolios (agreed objectives), complex projects (negotiated objectives) or programs (emergent objectives). Strategic programs should always be managed as a program.

3.2   Program Maturity

The previous section explained how organizations deal with the management of multiple projects and when to use program management. This section examines the difference between single project management and program management.

3.2.1   PROGRAM MANAGEMENT MASTERY AREAS

A project manager should possess in-depth knowledge of a number of project related areas; a program manager masters a number of program-related subjects. Many authors now agree that project management focuses on outputs and is performance-based, whereas program management involves the realization of business or social benefits and is learning-based. This means that the process groups and knowledge areas that are valid for a project cannot be directly transposed to the management of programs. In particular, managing project interdependencies in a complex environment is not like managing dependencies between activities in a fairly predictable context and requires different approaches.

As my practice of program management increased in range and depth, I experienced the need to draw from a much wider range of disciplines than when managing projects. This is also the case for many of my colleagues, some of whom have written well-known papers on the subject (Pellegrinelli and Bowman, 1994; Duggal, 2001; Partington, 2000; Cooke-Davies, 2002; Reiss and Rayner, 2002). During my three years, as Chair of the PMI UK Chapter Corporate Council, a group of senior managers in project organizations, I have witnessed first-hand the shift from technical skills requirements to leadership skills requirements for senior project managers and program managers. In addition, it was made clear that program managers are asked to understand business and strategy. Recently the PMI has come to similar conclusions and is now promoting the concept of a "Talent Triangle" (PMI, 2015) as a key aspect of professional development.

Obviously each program is different, but this section is intended to give clients and practitioners of program management an indication of the services that can be part of the program mandate and program sponsors an indication of what to expect. It can be completed with the roles and responsibilities of the different actors of the program, which will be discussed further in Chapter 5.

In order to help organizations understand how to migrate towards a program framework, this section aims to clarify the differences and similarities between a project and program perspective. Table 3.1 puts in parallel the *PMBOK® Guide* Fifth Edition (PMI, 2013a) knowledge areas structure with corresponding program mastery areas. The objective is to enable sponsors and practitioners to better define the services of program management against that of the more familiar project management scope. In general the program mastery subjects are of a broader range than that of the project knowledge areas.

TABLE 3.1   COMPARISON OF PROJECT AND PROGRAM KNOWLEDGE AREAS

Single Project	Program
Integration Management	Strategic Decision Management
Scope Management	Objectives Management
Time Management	Pace Management
Cost Management	Resource Management
Quality Management	Outcome Management
Human Resources Management	Stakeholder Relationship Management
Communications Management	Communication/Marketing Management
Risk Management	Uncertainty Management
Procurement Management	Partnership Management (Value Chain)
Stakeholder Management	Stakeholder Engagement

3.2.1.1   From integration management to strategic decision management

The *PMBOK® Guide* Fifth Edition (PMI, 2013a) states that:

> *The Project Integration Management Knowledge Area includes the processes and activities needed to identify, define, combine, unify, and coordinate the various processes and project management activities within the Project Management Process Groups (p. 63).*

The *PMBOK® Guide* takes a decidedly *transactional* approach for project integration:

> *Project Integration Management entails making choices about resource allocation, making trade-offs among competing objectives and alternatives and managing the interdependencies among the project management Knowledge Areas (p. 63).*

This view enables project managers to concentrate on what they do best: achieving high performance of clearly defined objectives within set parameters. Project integration management is based on the development and implementation of a baseline project plan. This involves a deliberate and planned strategy and a control process against the baseline plan with the underlying expectation that things should go as planned.

Programs, because of their lower degree of predictability and higher number of stakeholders with decision authority, evolve in a more complex environment. Continually changing circumstances require a deliberate planned strategy combined with emergent unplanned strategies. The program manager must control against a baseline, but also be open to change regarding the achievement of the ultimate benefits. Whereas projects require a transactional approach, the emergent nature of PgM requires more of a transformational approach with a combination of both learning and performance processes. This process is ideally supported with a sound business case process where expected benefits are outlined from the start and achievability must be demonstrated as the program progresses.

In programs, one should rather talk of *Strategic Decision Management*, a cyclic, benefits-oriented process capable of dealing with emergent inputs and continually evolving circumstances.

3.2.1.2   From scope management to objectives management

The *PMBOK® Guide* takes for granted that there is a defined scope of work for each project and that it needs to be determined as soon as possible, ideally, before the project starts. Typically, the project deliverables are defined and subject to approval by the project sponsor or customer.

As shown in Figure 4.2 the PgM process requires the combination of different disciplines like strategy development, value management and/or business analysis with project management. These disciplines are used to reduce ambiguity by identifying and agreeing upon the business and key stakeholders' objectives and translating them into measurable critical success factors (CSF) that will constitute the scope of the program. Strategy development, value management and/or business analysis are also used as a learning framework to address emergent changes and ongoing stakeholder objectives' management.

P2M explicitly states that the purpose of the program is to satisfy the demands of multiple stakeholders to create value for the organization. MSP argue that a key aspect of program governance consists of clarifying stakeholders' needs, forming a vision and agreeing objectives while identifying benefits and changes. These two standards clearly link the program scope to the realization of value for stakeholders. The Third Edition of the PMI Standard for Program Management considers stakeholders as both influencers on the program execution and contributors to its definition; some of the statements used in the

PROGRAM CONTEXT   *61*

standard are: agree on sought benefits, commit resources and maintain buy-in. All these standards insist on the role of the program manager as a leader capable of dealing with influence, power, motivation and other political issues.

In mature organizations, the program manager is clearly the initiator or sponsor of a project. PgM cannot therefore be content with simply "defining and controlling what is and is not included" (PMI, 2013a, p. 105) when talking about scope, but must take an evolving, systemic view of the business and stakeholders' needs and expectations to develop a program that will fulfil the business' expected benefits. Each project, that forms the program, is prioritized on the basis of its value, a combination of its contribution to benefits (CSFs) and its achievability.

Therefore, in mature program organizations, one would rather talk of *Objectives Management*: the management of the strategic objectives, represented by its stakeholders expressed in measurable terms (CSFs) and prioritized, the sum of which constitutes the program's purpose.

3.2.1.3   From time management to pace management

One of the key characteristics of projects is that they have a beginning and an end, usually set by the sponsor(s). Activities' duration and critical path control are the essential elements of project time management. The project manager typically breaks down the project into activities that are individually estimated in terms of time and cost, then, by identifying dependencies, forms the schedule of the project. The schedule allows project managers to estimate precisely how long the project will last and at which point what activity will take place.

P2M states that: "A program is defined as an undertaking in which a group of projects for achieving the program mission are organically combined" (PMAJ, 2010, p. 51). Program managers must possess a clear vision of the overall pacing of benefits realization and of all the component projects of the program that will contribute to this mission. At project level, they must give their attention to only the project deliverables that directly contribute to benefits (CSFs) as well as to the interfaces/interdependencies between projects. MSP promotes the view of projects as a "black box" and the focus on only key inputs and outputs to be able to schedule projects according only to their dependencies. They advocate the development of a benefits map that shows how benefits relate to each other and to the projects, as well as a dependency network to clarify dependencies between projects. Sometimes a small project can be critical not for its intrinsic value, but because it is a synergist or enabler for other projects. The benefits realization plan is a milestone-based schedule detailing when the benefits are expected to be realized. In the case of programs, the beginning and, more so the end, are usually "fuzzy". Because of the evolving, organic and complex context of programs, program managers need continually to re-evaluate project priorities and benefits delivery. In a program, the dependencies between projects will continually need to be updated as regards changes in the environment. The program manager will focus on benefits milestones and projects' relative pacing. Pacing includes prioritization of actions based on interdependencies and benefits delivery. It must take into account early benefits, positive cash flow and maintenance of the motivation of stakeholders.

Mature program organizations will focus on *Pace Management* rather than simple time management. The program schedule is a milestone-based roadmap rather than a Gantt chart and includes interdependencies and interfaces. It concerns the management of relative project priorities in accordance with emergent inputs and "optimal" benefits delivery, focused on the benefits realization. The formalization of the program pacing enables the measured delivery of benefits that are directly aligned with the strategic objectives and can be regularly accounted for. This enables the Program Board to make focused changes that support overall organizational value and greatly reduces the number of unpredictable changes that are often dictated by political or short-term financial reasons.

3.2.1.4   From cost management to resource management

In a project, cost, like time, is usually a pre-set parameter.

> *Project Cost Management includes the processes involved in planning, estimating, budgeting, financing, funding, managing, and controlling costs so that the project can be completed within the approved budget (PMI, 2013a, p. 193).*

In a project, the budget is approved at the beginning and must be met. On the other hand, the program manager is involved in setting project budgets and is usually asked to justify, or "re-justify" the program funding on a regular basis. Constant and regular funding of the program in regards of potential changes and realignments is essential to its success and must take into account the successful achievement of benefits.

Additionally, a program's budget includes elements of support activities and investment in supporting structures, which go beyond a simple delivery process. Program managers need to build long-term relationships and partnerships with their stakeholders, who can be either providers or customers, sometimes both. The management of funding and cash flow is directly related to the quality of these "partnerships", which also involve an aspect of stakeholder relationship management, when securing human resources for the program and negotiating commitments. Program budgeting is prospective, looking towards the realization of objectives, as opposed to cost management that is retrospective, comparing to a baseline. Typically, it will be part of a sound business case approach that focuses on both financial and non-financial benefits and rely on a much wider range of resources than simply monetary resources. Mature program organizations will depend on a broad *Resource Management* approach to tackle the above concept. It involves the long-term management of all the resources necessary to successfully carry out the program and is closely linked to pacing management and the achievement of a business case. Whereas project costs are estimated against the intrinsic value of the project deliverables, program resources are assessed against the whole program's expected benefits and their overall organizational value.

3.2.1.5   From quality management to outcome management

Project Quality Management is concerned with two things:

1.   the quality of the *project management process*; and
2.   the quality of the *product* being delivered.

Quality management includes:

> the processes and activities of the performing organization that determine quality policies, objectives, and responsibilities so that the project will satisfy the needs for which it was undertaken (PMI, 2013a, p. 227). Whereas the project process is generally linear and can be planned from the start, the program process is cyclic and needs to continually be reviewed in regard of results. It is directly linked to the achievement of outcomes rather than to a step-by-step process. PMI (PMI, 2013b) talks about Adaptive Change during the process to achieve outcomes in changing circumstances. In terms of the product, in a project, the final result is described in reasonable detail at the initiation level and refined during the planning process. Product quality measures are put in place to measure conformity to

the product description. In a program the final result is developed during the whole process and the products are adapted in time to achieve outcomes. The outcome management process is based both on a high-level baseline and on the results obtained to achieve the outcomes as the program progresses.

Benefits are the key success factors of a program and stem from the delivery of outcomes, as the final result or product is the key success factor of a project. Outcomes are tightly linked to business objectives as quality is to scope in projects. In MSP program quality management "ensures that stakeholders are satisfied that their planned benefits have the best chance of being realized and will meet their expectations" (p. 131). Quality management in a program focuses on the achievement of strategic goals, and these may change during the course of the program.

Benefits, expressed in CSFs, are both the program's objectives and the means by which achievement is monitored. The program manager should aim to keep the focus on the outcomes that will generate benefits, not on the provision of new products or production capacity, which are but means to an end. *Outcomes Management* is the management of the business capabilities that will lead to benefits over time so that ultimate impact of project deliverables and production improvement correspond to expected benefits that are a direct contribution to the strategic objectives.

3.2.1.6   *From human resource management to stakeholder relationship management*

While the *PMBOK® Guide* 2000 took a wider view of human resource management, stating that:

> *[It] includes the processes required to make the most effective use of the people involved with the project. It includes all the project stakeholders – sponsors, customers, partners, individual contributors, and others … (p. 107).*

The *PMBOK® Guide* 3rd to 5th editions narrow this view to include only the organization and management of the project team, which is fine for the management of single projects. The 5th Edition states that: "The project team is comprised of the people with assigned roles and responsibilities for completing the project" (p. 255). In a project it is assumed that stakeholder management is mostly focused on communications. In contrast, stakeholder relationship management and the resolution of their differences to identify expected benefits is one of the key roles of the program manager. In programs, stakeholder relationship management is a two-way connection that involves contribution of the stakeholders to the program and, in certain cases, the forming of partnerships, the equivalent of team development in projects, but on a much larger scale and with much less formal power.

Leadership in programs requires a facilitating or negotiating approach, since many of the stakeholders possess more formal power than the program manager. MSP, for example, state that leaders:

> *influence and persuade stakeholders to commit to the beneficial future*
> *… including considering internal politics, individual emotions and*
> *motivations (MSP Pocketbook, pp. 18–19).*

Program mature organizations will display strong *Stakeholder Relationship Management* competencies and the systems to support it (see Figure 3.2).

3.2.1.7   From communications management to communications and marketing management

Both the *PMBOK® Guide* and PRINCE2™,1 the UK project management method, define communication management as the processes required to identify communication paths, frequency, methods and reasons (OGC, 2005) and to "ensure timely and appropriate planning, collection, creation, distribution, storage, retrieval, management, control, monitoring and the ultimate disposition of project information" (PMI, 2013a, p. 287). PRINCE2 suggests that when the project is part of a program, the lines of communication and reporting structure between project and corporate or program must be made clear and that the communication plan should be part of the project initiation documents, not the project plan. Contrarily to project management, information and data management is just one aspect of PgM communications. As confirmed in the PMI PgM Standard, program management practice has seen the emergence of a new and crucial aspect of communications in programs: *marketing*. The MSP identifies both communication and marketing expertise as essential skills to successfully achieve stakeholder engagement (p. 54). Marketing is more than just advertising; good marketing encompasses

---

1   PRINCE2 is a Trade Mark of the Office of Government Commerce, UK.

strategic integration and not only follows strategy but drives it (Schmetterer, 2003). MSP also states that communication activities should ensure, not only that stakeholders are kept informed, but also engaged. In business, marketing is described today as a central element of value creation and its activities include value identification, provision and communication. Personal experience and research demonstrates that well-marketed programs are much more successful than those which solely rely on communication management, as described for projects. An integrated marketing strategy, supporting stakeholder management and engagement is an essential element of program success. *Communication and Marketing Management* could be summarized as: developing an interactive communication system aimed at gaining stakeholders' support in terms of the strategy and delivery of the program benefits. It includes the identification of the needs and expectations (expected benefits), clarification and communication of the way in which they will be delivered and measured, and the ongoing communication of their monitoring and delivery. Both to maintain the stakeholders' motivation and to make quick and sound decisions when required.

3.2.1.8   From risk management to uncertainty management

Although the *PMBOK® Guide* (PMI, 2013a) states that "the objectives of Project Risk Management are to increase the probability and impact of positive events, and decrease the probability and impact of negative events in the project" (p. 309), the practice of risk management in projects is still mostly a threat reduction process. In a paper presented at the PMI Research Conference in 2000, Chris Chapman and Stephen Ward, from the University of Southampton, made a strong case for the use of the term *Uncertainty Management* for complex projects and programs. They promote a much broader view: "an iterative, learning approach to understanding uncertainty" (p. 416) and insist on covering both threats and opportunities as well as taking a broader organizational view of risk assessment and impact. I tend to support this view, not only based on their argument, but also because of the negative image associated with risks, as expressed by many management writers, among whom is Peter Drucker (1989) who often pointed out that effective strategies should be focused on maximizing opportunities, and action should not be based on risks, "which are merely limitations to action".

Programs are very similar to strategies in that they focus on opportunities and are complex, therefore limiting the predictability of outcomes. The practice of risk management in a project environment is first and foremost an aid to decision-making. Project risk management is based on statistical analysis and rational decision-making, which is particularly useful at project level because by definition projects are usually set in a foreseeable future and outputs are fairly predictable. Although a rational decision-making process, based on statistical analysis and relying on historical data, is excellent at project level, its validity diminishes for more complex levels of decision where the number of variables increase and ambiguity is higher, as in programs.

Recent developments in mathematics and research results of the last few decades clearly demonstrated the limits of traditional probabilistic approaches. This is all the more true at higher levels of decision-making where the number of variables rises and the time span considered is less and less foreseeable. In complexity terms, this involves a move from what is called the "known-unknowns", the uncertainties you can identify if you look hard enough typically project risks – to the "unknown-unknowns", the uncertainties and ambiguities that you cannot predict because they are related to the turbulence of the environment – typically program uncertainties.

3.2.1.9   *From procurement management to partnership and value chain management*

Whereas in projects contractual relationships are usually built on a short-term basis, often with the lowest bidder, in programs it is essential to develop and maintain long-term relationships, which are not necessarily contractual, but based on mutual needs. Many of the contractors, consultants and suppliers that, in a project, would only perform a specific task will, in a program, be involved in more than one project and generally commit to larger, longer-term contracts. This creates a different kind of relationship and the power often shifts from the contract manager (project or program manager) to the organizational level. Often, the program manager has to deal with procurement stakeholders (external and internal) who hold a lot of power and clout. Therefore the standard procurement relationship promoted in project management standards cannot be appropriate anymore.

As shown in Figure 3.2 on the next page, a program can be considered as a value chain, involving a number of different stakeholders to generate internal or external outcomes. A learning flow conveys the information from the customer to the suppliers and a performance flow enables value realization through a number of stakeholder relationships. Value chain management involves much more than managing relationships required to procure goods and services; it is an organizational level process.

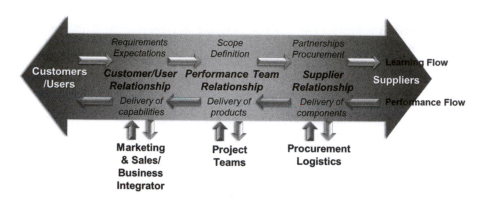

FIGURE 3.2   THE PROGRAM VALUE CHAIN

In fact, mature program organizations relate much more on *Partnership Management* than actual procurement management to acquire resources and support for the program from parties within or outside the performing organization. The ensuing relationships could be subjected to contractual agreement or not.

3.2.1.10   *From stakeholder management to stakeholder engagement*

Since project management has emerged a discipline, stakeholder management has been an issue. Until recently, stakeholder management consisted of acknowledging requirements and communicating through meetings and reports.

The new Knowledge Area of Stakeholder Management in the *PMBOK©️ Guide* Fifth Edition (PMI, 2013a) focuses on the identification of stakeholders and their management to create and maintain relationships that will enhance the project's success. Particularly, it is aimed at analysing the level of support required from stakeholders and ways to bring it to the desired level. It typically focuses on effective communication, building trust and minimizing resistance to change as well as facilitating agreement and consensus on objectives. This approach for project management is fairly recent and still needs to be integrated in practice.

Both the PMI Standard and MSP have a specific section focused on "Stakeholder Engagement", they state that the "leader must engage stakeholders so that benefits are identified, clearly communicated and understood, owned, and realized" (OGC, 2011) and that "the primary objective is to gain and maintain stakeholder buy-in for the program's objectives, benefits and outcomes" (PMI, 2013b, p. 45).

The objective of Stakeholder Engagement is to maximize the stakeholders' contribution to the ultimate delivery of benefits. The PMI® Standard for Program Management 1st Edition states that:

> the program manager must understand the position stakeholders may take, the way they may exert their influence, and their source of power.

The 2nd Edition adds that:

> where negative influence is possible, the program manager needs to ensure that the stakeholders see the benefits; something akin to marketing is often needed (p. 11).

The 3rd Edition states:

> Stakeholder engagement is a continuous program activity because the list of stakeholders and their attitudes and opinions changes as the program progresses and delivers benefits (p. 49).

As can be seen through these statements, stakeholder engagement has evolved from a reactive approach to a proactive and collaborative approach.

Important lessons can be drawn for program management from the Japanese approach which promotes full collaboration of all key stakeholders from the start and from agile methods that promote ongoing customer collaboration throughout.

3.2.2   PROGRAM CLASSIFICATION

In most of my consultancy mandates, the first thing I am asked is: "How can we distinguish projects from programs?" Over the years, I have used a number of qualitative approaches to answer that question and, from experience with a number of organizations, I have come to develop a more formal method to distinguish programs form projects.

The method is based on the distinction between project and programs described in Figure 1.3, which is based on predictability of outcomes and convergence of objectives. To this distinction I have added three additional factors that can distinguish programs from projects: Organizational span, level of change required and expected results. These five factors can be described as:

1. Convergence of objectives which measures the degree of *ambiguity* of the initiative:
    – *Agreed*: Alignment of stakeholders; typically few stakeholders; predictable interactions.
    – *Negotiated*: Likelihood or alignment; multiple internal stakeholders; predictable interactions.
    – *Emergent*: Challenged objectives; multiple internal and external stakeholders; unpredictable interactions.

2. Predictability of outcomes which measures the degree of uncertainty of the initiative:
    – *Likely*: Data/knowledge available enables to establish direct cause-effect relationship
    – *Unlikely*: Data/knowledge not readily available; indirect cause-effect relationship.
    – *Unknowable*: Unavailability of data does not enable cause-effect relationship.

3. Focus is the level at which the initiative is aimed. A wider focus increases the number of stakeholders and interdependencies between components, two factors that help distinguish a program from a project.
    – *Operational*: Typically focused on production within a business unit and does not require resources outside the technical area.
    – *Strategic*: Typically affects multiple business units and requires change in work processes. Requires resources coming from more than one sector.
    – *Contextual*: Spans the whole organization involving multiple business units. Typically related to competiveness and of strategic importance to the business.

4. Outcomes of programs generally affect broader areas of the business in more depth than projects:
    – *Technical*: Technical or operational deliverables.
    – *Structural*: Involves restructuring and new operational state resulting from the application of products or services.

- *Cultural*: Operationalization of new capabilities will affect the way people work together and require behavioural changes.

5. Level of change is a crucial factor that distinguishes programs from projects as a higher level of change management is required so that program outcomes actually deliver value for the business.
    - *Handover*: Simple handover of product to user or client. Some training may be required.
    - *Transfer*: Requires operational transfer activities such as piloting or testing of systems.
    - *Transition*: Full transition process over a period of weeks or months until benefits are achieved.

Each of those factors is set in a table and business initiatives are assessed on a scale from 1 to 3 to be classified as programs or projects. My experience is that this is best done by three distinct assessors to avoid skewing of results, typically:

a) the sponsor;
b) a representative of the PMO; and
c) a member of the portfolio management or strategy development team.

If the initiative's average score is between: 5 and 9 it is considered a project; if the score is between 10 and 15, it is considered a program.

TABLE 3.2   DISTINCTION BETWEEN PROGRAM AND PROJECT

Factor	1	2	3	Score		
				A	B	C
Convergence of objectives	Agreed	Negotiated	Emergent			
Predictability of outcome	Likely	Unlikely	Unknowable			
Focus	Technical	Structural	Cultural			
Outcomes	Operational	Strategic	Contextual			
Level of change	Handover	Transfer	Transition			
Individual scores						
Average Score						

3.2.3   MEASURING PROGRAM MATURITY

Over more than 20 years of practice and consulting with organizations worldwide, our organization has developed a program management maturity measure which enables us to identify areas of improvement and determine how to increase an organization's program maturity.

But, before introducing this measure, a few words of caution:

- The scores should not be taken at face value, but as an indicator of the areas that need improving.
- A detailed analysis should support any recommendation for enhancing maturity in order to provide a full picture of potential improvements.
- The analysis should include current methods, processes, as well as interviews of key program stakeholders at different levels of responsibility.
- The detailed analysis should identify areas of the organization that are more advanced and can be used as leverage.
- For better results, the analysis should cover all strategic initiatives, not simply initiatives that are labelled "program".
- Typically, mature project organizations score between medium and high overall but typically achieve such a score over a period of 5–10 years.

This measure has been developed on the basis of the Key Program Components (Elements 2, 3, 4 and 6) identified in the first edition of this book as well as the performance domains specified in the PMI Standard for program management (Elements 1 to 5) and implicit in the MSP Guide and P2M. In addition, I added decision and change management as well as organizational development and culture to the list of elements to be measured, following personal experience and consultation with colleagues.

The measure includes the following maturity elements:

1.   Strategic Alignment.
2.   Stakeholder Engagement.
3.   Benefits Management.
4.   Governance.
5.   Life Cycle.
6.   Decision Management.

7. Leading Change.
8. Organizational Development (including Cultural Issues).

Following completion of a questionnaire and following analysis, each element is scored on a scale of 0 to 5, 0 representing None and 5 representing Very High.

Element	None: Score 0	Very High: Score 5
1. Strategic Alignment	No program management.	All strategies executed through programs.
2. Stakeholder Engagement	Stakeholders not involved in program.	Key stakeholders involved in program on an ongoing basis.
3. Benefits Management	No benefits identification	Realization/sustainment of benefits part of the program scope.
4. Governance	Governance is focused on cost and schedule reporting	Governance board makes regular decisions in collaboration with Program Manager.
5. Life Cycle	Uses a simple review/ reporting system in lieu of a formal life cycle	Uses a cyclic program life cycle from needs analysis to value realization
6. Decision Management	Functional managers make most program decisions	Program manager has full authority on program. Consults PgM board
7. Leading Change	The program team executes a pre-approved plan	Transition and integration of change are considered part of programs
8. Organizational Development	Organization focuses on continuity and short-term value.	Focus is on transient competitive advantage and long-term value

The maturity measuring tool used in practice is much more detailed, but it is not the purpose of this book to describe this tool.

3.3 Practical Advice to Support Maturity Increase and Culture Shift

Most organizations are already undertaking program-like initiatives and just lack a formal methodology as well as a clear identification process as to what constitutes a program. Many elements of mature program management are often already in place, but distributed among different departments. The objective of any person aiming to improve program maturity in an organization or at a client's is to build on these existing elements to create a unified program methodology.

It must also be recognized that each business area will progress at a different pace towards the objective and that full maturity may not be required for all departments. One must identify internal stakeholders (typically the PMO) whose role it will be to define the required levels of program maturity and promote them using good practice methods and processes.

Most of the tools and processes that will be put in place to support the methodology should be initially applied at a lower level and their level increased as each area gains mastery of the process or tool. From experience, the major mistake managers make when implementing this type of process is to consider only the structural processes and tools and to neglect the need for culture change.

Within a program culture, project managers need to redefine their roles from tangible results managers to "tangible results-leading-to-business benefits" managers. Project managers will mature in this new role by redefining their respective projects in relationship to the overall program. Components of each project will be considered in respect to, and in comparison with each other – rather than in isolation, moving the locus of work to the program manager's level.

Depending on the organization's culture, program managers may come from the project or the management side of the organization. Organizations where program managers come from projects typically separate the definition, stage of the program from the deployment stages because project managers do not hold the necessary clout, understanding and authority to lead the initial part of the program. This is the view that more traditional organizations take. There is more fluidity between the stages in organizations that nominate business managers, or people who come from a management background, as program managers. Typically these people have the expertise to run the initial processes of the program and possess the necessary authority to deal with business stakeholders to define the program benefits. It is much easier to develop a strong, well-integrated program culture in such an organization.

My own experience, and that of many of my colleagues, is that the financial, chemical/pharmaceutical industry and government typically belong to the latter type of organization, whereas construction, IT and engineering firms typically belong to the former.

Simply transferring project management tools and techniques to the program level has led many program managers to frustration. These tools have been widely reported as inadequate to cope with the scope and complexity of program management and its need to continually adapt to a changing environment. Developing a program culture involves a shared understanding of the following objectives:

- Develop a common view and understanding of project and program management.
- Share program goals and objectives in order to focus around those goals and objectives.
- Develop program processes and procedures that are adapted to the program circumstances and to the organization.
- Develop project processes and documents that are meaningful to the project managers and useful to the organization.
- Define the contribution of each project to the program and identify the major elements of contribution.

This last point helps project managers take notice of their projects' ultimate objectives and focus on an integrated program approach, which has been an evolutionary tendency in project management practice in recent years, especially because of the interest of the project discipline in agile methods and business analysis. When coming into a new program, I typically ask each project manager to redefine the scope of their project in regards to its contribution to program benefits. I ask them to develop a "benefits-oriented" work breakdown structure (WBS) which is an extension of the program's benefits map. With a bit of practice, the "benefits-oriented" WBS will emerge as the key element of each project plan.

When coaching project managers to shift from a single project to a program culture, the following points emerged:

1. The project and program justification had to be clearly linked to the program's critical success factors (CSF) so that a common ground could be identified for all projects.
2. The list of stakeholders for each project was collated at the program level. Although the stakeholders' influence level and expected benefits varied from project to project, the overall list remained constant for all the projects.
3. We identified a need to clarify the contribution of the stakeholders to each project and to the program, not just the benefits of the program for the stakeholders.

4.   Once we distributed the stakeholder maps, stakeholders started identifying the need for interactions with other stakeholders, which was not obvious without the maps.

5.   We asked project teams to focus on the key deliverables that were directly linked to expected benefits. Milestones were set for each key deliverable and reporting was focused around these key deliverables/ milestones.

6.   Project managers were asked to identify key interdependencies between deliverables and between projects.

7.   The results of points (5) and (6) were then linked to the program's marketing and communications management plan in order to market the benefits to the stakeholders.

Figure 3.3 below shows the typical elements that should be included in any transformation program, like moving towards a program culture. In the transition stage, the goal is to establish the enablers, those elements that were discussed above and that will enable the organization to move towards a program culture. At the transformation state, the organization needs to measure the results and feedback to the enablers to modify them if required. This is an aspect of organizational change that is often neglected; organizations,

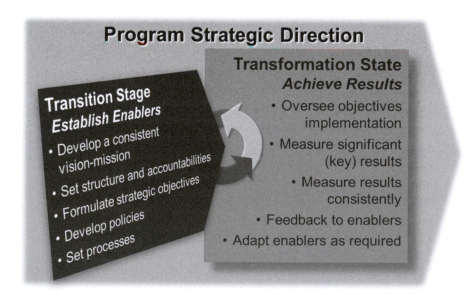

FIGURE 3.3   MATURITY DEVELOPMENT PROCESS

plan, execute and don't measure the achievement, or non-achievement, of their objectives.

The key element here is time. Sponsors of change typically want quick results; this does not happen in a culture change process. Changing culture takes time and requires a lot of sensemaking before it is acceptable. Sensemaking is the sum of interactions that enable individuals and groups to concur on the understanding of a situation, the clarification of its desired outcome and the consequences of the journey required to get there. A process of this nature could take anywhere from two to five years if it is to be sustainable, which does not mean that tangible results cannot be achieved before, but for the culture to be ingrained enough that it does not need a strong senior management support and a dedicated champion will take time.

3.4   From Program Maturity to Mastery

In this chapter, we examined the elements that make an organization mature in terms of its program management practice. Ideally programs should be deliberate, rather than ad hoc; we have seen that organizations that are project management savvy should also understand the essence of program management and how the two differ to become mature. In the next chapter I will discuss five key program functions: decision management, governance, stakeholder engagement, change management, and benefits management and how a good understanding of these issues will help both organizations and managers to make their programs succeed.

PART II
THE PROGRAM CONSTITUENTS

Part I has examined the context of programs and program management. It explained how program management is an essential tool for achieving strategic decisions, how program is viewed differently by different people and how program management became what it is today. It also outlined the relationship between programs and other components of the business and explained how developing project, portfolio and program management concepts can create synergy in the business and increase agility and competitiveness. Finally, Chapter 3 has described how a program culture can be developed and how organizations can increase their program maturity.

Part II examines the various constituents that make program management what it is. It builds on the concepts developed in Part I and explains in further detail what is required to manage programs effectively. In particular, Chapter 4 will discuss five key functions that can make or break a program. Program governance, stakeholder engagement and benefits management have already been identified as key aspects of a program, both in the literature and practice; this chapter explains how they will be most effective in a program culture context. The functions that have not been discussed as a key constituent of program management are change management and strategic decision management. Many books have been written on decision-making; most of them are based on research or theoretical enquiry and are aimed at graduate students and researchers. Many computer tools have been developed to help decision-making, but most of them are based on rational processes. This chapter discusses the steps required to make and implement decisions in a complex environment. As well, change management has always been seen as a soft skill limited to human resources, but in the last few years, it has developed as a true discipline aimed at implementing change successfully and sustainably. Chapter 5 concerns the roles and responsibilities of the different actors of the program. Both managers and practitioners will find their role described in detail, both in terms of the responsibility to lead and manage the key components and their role in each stage of the program's life cycle.

CHAPTER 4

Key Program Functions

In Chapter 3, we have seen how a program culture can be developed and how organizations can increase their program maturity. Chapter 4 explores five highly interdependent program functions and how they contribute to achieving program maturity and excellence:

1. *Decision Management* covers the making and implementation of strategic decisions;
2. *Program Governance* discusses the essence of governance and the different governance approaches;
3. *Stakeholder Engagement* lists the main program stakeholders and how they should be engaged;
4. *Change Management* consists of all the actions required to transform deliverables into benefits; and finally
5. *Benefits Management*, which is the core of program management, explains how to define, agree and deliver benefits through the program.

4.1   Program Functions in Standards and Guides

In its 3rd Edition, the PMI's *Standard for Program Management* identifies five "Performance Domains": Strategic Alignment, Benefits Management, Stakeholder Engagement, Governance and Life Cycle Management. The first four correspond to four of the functions I have identified inasmuch as strategic alignment is viewed as an active decision-making process rather than a passive alignment to an imposed strategy. Life Cycle Management is the actual management of the program activities, which I cover in Part III of this book.

In its 2011 version, MSP identifies seven "Programme Management Principles" that revolve around leading a major change in alignment with corporate goals. It also identifies nine "governance" themes, which could be compared to the PMI's *PMBOK® Guide* knowledge areas. They include some processes, some steps and some management functions. Strategic Alignment and Governance are key underlying concepts in MSP and Stakeholder Engagement and Benefits Management are two of the themes. Two aspects that deserve mention are the concept of leadership as an essential quality of program managers that is distinct from management and the concept of the program as a change leadership initiative, which is now well covered in the PMI's new *Managing Change in Organizations: A Practice Guide* (PMI, 2013c) and which I have included as a key function in this 2nd Edition.

The 2nd Edition of P2M of the Japanese standard views programs as an extension of the strategy into operations; they insists on a *Common View of Program Management*, which refers to the common understanding of program management that must be shared across the organization. P2M have identified four key program attributes: *Multiplicity* of context, *Scalability* by combination of a variety of elements, *Complexity* of interaction between components and, finally, *Uncertainty* from environmental changes. In order to deal with those attributes in an ever changing business context, they recommend that program activities be grouped under three key "platforms": *Organizational Strategy and Programs*; *Program Integration Management* (Mission profiling, architecture management and program execution management, including assessment of value) and; *Community Management*, which consists of creating a "common mental space where stakeholders communicate with each other [...] to create new values through concerted efforts" (PMAJ, 2010, p. 107). This latter element is really what distinguishes P2M from the two other standards/guides. P2M promotes the full engagement of all stakeholders throughout the duration of the program and is based on the empowerment of program human resources. This view is expressed in the networked governance approach further in this chapter.

4.2   Decision Management

Purposeful decision management has existed for as long as humans have roamed the earth. The concept of making a decision from a number of possible alternatives, implementing it and reassessing it in regards of results to modify it, if required, is as old as the human race itself. It is therefore surprising that the concept of decision management is quite new in literature. Many authors and researchers have written about decision-making, but very few have researched the implementation of decisions beyond the outlining of a process. Traditional decision-making literature is based on two central variables: the "efficiency" of the decision process (quality) or the "satisfaction" of the decision-maker with the decision (acceptance). Systemic decision-making literature is based on: the "group process" (participation). This limited perspective has reinforced the idea that, once agreed, a decision will automatically be implemented and resolve the problem. Reality is quite different as outlined by the recent trend of business and project management authors focusing on the "missing link" between strategy and results or the preoccupation that executives have with controlling execution because they often feel out of touch.

4.2.1   THE CONTEXT OF DECISIONS IN PROGRAMS

Increasingly, strategy is defined as "an integrated, mutually reinforcing set of choices ... that form a coherent whole [and that] can evolve and be adjusted on an ongoing basis" (Hambrick and Fredrickson, 2005). In such a context, decision management is intimately linked to maintaining the vision in a continually evolving context and, as such, it can be linked to PMI and MSP's strategic alignment, although the PMI Standard does not explicitly consider the turbulence of the program environment as part of strategic alignment whereas MSP clearly identifies "frequent changes of direction" as an integral aspect of aligning the program with a strategy (OGC, 2011, p. 17).

In Chapter 1, I have outlined the issue of uncertainty and ambiguity as a significant element in the decision to consider using program management. This section examines how the interdependent relationship between ambiguity and uncertainty, both of which were explained in Chapter 1, will affect the decision-making process and the implementation of the decision.

Whereas under low uncertainty decisions can be made based on accurate and reliable data; when ambiguity is high, decision-makers need to rely more on experience and intuition as the available data is often partial or unreliable. This situation requires a process where the results of decisions are continually measured and the objectives adjusted accordingly.

4.2.2   A DECISION MANAGEMENT FRAMEWORK

Figure 1.2 (p. 21) shows that program management is effective to manage change in organizations because it combines learning-based decision methods like value management, business analysis[1] or others (SWOT, Logical Framework, Soft Systems Analysis, etc.) and performance-based methods like project management, transition management and operations. Program management integrates learning and performance methods in a harmonized and coordinated way to combine both decision-making and decision-execution activities, into a full decision management process.

Figure 4.1 below displays this program decision management process. It is divided into two parts: the decision-making, or problem-solving part – a learning or analytical process, and the decision-execution part – a performance or action process. The learning part consists of identifying the need, stating the problem, generating alternatives and evaluating options and, finally, making a choice among the options. The execution part consists of planning and implementing the chosen solution(s), assessing (controlling) its results and recycling the data to realign the strategy, if needed.

Many studies have confirmed that projects often fall short because of their failure to provide sustainable business benefits to fulfil the stakeholders' needs or to align with the strategy; this focus on short-term financial results

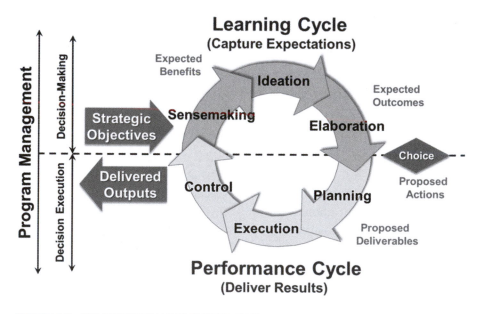

FIGURE 4.1   THE DECISION MANAGEMENT CYCLE

---

1   Whereas value management relies mostly on "soft" data analysis and translates it into measurable objectives, business analysis mainly relies on "hard" data that can be sorted to identify significant decision support information.

is exacerbated by the pressure to perform on the stock market, often to the detriment of long-term value maximization. This situation is definitely aggravated by the lack of understanding of the decision-making and decision management processes; especially the value creation aspect of the cycle and the need for ongoing appraisal and assessment of outcomes, based on the stated needs.

4.2.3   DECISION-MAKING

Many management authors argue that more detailed and accurate data increases the quality of decisions; whereas this reliance on hard data works in a low-ambiguity context, in complex situations, additional data can also increase complexity and ambiguity and therefore reduce the "quality" of decisions (Weick, 1995). Project management has been labelled as an uncertainty-reduction process (Winch et al., 1998) but, in its search for accurate data and predictability of outcomes, it often misses the complexity and ambiguity that is the feature of most organizational level decisions

In 1990, Henry Mintzberg defined a strategy development model based on the level of uncertainty. His model is interesting as it examines a context of decision-making very comparable to the uncertainty-ambiguity context displayed in Figure 1.2 (p. 21) and can therefore be easily related to programs. According to Mintzberg, a strategist/decision-maker operating in a low-uncertainty condition, where the rate of change is slow and complexity is low, will favour a rational decision-making model and use traditional decision-making tools. Under high uncertainty, when the rate of change is fast and complexity is high, rational decision models are not valid because data is not reliable and the situation changes too quickly, affecting the needs. Mintzberg suggests the use of a *radical model*, which consists of doing the best you can until the situation settles down. Although interesting, the radical model is not very helpful to managing programs. Since then, other authors, like Karl Weick (1995), have generated more advanced concepts like sensemaking and enactment, which rely on soft data. This approach consists of setting up a decision management system where key stakeholders take the time to discuss issues to agree a shared strategic vision and to make a series of small decisions on an ongoing basis in alignment with this vision. As the situation evolves, results are evaluated and new decisions are made that continually reinforce or realign the vision according to reality in a fashion similar to agile management. This is what I called a decision management system.

The project charter, or brief, and then the project plan create boundaries for single projects, which generates a low complexity environment. They could therefore be considered as either low uncertainty (low complexity-low rate of change) or low complexity – fast rate of change. In this case, decision-makers can rely on a rational decision process or use expertise to implement quick decisions based on realignment with the baseline plan. This is one of the reasons ill-defined projects often fail to deliver expected results when traditional methods are used.

On the other hand, programs are, in their essence, complex. According to Mintzberg, in cases of high complexity and low rate of change, which is typical of large-scale governmental or infrastructure programs, decisions are made in cooperation, so as to tap into the collective expertise of the team and make sure all the available data has been considered. Because it involves both stakeholder input and reliance on technical and operational knowledge, this process uses both soft and hard data. In this specific case, the rate of change is not fast, there is time to formulate the decision, and traditional decision tools can be used in an analytical approach. When the situation is both complex and fast-moving, traditional decision-making cannot be used, a sensemaking approach, producing mainly soft data, is the most effective in this case. The team would go through the steps of sensemaking, ideation and elaboration before making a joint decision to proceed with the implementation.

In Figure 4.1, the learning cycle represents a decision-making process. The first step, "sensemaking" relates to the need to make sense of the input that justifies the change. The second step, "ideation", consists of identifying as many alternatives as possible to increase the quality of the decision. The third step, "elaboration", consists of evaluating, combining and developing alternatives to create viable options from which to choose. and prioritizing these options. And, finally, "choice" is the action of selecting the best options. These steps will be examined in more detail in Part III, more specifically Chapters 7 and 8.

4.2.4   DECISION IMPLEMENTATION

The decision management process outlined in Figure 4.2 opposite shows how organizations are continually subjected to external or internal pressures to change (new competitor on the market, change of regulations, customer requirements, change in organizational structure, need to increase performance, new technology, etc.). These pressures, combined with the corporate strategy to stay competitive, generate ideas, problems or opportunities that the

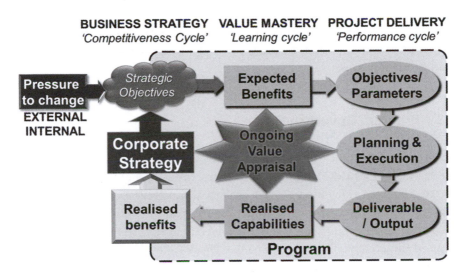

FIGURE 4.2   THE DECISION IMPLEMENTATION PROCESS

organization must transform into clear strategic objectives. The first step of the decision management process consists of clarifying these strategic objectives, which can stem from a SWOT analysis, a stakeholder needs analysis, or other methods. This step initiates the program definition process and will define its purpose. These high-level needs and expectations are then refined into agreed and measurable expected benefits that will lead to clear component project objectives; parameters are developed, based on the organization's means.

Based on this data analysis, projects are selected and undertaken to produce deliverables and outputs which will eventually lead to realized outcomes and increased capabilities. Sadly, most organizations stop at the project delivery stage and do not assess the business benefits of their projects. Mature program management has the capability to define and deliver appropriate strategic outcomes and to appraise project deliverables on an ongoing basis to assess ultimate outcomes at organizational level. It will also ensure that deliverables transform into added capabilities to produce benefits that will ensure that the program purpose has been achieved and the pressure is relieved. Program management is also a process by which strategic decisions can be evaluated on the basis of their actual results and strategies can be reformulated, based on these evaluations. This is the process described in Chapters 7 and 8, which cover the development of governance systems, appraisal system and measures of success (Chapter 8) as well as the delivery of project outputs and assessment of benefits (Chapter 8) and finally, evaluation of outcomes, change management and management of knowledge (Chapter 8). In the light of this perspective, program management can be seen as a strategic decision management process.

4.3   Program Governance

Governance is currently one of the most misused terms in the business. Since the scandals of WorldCom, Enron and others, the advent of Sarbanes–Oxley in the US and its worldwide spread, governance is mostly associated with disaster prevention, risk mitigation and consequently, tighter control. Legal issues of corporate responsibility are the main driver for the systems put in place to support this narrow vision of governance. These systems are stifling innovation and creating an oppressing culture in organizations where everybody feels that they should protect themselves rather than contribute to value creation, whereas a sound governance system is one of the most effective means for executives to communicate the purpose of the organization and ensure that results will match this vision.

The Organization for Economic Cooperation and Development in "Principles of Corporate Governance" states that:

> Corporate governance ... provides the structure through which the objectives of the company are set, and the means of attaining those objectives and monitoring performance are determined. (OECD, 2004, p. 11)

This view is shared by many prominent organizational authors; however, most organizations still focus on the monitoring and conformance process and neglect the forming of the mission and setting of objectives or the means of achieving the objectives and actual performance improvement aspects of the governance mission.

In parallel, the debate around governance theories is centred on two main perspectives: (a) the shareholders' perspective, which typically focuses on short-term financial performance, and (b) the stakeholders' perspective, which focuses on a wider range of long-term organizational measures. Recently a small group of authors advocated the idea of governance for "long-term value maximization" through innovation and intangible assets. In September 2006, Alfred Rappaport, the originator of the shareholder value concept (Rappaport, 1986) wrote in *Harvard Business Review*:

> *[...] despite SOX and other measures, the focus on short-term performance persists [...] Management's responsibility [...] is to pursue long-term value maximization [...] (Rappaport, 2006, p. 68)*

The fact that the initiator of the shareholder value concept makes such a statement shows that the short-term focused shareholder perspective is, albeit slowly, losing ground.

So, how does this affect program management? The mechanistic culture of organizations supports a shareholder approach of governance that favours short-term profit over long-term investment. It also favours a bottom-up approach to governance, focusing on controlling rather than the setting of objectives or putting in place the means of achieving these. The single project approach takes for granted that the sum of the parts is necessarily equal to a meaningful whole; in today's complex business environment, nothing is further from truth. In a recent study report on lost value by Booz & Co (Dann, Le Merle and Pencavel, 2012), the authors identified this bottom-up approach as flawed. They point out to the fact that teams are made accountable for results over which they have no control because they are not given the necessary authority to question decisions beyond the narrow business context to which they are confined. This controlling standpoint promotes a single project approach where monitoring is exercised precisely, but with a limited view, whereas a mature program approach can support the development of a clearly articulated, meaningful strategy and its realization.

4.3.1   GOVERNANCE PROCESS

Organizational purpose is what defines the long-term mission and objectives of the organization; it is influenced by legal issues and ethics, the organizational context and culture, as well as by its stakeholders. The most obvious manifestation of the organizational purpose is governance, which is the way significant components of the firm are organized to achieve the mission and how they are coordinated to deliver strategies (Dallago, 2002). The same can be said of program governance, which is a subset of corporate governance and ensures that the program purpose is well defined and achieved.

De Wit and Meyer (2004, p. 595) define three main functions for governance:

1. *Forming*: influencing the forming of the corporate mission.
2. *Performing*: contribute to the strategy process with the intention of improving the future performance of the corporation.
3. *Conforming*: ensure corporate conformance to the stated mission and strategy.

Program governance therefore consists of the three following responsibility streams:

a) developing the program vision and objective, based on the business strategy and stakeholders' needs;
b) putting in place the right structures and allocating the resources necessary to achieve the vision;
c) setting up appropriate monitoring and control systems to make the right decisions and realign the program if necessary.

These elements are discussed in more detail in Part III.

4.3.2   CONTROLLING APPROACH

Unfortunately, in the last 20 years, most organizations have focused on the "Conforming" aspect of governance: the collection, analysis and reporting of performance metrics, with the stated objective of ensuring visibility and control of services deemed necessary to do business. It is often focused on the management of service providers and vendors. In program management, this approach has often emphasized the gap between program and operations and programs are often isolated from the rest of the business, focusing on a traditional delivery role akin to that of project management, as seen in Figure 4.3.

Let us just say that it emphasizes the horizontal split between strategy and the delivery of program benefits In this case, the PMO will typically encompass a resource allocation and monitoring as well as a control role. The program office will focus on the inner program administrative and support tasks. This view, which characterizes the current focus of many large public corporations, was that promoted in the second edition of the PMI's PgM Standard.

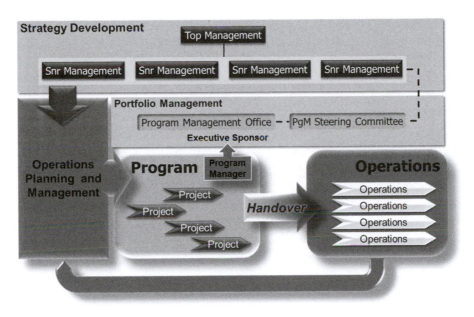

FIGURE 4.3   TRADITIONAL CONTROL-BASED PROGRAM GOVERNANCE STRUCTURE

4.3.3   INTEGRATED APPROACH

As stated above, three responsibilities govern the role of a program governance body:

a) Maintain direction (clarify vision, mission and strategy). This is a leadership role typically played by top management and portfolio and line management.

b) Put in place the structures necessary to ensure success (secure resources, define and support policies, processes, roles and responsibilities, arbitrate conflicts, etc.). This is a sponsoring role. This is the combined role of portfolio management, program and change management.

c) Make sure the stated objectives and benefits are achieved (control and monitor, evaluate and approve change, read and feedback on reports, etc.). This is a monitoring role. Responsibility for this role lies with the program manager and the business integrator.

In program management this translates through a collaborative process, which emphasizes constructive relationships rather than directive relationships.

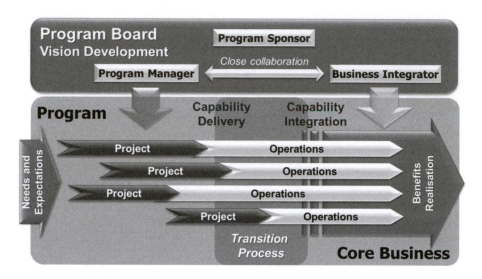

FIGURE 4.4   INTEGRATED PROGRAM GOVERNANCE STRUCTURE

Typically this approach will privilege a harmonization effort between program manager(s) and business integrator; the latter's role being to prepare the organization for change. This approach is displayed in Figure 4.4. This is the view promoted by the UK Guide: Managing Successful Programmes (OGC, 2011) and the PMI's third edition PgM Standard (PMI, 2013b) and Managing Change in Organizations (Practice Guide (PMI, 2013c).

This type of approach emphasizes the need for a strong collaboration between the program team and the business to deliver operational capabilities and requires an ongoing involvement of the program team in the actual benefits realization. If there is a program office, it will support the whole end-to-end process.

4.3.4   NETWORKED APPROACH

Recently a number of management authors have argued that governance focuses too heavily on facilitating the optimal utilization of existing productive resources and the sharing of residual wealth, but does not take into account processes by which resources are increased or transformed. Authors from various fields also claim that one of the major problems concerning the failure to deliver value lies with the mismatch between objectives and stakeholders needs and expectations, usually identified as benefits. In today's context, stakeholders are represented by a number of individuals or parties who exhibit different and sometimes conflicting interests. Rather than imposing tight controls, a value creation perspective of governance should focus on maximizing innovative capabilities and building sustainable relationships and trust with stakeholders.

The networked approach presented in Figure 4.5 represents a structure which fosters collaboration between the different stakeholders, through a number of "governance forums", to create and realize value. It involves a close-knit partnership between all parties to the program.

The networked approach is not easy to implement because it often requires a cultural shift that most organizations are not ready to accept. This view involves input from societal, technological and cultural actors to develop the vision and mission of the program and the support of structural, functional and operational actors to execute it, with strategy defining the execution and vice versa in a continuous loop of learning and performing. It also means that leaders empower rather than delegate and all parties take direct responsibility for their actions. The culture of such an approach is based on collaboration and sharing of information and knowledge in order to create value.

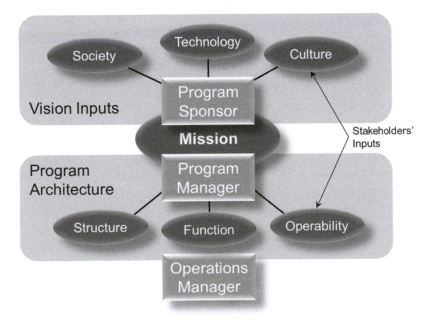

FIGURE 4.5   INTEGRATED PROGRAM GOVERNANCE STRUCTURE

P2M, for example, proposes the establishment of a program "community" based on an agreed context, creativity, collaboration, active communication, quality contents and concentration (PMAJ, 2010, p. 107). Its authors propose four principles of integration: "zero-based thinking" (thinking without preconception); "flexibility to changes"; "collaborative competence" and; continual and precise "value assessment" (PMAJ, 2010, pp. 59–60).

This view challenges the traditional Western view that strategy can be planned and executed, based on objective and simplified judgement of a situation; it takes into account the complexity and turbulence of today's business environment. More and more, this type of approach is gaining ground in concepts like "Agile Organizations" and "Intrapreneurship".

4.3.5   THE PROGRAM GOVERNANCE FRAMEWORK

In the integrated and networked approaches of governance, the business case is expected to focus less exclusively on financial predictions and more on improved organizational effectiveness and/or social outcomes, whether or not these improvements can be expressed in financial terms. In this context, programs sustain a value creation perspective, supported by innovation and empowerment; they focus on maximizing opportunities rather than reducing threats. Program sponsors also seek a wider set of success criteria and a drive towards sustainability over short-term results and, overall, develop an increased focus on the link between expected benefits and results.

If the goal of the organization is to use programs to be more flexible and dynamic in a highly turbulent and competitive context, management will look towards new product development and value management techniques to maximize the effectiveness of their investment and of their decision process. In the last five years, I have successfully put forward the concept of a tiered business case process (see Figure 4.6) inspired by innovation strategy (Moss-Kanter, 2006). With this process, a large number of potential programs and projects can be identified and examined at the portfolio level. An idea is submitted by its initiator to the potential sponsor or line manager. If they deem it worthwhile, they allow the person to spend a minimal time (a few hours to a few days) bringing it forward to the concept stage, which is re-evaluated by the sponsor or a sponsor group and then included in the portfolio for analysis. If approved, the formulation stage of the program is launched and the initiator develops a preliminary business case that is submitted to a potential program board. This Program Board evaluates the potential of the concept to support the strategy

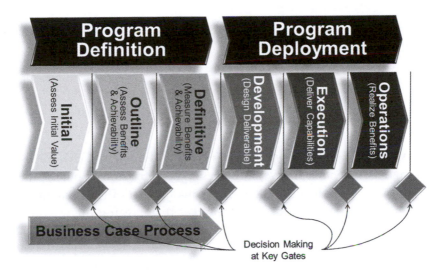

FIGURE 4.6 TIERED BUSINESS CASE AND GOVERNANCE PROCESS

and, if it is acceptable, they ask the initiator to prepare a detailed business case, drawing on all the required organizational resources (see Figure 7.1, p. 146). This method enables the portfolio and/or program team to look at a much greater number of innovative ideas without spending inordinate amounts of resources. Creativity and innovativeness are encouraged within the team and sustainability is ensured because many of these ideas come from the users. The business case process will be discussed further in Sections 7.2.6 and 8.1.3 (p. 165 and p. 179).

Research and practice have shown that it is very difficult to "kill" a project once it is accepted and resources are allocated to it. The APM Portfolio Management SIG (Special Interest Group) claims that:

> *Killing off a project is often viewed as "failure" whereas, in contrast, the PfM SIG sees it as a successful management action … terminating projects as early as possible are key measures of success.*

So, following the approval of the project, other stage gates are set that will enable the portfolio management team or program board to re-examine the value of a component project against expected benefits as they unfold. If deliverables and capabilities are well defined in measurable terms and intermediate deliverables are identified, the program team will be able to measure the progress toward that achievement of the business benefits. It then has the means to realign or stop the project if it is deemed that it will not achieve its stated objectives, or if the objectives change and the project deliverables are not required anymore. The PMI Standard promotes a similar view in their "Phase-Gate Review" process (PMI, 2013, pp. 59–60).

4.4   Stakeholder Engagement

A PWC survey from a few years ago (PWC, 2009) showed that CEOs see customers and clients as the "key influence on their decisions about the success of their business in the future" but, "information about their customers' and clients' preferences and needs" is perceived as their greatest information gap. This is still a frequent situation, therefore the importance of "good" stakeholder engagement.

The stakeholder concept was first used in a 1963 internal memorandum at the Stanford Research Institute. It defined stakeholders as "those groups without whose support the organization would cease to exist" (Freeman and Reed, 1983). A current generally accepted definition of stakeholders is: individuals or groups that can be positively or negatively affected by a process or its outcomes and have the potential to influence them.

Stakeholders' engagement is often confused with stakeholders' analysis. Whereas stakeholders' analysis consists mostly of identifying the different stakeholders, their influence and their needs in order to improve communications and understanding, stakeholders' engagement consists of the identification and analysis, influencing and engagement, and, finally nurturing and realignment of the different stakeholders and their needs. Whereas traditional business analysis may collect available hard data about the stakeholders, the goal of stakeholder engagement is to uncover, process and manage soft data about the stakeholders in order to understand how to influence their behaviour and gain their continued support for the program. Figure 4.7 displays this view and outlines the different processes that will be discussed further in Chapters 7 and 8.

Program level stakeholder engagement is not just about managing pre-set processes, but about influencing people and building rewarding relationships. Always think of stakeholders' engagement as a two-way street: what do you need from the stakeholder and what will you offer to them that they value? Figure 4.8 offers an example of a stakeholders' map that includes both the stakeholders expected benefits (expectation) and their expected contribution to the program. When such a document is shared with the stakeholders, it acknowledges the joint commitment between the program team and the other

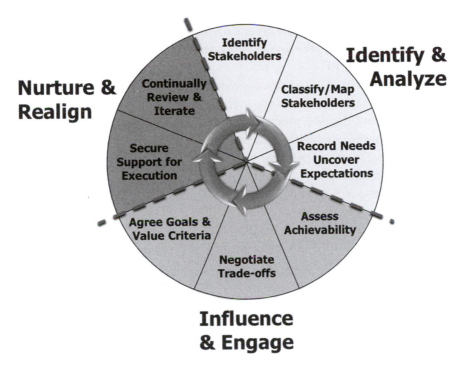

FIGURE 4.7 STAKEHOLDER ENGAGEMENT LOOP

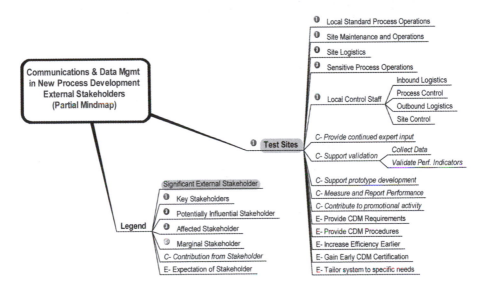

FIGURE 4.8 EXAMPLE OF STAKEHOLDER MAP INCLUDING CONTRIBUTION AND EXPECTATIONS

stakeholders, which enables the development of a sound and clear relationship. The use of the stakeholder map will be discussed further in Sections 7.2.2 and 7.2.3 (p. 150 and p. 152).

One of the issues of program stakeholder engagement is the level of authority that program stakeholders can have over the program manager. Both MSP and the PMI Standard describe processes by which stakeholders can be influenced and ensure that they are positively involved in the program. Both standards reject the word management to replace it with engagement, "because stakeholders do not like to be managed" (OGC, 2011), and insist on a process that will take into account perceptions, fears and concerns and focuses on the right message, rather than on the right method. As mentioned earlier, P2M promotes the creation of a program community focused on "collaborative competence".

As can be seen in Figure 4.9, most of the program stakeholders possess more authority than the program manager. Some of these stakeholders can even perceive the program as a threat to their authority. This requires that the program manager be able to take a facilitating, rather than an authoritative, approach to leadership, understand the organization's culture, speak the business language and be familiar with organizational politics.

FIGURE 4.9   MAIN PROGRAM STAKEHOLDERS

4.4.1   PROGRAM STAKEHOLDERS' ROLES AND EXPECTATIONS

The number and variety of stakeholders can vary greatly from program to program. Figure 4.9, identifies the typical stakeholders of most programs.

This diagram is adapted from the EFQM's Business Excellence Model (2001),[2] which outlines the key organizational partners for business excellence. This section describes the relationship that needs to be developed between these stakeholders and the program.

4.4.1.1 Top management

Top management is responsible for corporate governance. Their role is to establish the corporate vision, the purpose of the organization, and the strategy to achieve it. As such, they will exercise the required leadership to ensure that vision and strategy are clearly communicated to the rest of the organization. They are also responsible for ensuring that the necessary resources are available to implement the corporate strategy.

They will expect the programs to align with this vision and strategy and to put in place the necessary systems and processes to ensure that governance requirements are met. In order to achieve this, they will generally rely on line, or business unit, and portfolio managers.

4.4.1.2 Portfolio and line managers

Business unit or line managers are generally responsible for developing the business strategy. The business strategy is a subset of the corporate strategy. It is the organization's response to changes in its external environment: competitors, regulatory bodies, market, customers, technology, shareholders, etc. and its internal environment: personnel, restructuring, research and development, culture change, new technologies, etc. In that sense, the business strategy is much more dynamic than the corporate strategy. They are expected to define the policies, systems and processes that will support this strategy and allocate the necessary resources to support them. Portfolio managers share the resource allocation role with the line managers; they are also expected to coordinate the use of resources across the organization and ensure the alignment of the programs with the corporate strategy. Both the line and portfolio managers are often asked to lead program steering groups, committees or be part of the Program Board.

Programs are a direct response to the need to implement the business strategy, achieve a societal purpose or a cultural change. As such, the program team is expected to support the sponsoring group's strategy by

---

2   Available at: http://www.efqm.org/efqm-model/model-criteria.

delivering new capabilities and providing benefits that will provide value to its stakeholders.

4.4.1.3   Customers

Customers, whether internal or external, are at the core of the program management process. The ultimate purpose of the program is to create value for the customers. Customers can generally be divided into two categories: the sponsors (including external clients) – those that pay – and the users (including beneficiaries, and change recipients) – those that utilize. In many programs, sponsors and users are at odds with each other and one of the roles of the program manager is to try to reconcile these differences. This is the negotiating aspect of the stakeholder engagement process. Sponsors of programs are generally business unit managers or external clients; as such, they are responsible for providing the program team with clear objectives and expected benefits that are achievable and measurable. Users are expected to understand budgetary requirements and adjust the scope of their demands accordingly. Often, though, their priorities differ from those of the sponsors and prioritizing and realigning needs to available resources can be a demanding task.

Program managers are repeatedly required to play a facilitating role between different users and the sponsors to balance alignment with expectations and achievability of the program. It is the responsibility of the program manager to alert the sponsor to any discrepancy that may arise from the diverse stakeholders' demands and their consequences for the program. Once the expected benefits are agreed and their achievability has been established, it is the responsibility of the program manager to deliver them and that of the sponsors and users to review and approve them in a timely fashion.

Sponsors are also responsible for approving changes to the program and are generally required to coordinate change demands from the different users before passing them onto the program. Program managers have a responsibility to evaluate the consequences of changes on the program and to communicate them to the sponsor.

4.4.1.4   Human resources

Human resources can include both the program team and other personnel such as users. Users have already been addressed; let us now turn our attention to the program team, including project managers. The program team is expected to execute the tasks they were made responsible for and deliver the products or services they have committed to.

One of the key aspects of program management is that it is usually longer-term than project management and therefore constitutes a larger commitment on the part of human resources. In order to keep their team motivated, the program manager should make sure that the different resources involved understand how the program constitutes a career opportunity for them, or if they are users, how it will benefits them. This can be done in collaboration with the human resources department and, if the organization is based on a matrix structure, with their direct line manager.

4.4.1.5   Partners

Relationships with partners are often guided by legal agreements. Mutual expectations and obligations are well defined in a contract and the means to ensure that these are fulfilled clearly stated. This section discusses the relationship beyond the contract and looks at two specific procurement approaches that enhance the long-term relationship required by programs.

Partners can include both business partners and suppliers. Business partners usually share similar expectations as the sponsors and are bound by the same type of obligations towards the program. The suppliers can include contractors, consultants, and goods and equipment suppliers; again here, the key point to remember is that a program is a longer-term relationship than a project. Instead of focusing on the lowest bidder approach, the program team should focus on building long-term, mutually beneficial relationships. These relationships need to be set early, as partners could be asked to contribute to the development of the business case for the program. Because programs are complex, they can be difficult to estimate precisely and only the people that are directly involved in its delivery may possess the right supporting data. If one uses selected partners to help with the business case and there is a possibility that they be involved later in the program, it is often useful to consider two levels of request for proposal in a program: the first for a consulting mandate during formulation and organization and the second for the deployment stage, where the suppliers involved in the first phase are invited with others to submit a new proposal. This is a method used regularly in the oil and gas business and known as front-end design.

Another useful procurement approach in program management is the "framework contract", which is designed to allow a client to invite proposals from partners to carry out work on a "demand" basis over a set period of time. Because the program is complex, needs are not always well defined during the initial phases and changes will occur on a regular basis. The framework contract enables the program manager to react rapidly to unexpected situations without having to repeat the whole, and often lengthy, procurement process. It also encourages the development of longer-term relationships with the best partners.

4.4.1.6   Regulatory bodies

Many organizational activities are undertaken for conformity reasons; these activities are usually mandatory and therefore offer little room for interpretation. Whole programs or only some program activities are sometimes subjected to regulatory requirements. Usually, regulatory requirements are not negotiable; in many cases they are also subjected to tight deadlines or milestones. Regulatory stakeholders can be external, like governmental bodies, health and safety officers, quality certification bodies or others, or internal, like finance, procurement or quality auditors. When regulatory stakeholders are involved in a program they usually require that the program and its deliverables conform to issued rules and regulations. Their role is to ensure that the latest and updated rules and regulations are available for the program. The role of the program team is to confirm adherence of the program to those rules and regulations and prepare the necessary reports to gain certificates of conformity, if required.

4.4.1.7   Community

Whereas most organizations' operational departments and most projects do not have to deal with the community, many programs, because of their scale or focus, have to involve community stakeholders. Community stakeholders are usually part of the user group or their representatives, like NGOs (Non-Governmental Organizations), charities, political entities, pressure groups, sometimes supported by the media, and often governments, especially local governments that can play three stakeholder roles: sponsor, regulatory and community. Typical user groups are the staff of the company and the external community – residents, users and consumers.

   This group finds itself very interested in the outcomes of the program, but often has little authority to enforce their views, except through their organized representatives. It is the role of the program team to communicate regularly with these stakeholders. Although they cannot always be fully satisfied, regular consultation and communication explaining why the program is managed in a particular way and how its outcomes will affect them will generally produce positive feelings and often result in collaborative behaviour. On the other hand, when they are not consulted and if communication is deficient, they will quickly find ways to organize into pressure groups that will gain power and potentially derail the program, even if they were originally positive towards it. People who resist change are not always negative and whenengaged, they can prove invaluable in finding viable alternative solutions. The key word here is "respect".

4.4.1.8   Program and project managers

Program and project managers are at the core of the program stakeholders' dynamics. Program managers accept the responsibility for delivering the program benefits. Depending on the structure chosen to manage the program (see Figures 4.3, 4.4 and 4.5) the program manager will be responsible for the development of the program concept, ongoing realignment, delivery of project outputs, program benefits, business value, or all of these. The program manager would be right to expect full collaboration and openness from the key stakeholder, especially sponsors. The program manager will also act as the sponsor of the projects within the program. This may cause friction if some of the projects already existed before the program and were initiated either by line managers or other senior managers. Section 7.2.4 will establish the importance of the critical success factors to manage this issue. The program manager would also logically be responsible for the allocation of resources, human, financial and other, within the scope of the program. Again this may cause friction where the organization is more traditional or set up as a matrix.

Project managers are mainly responsible for delivering the expected project deliverables. Additionally they must understand their role as team members that need to collaborate for the program's success. This is not easy because, traditionally, project managers are isolated in a single project role approach and have a strong performance focus. Project managers need to ensure that interfaces and interdependencies with the program and between projects are identified; they also need to report on their key deliverables to the program manager. In return, they could expect the program manager to be fair and act as a buffer between the higher-level stakeholders and their projects. Their role is to deliver on time and on budget – that of the program manager is to manage the stakeholders' needs and expectations, expressed as scope and quality on one side and time and cost on the other. It is not the role of the project manager to set these variables and they would be right to expect clear parameters from the start.

4.4.2 STAKEHOLDER ENGAGEMENT PROCESS

The stakeholder engagement process is so integrated in the program management life cycle that it cannot be discussed independently. It will be covered in detail in Part III, and particularly in Chapters 7 and 8: Definition. However, at this point it could be useful to outline its main steps.

4.4.2.1 *Identify stakeholders (see also Section 7.2.2)*

The stakeholder identification consists of identifying as many programs' stakeholders as possible, working first at the group level, then down to the individual level for key stakeholders. It is necessary to identify subgroups or individual stakeholders only if it is believed that their needs and expectations will be significantly different from the rest of the group or that their level of influence on the program can be major.

4.4.2.2 *Classify/map stakeholders (see also Section 7.2.2)*

There are many methods to classify or map the stakeholders; typically they are first mapped in a "Stakeholder Constellation" or stakeholders map. They are then classified by power level (preponderant to affected party); level and area of interest (financial, technical, regulatory ... or structural layer (regardless of direct influence) or a combination of these.

Following this first classification, the program team identifies the "key" stakeholders of the program; those that will be most involved in the program decisions. One of the most popular methods of stakeholder classification advocated in management books is the "Influence Grid" or "Power/Interest Matrix", originally developed by Mendelow in 1991 (see Figure 7.2); this is the method promoted by the PMI in their standards. It measures power level and level of interest, both positive and negative and classifies stakeholders in four categories from key to marginal. Another interesting method is the "Social Risk Assessment" that measures the level of resistance and level of instability of each stakeholder and then the quality of their interaction and the level of control you have on this interaction. The resulting grid classifies the stakeholders from positive and reliable stakeholders to uncontrolled and negative stakeholders.

4.4.2.3   Record needs and uncover stakeholders' expectations (see also Section 7.2.3)

In the project management world, needs and expectations are considered as two separate issues. Most project management books and manuals define a need as an explicit requirement, whereas typically, expectations are undefined requirements. On the other hand, the European Value Management Vocabulary Standard defines needs as: "what is necessary for, or desired by the user ... A need can be declared or undeclared; it can be an existing or potential one" (BSI, 1997). As failure to satisfy stakeholder needs and expectations is one of the major causes of project failure, program management, like strategy, cannot afford to consider only existing and declared needs, but must also strive to uncover undeclared and potential needs, usually labelled as expectations.

This involves determining both defined and undefined stakeholders' requirements; at individual level for key stakeholders and group level for others. In order to ensure success, benefits and expectations must include and consider both hard benefits (economic, technical, operational, etc.), usually disclosed, and soft benefits (power, politics, communications, etc.), often undisclosed. Soft benefits cannot always be expressed openly for political reasons, but they have to be acknowledged by the program management team. Expectations may be assumed; if this is the case, these assumptions must be documented and communicated to the concerned stakeholders to elicit a reaction which will either confirm that the assumption was right or that it needs to be revised.

4.4.2.4   Assess achievability – negotiate trade-offs – agree goals and value criteria (see also Sections 7.2.3 and 7.2.4)

Once the needs are identified, their achievability is assessed against resource availability and capabilities, these can include financial, human, time, and more intangible aspects like readiness, competence, expertise, etc. Any discrepancy is identified and trade-offs negotiated with the different stakeholders. In this case the classification effort becomes valuable because, as it is impossible to fully satisfy every stakeholder; obviously, the key stakeholders have more weight than the marginal ones. The objective is to make stakeholders aware of the consequences of their choices and to find solutions that will satisfy as many of them as possible. Value management, practised according to the European Standard BS EN 12973: 2000 (BSI, 2000) can be an essential element of this process because of its focus on the group decision process. Following these negotiations, the program sponsoring group, business integrator and program management team agree on the program's goals and the benefits it is expected to realize. These are generally expressed in qualitative terms as critical success factors (CSF) and their quantitative subset, key performance indicators (KPI). The process required to define expected benefits and select CSFs is discussed in detail in Section 7.2.4 (p. 157).

4.4.2.5   Secure support for execution – continually review and iterate (see also Sections 8.1.1 and 9.2.1)

As the program team implements actions (projects, operational and support activities), it will make sure stakeholders stay committed to the program's objectives. The team will reassess the relative status of stakeholders as it may change over time and new stakeholders may appear. Some of the needs may change or disappear and new needs may appear, either in regards of market changes, technology development, social transformation or other factors. The team will therefore actively aim to identify any change in stakeholders' needs and expectations, especially those that are based on assumptions and will make sure that continued support is maintained for the program. As a rule, stakeholder engagement is an ongoing process and the stakeholder analysis and engagement process should be reiterated regularly.

4.5   Change Management

As the role of project and program managers expand, change management is becoming an essential aspect of the management of programs and projects. The creation of change management professional associations and the publication of a change management guide by the PMI have established change management as a function to be considered in program management. This is especially true in the context of programs extending their traditional scope to include the transition and integration of capabilities into the business.

4.5.1   WHAT IS A CHANGE MANAGEMENT?

Change management can be defined as:

a comprehensive, cyclic, and structured approach for transitioning individuals, groups, and organizations from a current state to a future state with intended business benefits. (PMI, 2013c, p. 7)

Change can be desired or not and the scale of change can range anywhere from continuous improvement to radical transformation. In the organizational context, change is a combination of behavioural change, from incremental to fundamental, and structural change, from minimal to extensive. Projects and programs do not usually include unplanned change: whether it is radical transformation caused by unpredictable, often external, events or continuous improvement triggered by the need for better operational performance. Project and program management essentially cover planned change, in which both the degree of structural and behavioural change can be reasonably managed. Figure 4.10 below displays this relationship between change, projects and programs.

Change processes and approaches can vary. From a theoretical point of view, project management can be associated to life cycle change management: "a linear and irreversible sequence of prescribed stages" (Van de Ven and Poole, 1995, p. 514), whereas program management would be more associated to Teleological or Goal-Based change management process: "recurrent,

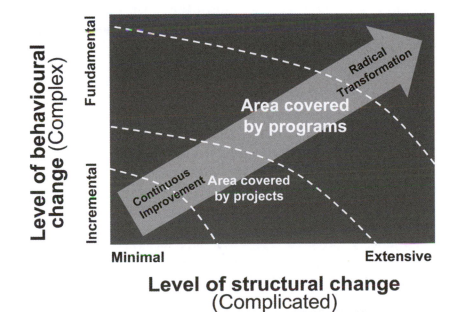

FIGURE 4.10   AREA OF CHANGE COVERED BY PROGRAM MANAGEMENT

discontinuous sequence of goal-setting, implementation and adaptation of means to reach end state" (ibid.).

4.5.2 MANAGING CHANGE

The management of change essentially covers three areas in program management:

1. the management of the change in regards of the context;
2. the mastery of the change process during the course of the program; and
3. the management of adaptive changes to the program.

Change management is the joint responsibility of the program manager and business integrator. It is good practice to set up change agents' groups to alert the program manager and business integrator to any issues regarding change.

4.5.2.1 The change context

The Change Management Institute (CMI) define change in relation to its broader context: "Change in organizations can have wide-ranging implications. Change must be understood thoroughly for it to be successful" (CMI, 2013, p. 37). It explains why program managers need to have a good understanding of change management. The analysis of the organization's readiness and the pacing of the program have a direct impact on the successful implementation of change.

The pace of the program is directly related to a good understanding of the program within the greater context of change. Program cycles are defined according to the client or own organization's readiness for change and the urgency of the change (see Section 8.1.3.1). The higher the readiness for change, the bigger the scope of each cycle can be, the longer the cycles and the shorter the periods of integration are. If the readiness is low, cycles should be shorter with longer periods of integration and a smaller scope for each cycle (see Figure 8.6). This approach should also be balanced with the urgency of the change to ensure maximum success.

As stated above, change can be expected or unexpected, the purpose of change management activities is to reduce the amount and impact of unexpected change. It has been shown that sensemaking is an important aspect of successful change management (see Section 10.1.1.2). Another requisite of successful change is to provide enough time to absorb the change.

4.5.2.2 Change mastery

The purpose of change activities is to support business integration by ensuring full acceptance and sustainability of the program benefits into the business.

In coordination with the business integrator, the program manager identifies any integration activities required to ensure full sustainability of the benefits during the preparation stage of the program. During deployment, the program team conduct change management activities (information and decision meetings, interviews, and workshops in addition to communication, training, coaching, and consultation) in order to ensure that the change can be sustained. They monitor the transition and integration process to identify any resistance to change, change of pace in delivery of benefits, perception of benefits value, level of performance, or change in priority of CSFs. If necessary they plan and implement additional activities.

In addition to the component transition and change management activities, the program may need to include some operational activities like: service management, user engagement, customer support, operate and transfer or others. These activities must be clearly identified at the planning phase of components, or in the preparation phase of the program. The risk of not identifying these activities is to invite scope creep.

The program manager and business integrator, or client, negotiate the activities required to ensure sustainable change. The sponsor approves them and the program team executes them.

4.5.2.3 Adaptive change management

This process concerns the management of controlled and emergent changes to the program. It includes the monitoring of the program context (technology, business and market) and key stakeholders (sponsors, clients and change recipients) to identify any potential change early. The process consists of gaining agreement from key stakeholders on objectives and expected benefits of the change and applying the agreed scope change process.

In a program context, change should be viewed as an opportunity to respond to new situations, not as a threat to the baseline. Change can be planned or unplanned, the purpose of change management is to reduce the negative impact and maximize opportunities of any unplanned change. The program manager is responsible for the wider impact analysis and for approving changes that are within the scope of the program, the program sponsor and integrator are responsible for approving changes that impact the scope of the program.

4.6 Benefits Management

In Section 4.4 (Stakeholder Engagement), I outlined the process required to identify needs and expectations. The benefits are the tangible improvements that will fulfil those needs and expectations. Benefits management is complementary to stakeholder engagement; only a good stakeholder engagement process will enable the identification and realization of significant benefits.

4.6.1 WHAT IS A BENEFIT?

First, we need to define what a benefit is. The PMI® Standard for Program Management states: "Programs and projects deliver benefits by enhancing current capabilities or developing new capabilities that support the sponsoring organization's strategic goals and objectives" (PMI, 2013b, p. 34). It defines a benefit as: "an outcome of actions, behaviors, products, or services that provide utility to the sponsoring organization as well as to the program's intended beneficiaries" (PMI, 2013b, p. 165). Managing Successful Programmes defines a benefit as "the measurable improvement resulting from an outcome perceived as an advantage by one or more stakeholders, which contributes towards one or more organisational objective(s)" (OGC, 2011 p. 75). In layperson's terms, a benefit is a positive outcome that stems out of the use of a product or capability; it is an outcome of the execution of the strategy. P2M focuses on overall value rather than benefits. Benefits are simply seen as value indicators representing the values of the different stakeholders of the program. It is the role of the program team to balance the stakeholders' values and increase the overall value the program will provide.

Financial benefits are generally expressed as cost reduction, cost avoidance or revenue uplift. They include, but are not limited to, reduction of maintenance costs, capital investment, unit price, number of required units; avoidance of required work, equipment purchase, resource hiring; or any combination of the above. Every financial benefit needs to be easily monitored and expressed in monetary value. For example, "performance improvement" is not a financial benefit, except if there is a direct traceable cause-effect relationship between performance improvement and cost reduction, cost avoidance or revenue uplift.

Non-financial benefits are all the benefits that cannot unambiguously be put in the financial benefit category. In a program context, non-financial benefits must be measured. For example performance improvement could be measured through number of additional units produced, reduction of processing time, client satisfaction, social impact or other similar measures (see Section 7.2.4 for discussion on performance indicators).

In program management, benefits are tangible improvements that contribute to the overall value of the organization or have a positive social impact. Benefits are aligned with strategic objectives but are always measured at operational level. There may be negative outcomes, drawbacks, stemming from the implementation of the program, but there is no such thing as a negative benefit and, in that sense, I would disagree with MSP's use of the term "disbenefit" in program management, even if, from a dictionary definition point of view, the term may be right.

4.6.2   IDENTIFYING AND SELECTING SIGNIFICANT BENEFITS

One of the difficult tasks for the program team is to identify what should be considered as benefits and to establish a hierarchy from the purpose and strategic objectives of the organization to the delivery of new products or capabilities to enable the measurement of the benefits that have been achieved. This is the purpose of the Benefits Map which will be discussed further in Section 7.2.2.3. The benefits identified as such in the benefits map are derived from the stakeholder analysis and, ideally, every "expected benefits" expressed by the stakeholders should be identifiable in the draft Benefits Breakdown Structure (BBS) (see Section 7.2.2.3); some at lower levels and some at higher (corporate or business) level. The reason for this is to get buy-in from the stakeholders. Ultimately, the final BBS will elicit only the benefits that have been agreed.

4.6.2.1   *Functional-based versus technical-based specification*

Many organizations still use technical-based specifications to describe the program "product". By definition, a technical specification describes the product in detail and offers little opportunity for transformation or innovation. By contrast, the functional specification is performance-based; it describes what a product or capability is expected to do rather than how it should be built and offers more opportunity for creativity and innovation, but requires more involvement from the stakeholders in the decision-making process.

A program, being subjected to ambiguity, should be defined by its expected benefits and described in functional rather than technical terms. There would generally be three types of benefits to describe: value improvements (increase or maintain competitiveness), performance improvements (business as usual and operational), and social improvements (culture and society).

The PMI uses the concept of program vision to describe the future state that is envisioned at the end of the program. It is a high-level framework of the objectives and intended benefits of the program (PMI, 2013b, p. 28). MSP uses the concept of the "blueprint" as the detailed description of the future capabilities of the organization described in the vision statement (OGC, 2011). P2M (PMAJ, 2010) uses the concept of *Common View*, which involves high stakeholder engagement to share and agree envisioned values for the program. All three organizations promote the use of a vision document throughout the program to maintain the focus on the expected new capabilities delivery. My experience is that many programs are defined by capabilities described in technical terms too early in the process. The program's strategic objectives should drive the benefits definition and component projects should be described through their expected benefits at the program level; technical specifications should be defined only once stakeholders' requirements have been agreed at program level. In the process outlined in Figure 4.6, any project, product or capability specification is described functionally until the end of the business case process. It is only at the development stage that the design team use the detailed functional specification to describe the product in technical terms.

The blueprint is based on the achievement of benefits and described in functional terms, at least until the end of the definition stage, and ideally into the development stage. This method enables the program team to achieve maximum flexibility for the technical or operational aspects of the product, including benefits/cost ratio, and enhance its ability to respond to changes in the market or stakeholders' needs and expectations. Section 7.2.5 (p. 162) develops the concept of blueprint in more detail.

4.6.3   BENEFITS MAP AND BENEFITS BREAKDOWN STRUCTURE (SEE SECTION 7.2.3.3)

In 2008, for the third year in a row, a CIO magazine survey (CIO, 2008) identified project alignment with the strategy as CIOs' number one management priority, whatever their position, and integrating systems and processes as their number one, or two, technology priority. Value management offers a powerful technique called function analysis that can be used to link a rather abstract vision to measurable outputs and ensure the alignment of the firm's actions with the strategy (Thiry, 2013).

Function analysis consists of identifying the "functions" of a product rather than its technical components to focus on functionality rather than features and then to classify them using the function diagramming technique, which is based on a "How-Why" logic. In organizations, the benefits are synonymous with the functions in a product; by putting the focus on benefits, rather than products, the team makes sure that the strategy will be supported and that products correspond to a real need. For its use in programs, Thiry (2004) has labelled the function diagramming method: benefits breakdown structure (BBS). MSP (OGC, 2007) uses a similar methodology that they labelled the benefits map. PMI describes "benefits mapping" as a variant of the benefits register. The term benefits map is probably more familiar to people with a management background, whereas BBS would be more familiar to people

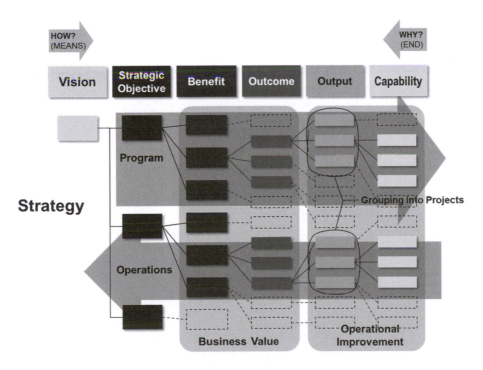

FIGURE 4.11   BENEFITS MAP/BENEFITS BREAKDOWN STRUCTURE CONCEPT

with a project background. MSP does not include the "how-why" logic in their description of the benefits map. The use of the "how-why" logic in the classification of the benefits helps remove some of the subjectivity and politics involved in the prioritization process. Figure 4.11 on the previous page shows the concept of the benefits map/benefits breakdown structure.

Within this framework, the vision is implemented through strategic objectives, which, in turn, are implemented through benefits, and so on until the deliverables of projects and other actions produce measurable outputs that enhance capabilities. Capabilities are measured at operational level. In the reverse order, new capabilities produce outputs that, in turn, produce outcomes, which contribute to business benefits, strategic objectives and, ultimately, to the vision. Note that outputs are grouped into projects for management purposes and become project deliverables.

4.6.4   ASSESSING THE BENEFITS

Business organizations aim to make a profit, or to increase their revenues, their objective is typically to invest as little as possible to reap the highest possible benefits. Social organizations aim to increase wealth or satisfaction of communities, they are less concerned with financial factors but will aim to measure environmental, ethical or societal impact. I outlined, in the previous section, the importance of identifying and classifying benefits in accordance to their significance for the achievement of the organization's strategic objectives, whatever they are.

4.6.5   REALIZING BENEFITS

Benefits realization is the fundamental purpose of program management. Benefits cannot be realized if the actions that enable them are not achievable. Achievability assessment is discussed in detail in Sections 7.2.6.2 and 8.1.2 (see p. 167 and 179). Benefits can be measured only after the new capabilities that the program is providing are implemented, therefore benefits appraisal is an operational level process. There is usually a delay between the delivery of the individual project outputs and the benefits assessment and often the responsibility for realizing the benefits is not clearly outlined between the program manager and business integrators, business managers or sponsors. In organizations that are not mature, program managers are accountable for the coordinated management of projects and therefore for project deliverables but are not accountable for the operationalization of the benefits. On the other hand, business integrators, managers and sponsors do not feel accountable for any failure to integrate the project deliverables into the business and often blame it on outstanding work or omissions of the projects, mostly if they were not fully involved in the program process. Without a clear responsibility assignment benefits are likely not to be realized fully. For a more detailed discussion of the roles of program actors, see Chapter 5 (p. 117).

4.7   From Program Mastery to Function Mastery

In this chapter, we have examined the five core functions of program management: decision management, governance, stakeholder engagement, change management and benefits management. These five functions describe essential concepts that distinguish program management from other management methods. In the next chapter, I will aim to clarify how the different program actors can contribute to program maturity and support the program in these five core areas and at each stage of the program.

CHAPTER 5

Program Actors

In the previous chapters, we looked at different views of program management, at the program management context, at how to structure programs in different contexts and finally at the key functions of a good program. This chapter describes the roles of the main program actors for each of these program functions and the role of the program manager at each stage of the program. I will take a broad view of those roles and responsibilities by encompassing the views promoted by different organizations.

5.1   Roles and Responsibilities

It is essential to acknowledge the full range of interests of stakeholders in the success (or failure) of the program. The successful conclusion of a program, or its realistic termination, is highly dependent on negotiations between those interested stakeholders, especially when changes are necessary. A significant amount of the stakeholders' interactions will take place at the interfaces and in the interdependencies between projects, therefore the recognition of their roles and responsibilities at these points becomes particularly significant.

Both MSP and the PMI Standard define a number of program stakeholders. I have extracted eight roles from these standards. These correspond to roles that I and my colleagues encountered in our practice. Table 5.1, on the following page, defines these roles. Most roles are similarly described in both standards, albeit with different designations.

The role of the Executive Sponsor (PMI) or Sponsoring Group (MSP) is clearly defined as championing the program initiative and providing the investment decision and top level endorsement.

The PMI attributes the responsibility of ensuring that program goals are achieved to the Program Sponsor and Program Governance Board; MSP labels these roles as responsibility of the Senior Responsible Owner (SRO) and Programme Board. Practice shows that either the individual or the board can

TABLE 5.1 MAIN PROGRAM STAKEHOLDERS AND THEIR ROLES

PMI (2013, 3rd Ed)	MSP (2011)	Role
Executive Sponsor	Senior Responsible Owner (SRO)	The individual with executive ownership of the program and overall responsibility for ensuring that the program meets its strategic objectives.
Program Sponsor	Sponsoring Group	The individual or group who champions the program initiative, provides resources and is ultimately responsible for benefits.
Governance Board	Programme Board	The decision-making group responsible for ensuring that program goals are achieved and providing support to the SRO/Executive Sponsor.
Program Manager	Programme Manager	The individual(s), responsible for the set up, leadership and management of a program as well as delivery of new capabilities
Program Management Office (PMO)	Programme Office	The function defining and managing program processes and providing central administrative support program mgmt teams
Program Change Manager (Integrator*)	Business Change Manager (BCM)	Person(s) responsible for benefits realization by ensuring the implementation and embedding of new capabilities delivered by the program.
Project Managers		The individuals responsible for managing the individual projects within the program
Customer		The individual or organization that will use the new capabilities/results of the program and derive the anticipated benefits.

have that responsibility and that the choice of one or the other depends on the delegation of authority in the organization and the seniority of the Sponsor/ SRO. In any case, either the board, collectively, or the individual that exercises this role are required to have a thorough and broad understanding of the organization and to work hand in hand. MSP states that the Programme Board is appointed by the SRO who has full authority over it. In the book, I will use the PMI term Program Sponsor.

The Program Management Office (PMI) or Programme Office (MSP) has an administrative role to provide support to the program. Typically, this involves management of program governance processes, procedures, templates, reporting or other similar activities.

Because MSP was initially developed for government work, it identifies the business change manager's (BCM) role mainly as that of an internal customer. PMI separates the role of the Program Change Manager from that of the customer. In PMI's view, the customer is viewed more as a sponsor, an important stakeholder independent from the core team, who defines the needs and validates the program's outcomes. The Program Change Manager is mainly responsible for the transition activities that will lead to full integration of the program outcomes into the business. I have decided to use the term Business

Integrator (BI)[1] for this role, in alignment with the label used in the new PMI Practice Guide: *Managing Change in Organizations*. My own experience, and that of many of my colleagues, brings me to promote the role of the business integrator, business sponsor and customer as intimately linked in order to ensure a successful integration of the program outcomes into the organization. This approach challenges the traditional "Command and Control" view of most organizations, but is necessary to ensure successful transition and integration of benefits. It aligns with the Networked Governance perspective presented in Section 4.3.4.

The project managers are described as stakeholders only in the PMI Standard. MSP attributes the responsibility of appointing the project managers and the authority over them to the Program Manager, which is more effective from a program point of view. If this authority is not clearly defined, it becomes very difficult to run the program. I will elaborate on the detailed role of the project manager in Section 9.1 "Capabilities Delivery."

In the rest of the book, I will primarily use the PMI terms as my experience and that of my colleagues is that they are more widespread and therefore more pertinent for a worldwide application, including that of the business integrator (BI) as an essential role in the success of a program.

Table 5.2, on the following page, presents some more specific responsibilities for each of the roles previously described within a number of program functions. I have integrated the customer's role with that of the BI and therefore will not describe it in detail. When customers are external, the relation is essentially subjected to contractual arrangements. I will not cover the role of the Project Manager either as it is well described in standards like the *PMBOK® Guide* (PMI, 2013a).

In a commercial or consulting environment, program managers will also have a sales role. Since they already manage and influence stakeholders' expectations they can help build or maintain strong and effective client relationship. Good program managers will participate in client/sales meetings, making sure they know the customer's account and understand the customer's strategy. In a Not-For-Profit environment, they will participate in stakeholder groups' meetings and make sure they understand their needs, issues and concerns. They are proactive in identifying emergent project opportunities early by using current projects to uncover future needs. They will verify that needs are clearly defined by clarifying existing expectations and uncovering

---

1   Another label that could be used for the business integrator could be that of Capability Integrator, especially in Not-For-Profit organizations.

TABLE 5.2   SPECIFIC RESPONSIBILITIES OF MAIN PROGRAM ACTORS

Process	Executive Sponsor	Program Sponsor	Program Manager	Business Integrator	Program Office
Outcomes	Define Direction of Business	Own the vision (Champion)	Deliver integrated capabilities	Realise, embed benefits	Administer and support
Governance	Endorse, advise C-Level	Accountable governance arrangements	Define governance framework	Compatibility of new capability	Process quality control
Investment	Provide investment decision	Secure investment	Manage program budget		Financial accounting
Definition	Program Mandate	Program Charter/Brief, Business Case	Plan & design program	Prepare organization for change	Set up monitoring and reporting
Deployment	Approve vs strategic objectives.	Maintain alignment	Ensure overall integrity & coherence	Monitor outcomes vs predicted	Tracking & configuration management
Risks & Issues	Assess business risks	Manage strategic risks	Manage program risks	Manage operational risks	Risk and issue tracking
Change Management	Define change framework	Lead change process	Initiate change activities	Measure change impact	Control change process
Benefits Appraisal	Continued commitment and support	Commission and chair reviews	Demonstrate results and progress	Optimise timing of release	Health checks
Closure	Confirm success and sign-off	Ultimate accountability for outcome	Ensure meeting of requirements	Lead transition management	Control dissolution process

expectations that their organization can fulfil and then, help the customer/user develop their requirements to initiate new projects that support the program manager's organization's capabilities.

Accomplished program managers will also improve their team's career development opportunities by ensuring that the core team members gain satisfaction from their role, recognizing their contribution and allowing them to gain valuable experience.

5.1.1   PROGRAM RESPONSIBILITY STRUCTURE IN TRADITIONAL AND INTEGRATED ORGANIZATIONS

As a growing number of organizations are adopting project and program management as a way to manage strategic initiatives, organizational structures are evolving to accommodate a project approach. Most organizations maintain a traditional siloed and controlled approach though, and do not use all the capabilities that a project/program approach can offer. In particular, they clearly separate the project functions from the operations and focus on the management of a "handover" period to integrate the capabilities that projects deliver. No wonder then that many research studies show that projects are not well integrated. These organizations typically use an ad hoc program perspective where projects are defined before the program is formulated, therefore losing the opportunity to integrate the program outcomes and the project outputs in the business. Figure 4.3 displays such a structure. On the other hand, a mature and well-integrated organization will use all the flexibility and dynamism that a project and program approach can generate. The program board will consist of the sponsor, program manager, business integrator and business managers that are concerned by the change that the program brings about. As the members of the program team will be responsible for the realization of the benefits, they will ensure a good integration with the operations. The operations users, under the guidance of the business managers, will prepare the business for the new capabilities that will be delivered and give constructive feedback to the program team. In this sense, the program will become like the value chain described in Section 3.2.1.9. This approach is more effective when using a deliberate approach, but can also be achieved with an ad hoc program if there is a firm dedication to the success of the business and a commitment to an end-to-end process that spans business units or departments. Figure 4.4 graphically depicts this situation.

In the next three sections, I will discuss the responsibilities for realizing benefits, governance and stakeholder engagement; each of these will be further developed in Part III.

5.1.1.1   The responsibility for realizing benefits

A number of organizations consider that it is the responsibility of the program manager to deliver benefits to the business, but this requires authority over the resources necessary to do so. MSP recommends that the Program Manager be responsible for delivery of capabilities and governance of the program, the "Business Change Manager" (MSP), or Executive Sponsor (PMI), being responsible for the benefits realization and integration in the business. The full collaboration between organizational managers and the program manager is essential for successful benefits realization since one of the main reasons for using program management is to integrate the horizontal strategic decision management process. MSP recommends the formation of a Program Board, which may compensate for this gap, but many programs do not require the increased overhead that comes with it. The PMI Standard, makes the following statement:

> *The program manager, in collaboration with the customer/sponsor,*
> *agrees and secures resources to undertake the component transition*
> *activities. (PMI, 2013b, p. 87)*

It views the equivalent of the Business Manager as the customer or executive sponsor, who then has only an approval role.

In our experience the traditional handover process is not really effective for programs that deal with organizational change, and the role of the program manager should extend beyond the delivery of project outputs. The ongoing collaboration of the program manager and the business integrator is essential, but the program manager should take the responsibility, and be given the authority to realize the benefits. When programs involve major organizational change, the role of business integrator is essential in preparing the organization for the change and maintaining the right level of performance, which the program manager usually does not have the authority to do.

In cases where the program manager does not have full authority over the transition and integration process, the business integrator should be involved as much as possible in all program decisions from the start to support the program manager. In any case they should work as a cohesive team.

5.1.1.2   The responsibility for governance

Both the PMI Standard and MSP recognize that the governance of the program needs to be embedded within the corporate governance system. The MSP defines overall program governance responsibilities as the design and approval of, and compliance with the corporate controls, governance strategies and assurance reviews. Although MSP has a program definition phase, in their processes, they focus on the compliance and control aspects of program governance. The 3rd Edition of the PMI Standard defines governance activities as defining, authorizing, monitoring and supporting the program controlling the program and its strategy. This view is aligned with the approach described in the previous chapter for program governance (Section 4.3.3). P2M insists on the development of the program vision as part of the program process; although they don't specifically outline governance processes, the whole program process is based on team consensus and strong support from management. The APM (Association for Project Management, UK), in their *Guide to Governance of Project Management*, identify four components to project governance:

a) portfolio direction;
b) project sponsorship;
c) project management effectiveness and efficiency; and
d) disclosure and reporting (APM, 2004).

Only efficiency, disclosure and reporting concern control. Direction concerns leadership; sponsorship is a mix of leadership and support and effectiveness is related to strategic alignment; in that sense they are close to the view of governance outlined in the PMI Standard and in this book, which shows a growing alignment of concepts.

This is not meant to say that the conformance aspect of program governance is not a required and essential part of the process, but emphasis should also be on setting the program purpose and objectives and ensuring that the means to realize value are in place. In fact the P2M life cycle closely follows the concept of three main functions for governance "forming-performing-controlling" as defined by De Wit and Meyer (2004) (see Section 4.3.1) with the first three phases focused on defining and sharing the vision and the last two on performing and conforming (see Table 6.1).

Often strategies and strategic objectives are communicated in ways that are not clear and leave a lot to interpretation. Setting strategic objectives involves that the person responsible exercises leadership by consulting with the main stakeholders to identify their needs and expectations to define what constitutes value for them. This is a sensemaking process that is defined in P2M as "acquire a common view" and "understand common view". The management of the sensemaking process is typically the role of the sponsor, who can delegate it to the program manager when they have enough clout. Following this process, the sponsor will need to formulate and clearly communicate the program strategy in measurable terms; this is usually done through the program mandate which is clarified in the business case. When a Program Board is set up, the Program Board may take up this responsibility.

Management has to commit, not only to clear, measurable objectives, but also allocate the necessary resources – financial, human, technical and time – to achieve them. The sponsor and Program Board have a responsibility to use their expert knowledge to assess the achievability of these objectives and correct any discrepancies. They bear the responsibility to provide the program with the necessary resources to deliver the benefits and to authorize changes in the program. This role is well described in the PMI Standard, but not in MSP.

MSP describes the stakeholder engagement aspect of governance as part of the program manager's role, the PMI Standard argues that stakeholders cannot be "managed", but need to be "engaged" (PMI, 2013b, p. 45), which means they should be seen as an important part of the program management process, not merely "to be dealt with". My personal experience, as well as that of many of my colleagues, is that this whether you call it management or engagement, it an ongoing sensemaking process and should be the responsibility of the program manager, with the potential to refer to the Sponsor or Program Board when additional authority is required or if decisions involve potential conflict between board members.

Monitoring the achievement of the program objectives is currently viewed by many organizations as a rigid system, focused solely on bottom-up reporting in a standardized and imposed format. The purpose is often to protect managers from any legal consequences that their decisions could have. Such a system can be bureaucratic and kill accountability, initiative and creativity. In an innovative fast-moving environment this can make the difference between competitiveness and stagnation. So, what is the answer? To be dynamic, and at the same time make sure that legal accountability is not compromised, program governance should ideally integrate the three elements of governance through a system that enables strategic decisions to be reformulated in order to adapt to changing circumstances. This means that monitoring is not done solely for verification purposes, but also to provide data for management to make the right decisions, if and when changes are required. In this way, legal accountability is not compromised and the organization retains its flexibility to adapt to changing circumstances.

Governance is essential to integrate corporate and business strategy with programs and projects and to communicate strategy to program and project managers. It is also an essential element of decision and change management.

5.1.1.3   The responsibility for stakeholder engagement

Both MSP and the PMI Standard explicitly identify a range of program stakeholders and put the emphasis, not only on sound communication, but also on commitment and support. The PMI takes an objective approach to stakeholders, describing them as individuals, groups or organizations that are affected by or may affect the program; in comparison, MSP insists on the emotional aspect of stakeholder engagement and states that "stakeholders are people with feelings, perceptions, desires and influence" (OGC, 2011, p. 60). MSP describes stakeholder engagement as a way of achieving influence through the effective management of relationships. This is very different from the management of communications. Some of the supportive activities that are recommended are workshops, transformational leadership and a range of adaptive behavioural attitudes, which the PMI has described as sensemaking activities in their Managing Change Guide (PMI, 2013c). MSP also insist on the changing aspect of stakeholders over the course of the program and therefore the need to constantly review and work on the relationship.

In terms of stakeholder engagement, the PMI's PgM Standard defines the role of the program manager as communicating a vision of the need for change, specific program objectives and resources required, as well as setting clear goals, assessing readiness and planning for the change while monitoring the impact of the change. MSP considers that the role should be shared between the program manager and the business change manager. Additionally, the program manager develops and implements the stakeholder engagement strategy and the business change manager engages and leads those affected by the change through the transition. The PMI's Managing Change Guide has described a similar role for the integrator who is responsible for the preparation and integration of the change into the business. In our experience, stakeholder engagement is a crucial part of program management; key stakeholders will support, fund, contribute to and market the program. They need to constantly be motivated and re-motivated and negative stakeholders need to be influenced. It is the program manager's responsibility to attend to this responsibility on an ongoing basis. The business integrator, if there is one, will focus on the operational stakeholders, those that will implement the new capabilities. The sponsor will make sure that the key stakeholder are initially engaged and support the program manager if additional authority or influence is required.

5.2   Leadership and Competencies

One of the functions of program management is to transform an abstract, often ambiguous, strategic purpose into a clear program statement supported by well-defined critical success factors. These CSFs are translated into project deliverables that will increase the organization's capability and produce benefits, which in turn help achieve the strategy. This is clearly the view promoted by P2M. The successful implementation of the strategy requires empowerment of the people that will interpret strategic objectives and translate them into specific deliverables.

Many organizations leave the translation of the strategy, which has been elaborated by senior management, to a group of analysts or middle managers that, in turn, write a scope statement for the different programs. Whereas this process is not wrong in itself, it is most likely representative of an agency approach, which is built on shareholder interest. In the agency relationship, one party (the principal) delegates work to another (the agent), who performs that work. To make sure agents align their interests with the shareholders and their representatives, they are motivated through executive compensation schemes and controlled through governance structures. Agency-based structures advocate a high level of control over the agent(s). In the agency approach, there is no purpose to build relationships and develop trust since it is rooted in McGregor's (1960) Theory X that assumes workers inherently dislike working and would avoid it if they could. It is very difficult to develop a good program culture within this perspective where program managers are expected to be "super" project managers that follow a written script. In an agency context, projects are often initiated by line managers who "own" them; program managers are just asked to deliver them. To do so, the program manager exercises a transactional style of leadership and focuses on explicit knowledge, which is displayed by the left-hand side of Figure 5.1.

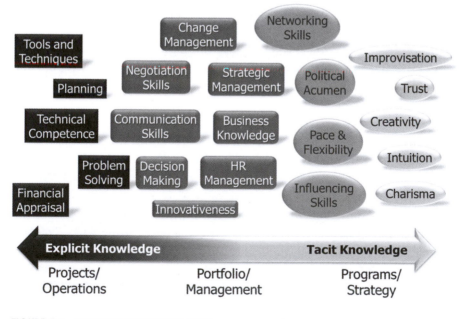

FIGURE 5.1   LEADERSHIP SKILLS VS ROLE

On the other hand, more progressive organizations favour an innovative approach based on the empowerment of their managers, set some guiding principles that will empower people and help them make decisions under uncertainty. This approach has been proven to be more effective with non-repetitive tasks that require decision-making skills. The stewardship approach is based on an extension of McGregor's (1960) Theory Y, by which workers are committed to the goals of the organization if they find value in their work. The stewardship approach promotes the concept that employees can have higher motives than simple self-interest. Stewards are motivated by higher order needs than agents, their relationships are longer-term and subjected to intrinsic factors, rather than extrinsic factors; they identify with the organization and commit to it. They are more likely to use personal power than institutional power and are more prone to find themselves in involvement-oriented situations than control-oriented situations. This perspective is gaining ground and is now adopted by many organizations such as Netflix, Apple, Google, W.L. Gore and others.

In this scenario, program managers will be expected to develop the program objectives from the strategy, to identify the program benefits from consultation with the stakeholders and to initiate the projects that will form the program. They would also be expected to be capable of managing both uncertainty and ambiguity and have the authority to make decisions in a changing context. This approach requires a transformational leadership approach, based on tacit knowledge and is displayed by the right-hand side of Figure 5.1.

The control-based approach separates the thinking and controlling part of the work from the doing part, whereas the empowerment-based approach integrates thinking, controlling and doing and relies more on self-control and self-management. Organizations that promote the latter approach need to let people experiment and build on mistakes and therefore enforce few rules. The organization will want to encourage team accountability and support it with clear shared goals and frameworks and ascertain that accurate and relevant data is available and shared to promote innovation and creativity.

In the next section, I will outline more specific competencies and skills that are required from program managers. It is not expected that every program manager possesses all these skills, but they can offer a framework for job description and personal development. The skills that are outlined below are more representative of a stewardship approach as they are often associated with empowerment. It is unfortunate, though, that many organizations require skills associated with empowerment and creativity from program managers when they hire them, only to cage them in an agency and control setting. This creates unnecessary frustration and potential conflict; it is much better for the organization to honestly describe the role of the program manager, whether agent or steward, and hire the person that will feel most comfortable in the described role.

5.2.1   SPECIFIC COMPETENCIES OF THE PROGRAM MANAGER

The following list of skills is provided as a guide of what is to be required by program managers for each stage of the program: Definition; Deployment and Closure. It may vary according to the context and the expected role of the program manager.

5.2.1.1   Definition stage (formulation)

A competent program manager will be able to:

- Understand and interpret a corporate vision and mission and translate it into clear strategic objectives for the program.
- Analyse financial and organizational data, more specifically, business case data and market data.
- Interview various level of management, sponsors/clients and users to understand their needs and expectations.
- Help resolve conflicting interests and negotiate with the different stakeholders to reach agreement on the program objectives and resources.
- Use a variety of financial tools to perform cost-benefit analyses.
- Collaborate with Business Analysts and Value Managers.
- Understand business benefits beyond economic factors.
- Develop strategic plans and business cases, including long-term budgeting and short-term estimating (understanding of basic financial models).
- Identify and prioritize the program critical success factors that support the strategy.
- Communicate effectively in verbal and written form to present strategic concepts in a clear manner to a wide range of managers and their team.
- Understand marketing issues in presenting their program for approval.
- Be capable of reformulating the program, based on appraisal feedback.

5.2.1.2   Definition stage (preparation)

A competent program manager will be able to:

- Collaborate with various levels of management across the organization.
- Evaluate and build relationships with potential partners.
- Create a strong structure for the program across different organizational departments.
- Evaluate the organization's workload and capability to undertake new activities.
- Appreciate organizational politics.
- Realize how to pace the program in regards to the organization's readiness for change and the urgency of the change.
- Prioritize the organization's resources in regards to the program's strategic objectives.
- Use all the available resources while maintaining strong relationships with the different departments involved.
- Gather, analyse and integrate data from a variety of sources.
- Develop a good governance structure for the program as a subset of the corporate governance system.
- Understand reporting needs for both program and projects and organize consistent and effective reporting system to support decision-making.

5.2.1.3   Deployment stage (deliver capabilities)

A competent program manager will be able to:

- Analyse and clarify requirements to translate them into key project deliverables.
- Distinguish project deliverables that directly contribute to benefits and giving them the necessary importance.
- Have a systems view of the program.
- Maintain monitoring and reporting at the program level without dwelling in at project level – typically milestones and key deliverables.
- Recognize the knowledge and skills required from key program resources, more specifically project managers.
- Understand project best practice and promote the organization's standards.

- Match resource experience and competencies with significance of task (project).
- Negotiate program resource commitments, specifically in matrix and functional environments.
- Act as the project sponsor, including delegate and empower, mentor and coach project managers.
- Manage program level and "aggregated" risks (project level risks that affect more than one project); lead management of project risks.
- Understand the organization's procurement rules and legal issues and lead procurement effort both at program and project level.
- Facilitate conflict resolution between line and project managers, as well as between program stakeholders with different interest.
- Exercise leadership and communication skills to manage all stakeholders, whatever their hierarchical level.
- Analyse project managers' and other key resources' competencies and take appropriate measures if needed.

5.2.1.4   Deployment stage (transition program)

A competent program manager will be able to:

- Clearly define program objectives and expected benefits.
- Clarify the roles of program manager versus business integrator for new capabilities and business change integration.
- Develop program accountability for key resources, specifically project managers (capable of influencing and communicating a vision).
- Sell program benefits.
- Lead customer (sponsor and user) project reviews.
- Assess capability of the organization to absorb change, in collaboration with business managers.
- Pace and prioritize projects and benefits delivery.
- Manage change and revised stakeholder priorities.
- Prioritise and reprioritise resources across projects on an ongoing basis.
- Lead project closing process and secure deliverable acceptance by customers.

5.2.1.5   Deployment stage (appraise benefits)

A competent program manager will be able to:

- Facilitate program level reviews with executive level stakeholders.
- Exercise both "baseline" evaluation (based on baseline variance) and "opportunity" evaluation (based on objectives' realization).
- Identify significant data and the methods and format necessary to collect it on time and use it effectively in line with organizational requirements.
- Interpret complex information and present it effectively.
- Understand basics of statistical quality control methods.
- Understand how project management information systems can generate appropriate data; be capable of interpreting it and visualize trends.
- Generate appropriate financial data and interpret it.
- Manage of both risks and value data.

5.2.1.6   *Deployment stage (transition to next cycle)*

A competent program manager will be able to:

- Measure benefits and capabilities realization against blueprint.
- Manage project knowledge through lessons learned and data recycling.
- Identify and recommend feasible solutions for next cycle based on benefits appraisal.
- Apply creative processes to issue resolution.
- Lead change management and decision-making, including analysing change drivers and facilitating decision process.
- Make recommendations for review and /or update of value proposition.
- Review and update program documents in preparation for next cycle.

5.2.1.7   *Closure stage*

A competent program manager will be able to:

- Ensure that all the program objectives and benefits, including operational integration, are achieved.
- Coordinate outstanding integration work and transition plan with appropriate managers.
- If the program has been stopped before its natural conclusion, analyse reasons and draw conclusions for future use; ensure that maximum benefits are drawn from both dissolution and report. This requires a capability for self-assessment.

- Collate and archive all program data in comprehensive and organized manner.
- Analyse data to draw conclusions and produce performance summaries.
- Communicate program results effectively, both at executive and team level.
- Manage release of program resources.
- Support the program team in career development opportunities.

5.3   From Program Understanding to Doing

In the first five chapters of this book, we set the scene for the management of programs by examining the main concepts and issues regarding the management of programs in organizations. This chapter has described the roles and responsibilities of the different program actors regarding the key program components, as well as the more specific leadership and competency requirements of the program manager at various stages of the program. In Part III, I will illustrate how to put these concepts into application by going through the step-by-step process of managing a program.

PART III
THE PROGRAM LIFE CYCLE

In Parts I and II of the book, we have discussed the context, issues and key concepts that make program management an ideal method to deliver organizational strategies. We have seen that the program environment is complex: there are multiple stakeholders with differing and often conflicting needs, emergent inputs are always affecting the process and ambiguity is high.

The program management life cycle must reflect the rhetoric and concepts of strategic long-term management, rather than the product-centric short-term view of traditional project management in order to gain executive management support and truly be able to support strategic decision management. Part III describes in detail all the steps required to successfully deliver a program from its definition to its closure. It covers the detailed roles of the main program stakeholders from executives to project and operational managers and describes a number of tools and techniques to manage programs effectively.

Chapter 6 outlines the three main program stages: Definition, Deployment and Closure. Chapters 7–11 present a step-by-step program management methodology based on practice and emphasize the iterative and cyclic nature of the program by linking all the program processes and tools through its three main stages.

CHAPTER 6
Program Life Cycle Outline

Many older books and guides on program management have suggested program "phases" which are simply transpositions of the project perspective. We have seen in the preceding chapters how this view can jeopardize the effectiveness of program management and its capability to deliver strategies. Although it has been agreed for a few years now that the objective of programs is to produce organizational level benefits by aligning a number of program components with strategy, it is only in the last few years that management rhetoric has made its way into the program management literature and practice. In this chapter, I will compare life cycles described in the main program management standards and outline a proposed life cycle based on current practice.

6.1   Comparison of Program Life Cycles

In order to ensure the realization of strategic objectives, the program life cycle must enable regular assessment of benefits, evaluation of emergent opportunities and pacing of the process; it must take into account the "interdependence" of component projects in order to ensure strategic alignment. To achieve this, a program life cycle must be iterative, rather than linear, include periods of stability for benefits integration and learning, and have a systems perspective. Executives and sponsors become change leaders by taking responsibility for three steps that underlie every program decision: value creation, transition and value realization.

The phases outlined in the three dominant standards (PMI, MSP and P2M), although their names differ, are relatively consistent. Every standard agrees on a formulation/definition stage which is completely distinct from the deployment/execution stage. The definition stage is meant to identify the needs, understand the program's basic objectives and prepare the business case for the program. The standards also agree that there will be phase-gates between each of the stages.

The deployment stage of the program is handled differently by different standards. The PMI calls this stage "Benefits Delivery"; it is essentially the component (projects) management and transition. This component transition step includes the transition and integration of deliverables as well as the measurement of benefits. MSP does not focus on the program components, but rather considers a higher level of management including managing the tranches (or cycles), delivering capabilities to the business and realizing benefits. P2M, like MSP considers integration management (managing the program cycles and component integration) and adds assessment management as a distinct stage, which is implied in the two other standards.

Both the PMI Standard and MSP include a closure stage where the program is wound down, feedback is collected and resources reallocated. PMI includes the final program transition in that stage; it is defined as the handoff of outstanding program activities to other programs or to the business and a transition of stewardship. P2M does not explicitly identify a closure stage, but it is implied that, when value is achieved, the program resources will be reallocated and post-program assessment will be carried out.

In Table 6.1, the three guides are compared to the life cycle that forms the framework of this book, for reference purposes. The PMI Standard's life cycle is the one described in Section 2 of the Standard (PMI, 2013b). MSP's is

TABLE 6.1　COMPARISON BETWEEN STANDARDIZED LIFE CYCLES

	PMI (2013)	MSP (2011)	P2M (2015)		Thiry (2015)
Definition	Formulation	Identifying Programme	Mission Profiling (Strategic Goal Management)	**Definition**	Program Formulation
	Preparation	Defining Programme	Program Design (Agree Program Architecture)		Program Preparation
Benefits Delivery	Component Planning & Authorization	Manage Tranches	Integration Management of Program Implementation (Program Launch, Management of Goals, Closing)	**Deployment**	Capabilities Delivery (Manage Components)
	Component Oversight & Integration	Deliver Capabilities			
	Component Transition & Closure	Realise Benefits			Capabilities Transition
			Value Assessment Management (Ongoing Measurement of Results)		Capabilities Integration (Benefits Realisation)
					Benefits Appraisal
Closure	Program Transition	Closing Programme	*No identified closing phase*	**Closure**	Value Realisation Assessment
	Program Closeout				Program Completion Management
					Lessons Learned Finalisation

the outline of what they call the Transformational Flow: "a series of iterative and interrelated steps" (OGC, 2011, p. 143). Finally, P2M describes a series of steps outlined in Section 3.2 Program Integration Management (PMAJ, 2015, pp. 36–7).

6.2   An Agile Program Life Cycle

In previous writings, I have summarized the program management life cycle through five generic stages or processes (Thiry, 2002, 2007, 2010); in this second edition, I have decided to align it closer to professional standards because those standards have all evolved closer to one another and because I believe the project management community should have a unified program management language. I will therefore describe three stages: *Definition*, *Deployment* and *Closure*, each divided into sub-stages.

I use the word "stage" instead of "phase" because it expresses a different concept. Typically, a phase is defined as a distinct period in a sequence of events or change. A phase generally represents individual aspects of a sequential process, as in a project. On the other hand, a stage is defined as a distinct step or period of development, growth, or progress in any series or cycle of changes. It represents intervals between measurable steps of development and is generally associated with a cyclic process like program management. The end of a stage also generally corresponds to step from which to reach a further level; in management, a decision point or gate (In the PMI Standard, they are called "Phase-Gates", which is a standard project term; the new product development industry, which is more akin to program management, typically uses the term "stage-gate").

6.2.1   DEFINITION STAGE

The primary purpose of this stage is to progressively elaborate the strategic objectives and expected program outcomes; to seek a common view of the program's mission and get approval for the program deployment. The program business case is the main output of this stage. It outlines these elements as well as the set-up of the program architecture, strategy and assignment of roles and responsibilities.

The definition stage is commonly funded independently from the rest of the program since its purpose is to gain funding for the program deployment.

Therefore, in practice, the program manager for the definition phase is often not the same person as the program manager of the deployment and closure phases. They are usually more senior and able to negotiate agreements with key senior stakeholders.

This stage aligns with the three standards' phases and its purpose is the same. The program *Definition* stage includes two sub-stages: *Formulation* and *Preparation*, these terms are in alignment with the PMI Standard.

6.2.1.1   Program formulation

Formulation is associated with the translation of strategic objectives into program outcomes and the assignment of a sponsor. The sponsor will be responsible for assigning the program manager.

Because programs often exceed the typical organization's budget allocation period, formulation is repeated at regular intervals in each of the main cycles of the program. It allows the program team to redefine the program more precisely as results are being measured and its ultimate value better defined.

The business case process overlaps the formulation and preparation stages, going from preliminary to detailed as more data becomes available. Together the sponsor and program manager clarify the objectives of the program, secure financing, develop the preliminary blueprint, as well as the management strategy and roadmap, which will all be included in the program mandate, or preliminary business case.

6.2.1.2   Program preparation

Preparation consists of setting up the governance system, defining the program architecture, deploying the initial team and finalizing the development of the business case and program plan. It is also during this process that proposals are made for candidate components (projects and other actions). The ultimate purpose of this stage is to get approval for the program deployment.

Preparation is iterative with formulation, it will enable the team, to plan and pace benefits realization and finalize the program scope for the next deployment cycle. This process requires the engagement of the key stakeholders around the program's critical success factors (CSFs) and the structuring of the program.

The scope of the program and benefits realization strategy are initiated during the formulation stage, refined in the preparation stage and reviewed and updated as necessary at each program cycle.

6.2.2   DEPLOYMENT STAGE

Deployment consists of the harmonized governance of a number of aligned components. It includes the management of the interdependencies between components as well as transition and integration activities. It includes the ongoing appraisal of benefits. The objective of this cyclic process is to deliver benefits in a controlled sequence.

The key to successful deployment is the harmonization of all the resources and constituents of the program to realize benefits consistently through the delivery of usable capabilities and sustainable change.

The program *Deployment* stage includes four sub-stages:

- *Capabilities Delivery*;
- *Capabilities Transition*;
- *Capabilities Integration*; and
- *Benefits Appraisal*.

It also includes the transition from one cycle to the next. I have made the decision to keep the term Deployment for this stage because I believe the PMI term of "Benefits Delivery" does not represent the processes of this stage but rather its outcome. The P2M term "Integration Management of Program Execution" is representative of the processes taking place in this stage, but it is too long. The MSP term "Tranche" is limited in meaning, but MSP divides it into meaningful sub-stages: "Delivering the Capability" and "Realizing the Benefits". Deployment is a well-known term used in business and therefore universal and representative.

In the sub-stages, I have decided to focus on the processes that I have experienced in real-life and adopt the MSP term capabilities delivery. Capabilities are delivered through the management of program components (projects and other actions). These capabilities are integrated into the business through a series of transition activities that enable benefits to be realized. Benefits must then be appraised to assess the need to realign the program strategy for the next cycle.

6.2.2.1   *Capabilities delivery (components management)*

This is the stage where the initiation, planning and execution of projects and other activities are coordinated and monitored to ensure the consistent delivery of capabilities that will eventually produce benefits. This includes any component interdependencies activities required from the program team and component managers.

6.2.2.2   Capabilities transition

This sub-phase consists of the transfer of capabilities and the closing of components. Activities include the delivery of component outputs and any transition activities that are part of the components' scope as well as specific program transition activities, in particular those that pertain to stakeholder engagement. One important aspect of program success is to market benefits to the key stakeholders to keep them engaged and gain their continuous support.

6.2.2.3   Capabilities integration (benefits realization)

There is a difference between transition and integration. Whereas transition is generally associated with a series of activities to help recipients accept change, integration requires a full sustained acceptance of the change. Integration of project deliverables and capabilities into operations is often neglected, or limited to finite "transition" activities, when managing a program. It is part of the change management process and usually overlaps the delivery of capabilities because many of the activities required to transition and integrate capabilities into the organization start as soon as the component is initiated. Integration often triggers the need for adaptive change in the program.

6.2.2.4   Benefits appraisal

The appraisal of benefits realization is an ongoing process which both the PMI and MSP have clearly acknowledged. It requires not only the measurement of the delivery of capabilities but also the measure of the achievement of the benefits that stem from their integration into the business. Communicating progress to stakeholders in order to maintain their ongoing support is part of the activities included in this sub-stage.

6.2.2.5   Transition to next cycle

As part of the Deployment stage the program team needs to prepare for the next cycle, this requires: measuring realisation against blueprint; drawing lessons learned from the current cycle; analysing the need to realign the program; reviewing and updating program documents. The end of a cycle is also the best time to realign objectives and review the value proposition, if required. Although not a sub-phase as such, the activities pertaining to the end of a cycle and the authorisation of the next have to be outlined and managed.

6.2.3   CLOSURE STAGE

During the closure stage, ultimate benefits realization is measured against the blueprint. Outstanding work is agreed and completed; any residual work is transferred to the organization or to other programs. Lessons learned are drawn and communicated before closing the program.

Program closure consists of three sub-stages: *Value Realization Assessment, Completion Management,* and *Lessons Learned Finalization.* In the standards, lessons learned is included in the closing process, I have decided to make it a distinct sub-phase to emphasize its importance in developing program maturity in the long term. I have used value realization, in alignment with P2M in order to emphasize the fact that programs are meant to help an organization realize benefits, but that the ultimate purpose is to realize value for the organization.

6.2.3.1   Value realization assessment

Ultimate benefits, the sum of which represents the value that the organization was initially seeking, are measured against the blueprint, which represents the desired future state of the business at completion of the program. Any discrepancies are noted and addressed in completion management.

6.2.3.2   Program completion management

Following the measurement of value realization, any outstanding work required to achieve the initial or current strategic objectives is identified and agreed, resources needed to complete the work are agreed and assigned, and any residuals are transferred to other programs or to operations.

6.2.3.3   Lessons learned finalization

In a program, lessons learned are an ongoing process as data is analysed continually to prepare for the next cycles. At the closure stage, final lessons learned are prepared, including a summary of lessons learned at each cycle; they are communicated to key stakeholders and made available to the organization.

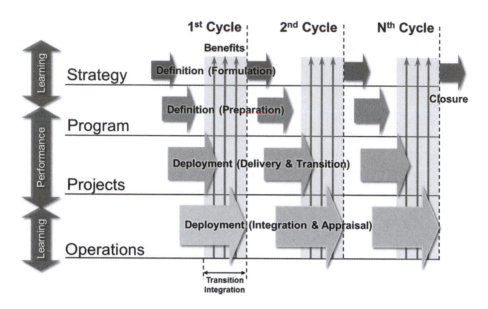

FIGURE 6.1   THE PROGRAM LIFE CYCLE

Figure 6.1 displays the three generic stages and sub-stages and the organizational level at which they occur. The organizational level is related to the decision management process and displays the level at which the decision authority for each stage sits within the organization. In addition, on the left-hand side of the diagram the learning and performance cycles are also displayed (see Figure 4.1, p. 84). The *formulation* and the strategy development part of the *preparation* stage are learning cycles, as are the *integration* of capabilities and *appraisal* of benefits realization. These stages require the application of business analysis and value management tools and techniques. The structuring part of the *preparation* stage as well as the *capabilities delivery* in the *deployment* stage, are performance cycles where project management tools and techniques can be appropriately used.

This diagram also illustrates the cyclic nature of programs where benefits are appraised on a regular basis and the resulting operational outcomes are used to realign the strategy, if required. Typically the cycles of the program life cycle also correspond to periods of transition and integration that enable the organization to absorb change at a rhythm that corresponds to its readiness. These periods of stability, which usually correspond to stage gates, are typically determined when pacing the program.

During the whole program life cycle there are three underlying aims that define every program decision from definition to closure, and in particular when managing changes to the program.

- *Value creation*: making sense of the change and agreeing to a value proposal. One of the main characteristics of change is ambiguity, which is often associated with complex situations and multiple stakeholders. Whereas uncertainty is easily dealt with through "good management", ambiguity requires leadership and vision. The change management team and the stakeholders must first make sense of the impact of the change and agree on the expected benefits. This is the definition stage of the program.
- *Transition*: committing resources and managing the change process. During the transition stage, both ambiguity and uncertainty need to be managed to achieve success. Program management is ideal to deal with unexpected events whereas uncertainty reduction is the domain of project management. Program management helps define and keep the vision, adapt to changing circumstances, and prepare the organization for the change; this is the benefits realization plan.
- *Value realization*: integrating change and achieving a sustainable transformed state. When project deliverables are transferred into the organization to create new capabilities, it is the role of the program management team, in collaboration with the business management team, to ensure that the organization is ready for the change. It is useful to run workshops with change agents – people who will help integrate the change sustainably at all levels of the organization. Communication is an essential tool for the integration of change.

Ideally, executives and sponsors take responsibility for leading change by providing the framework and resources to integrate program and project management results and day-to-day operations to realize value during organizational change management.

6.3   From Life Cycle to Management of the Cycle

In this chapter, we have examined how different program guides and standards view the program life cycle. The chapter has then outlined a program life cycle linked to the management of the whole strategic decision process, including the making of the decision and its implementation. The next chapters describe in detail a step-by-step methodology within each of the stages and identify the different actors' roles in the process. The important thing is to remember that programs are complex and that they will require regular adjustments and realignments, therefore this step-by-step process is not linear or sequential, but cyclic and iterative and there are overlaps between the different steps which can often be conducted in parallel. Figure 6.2 represents the next chapters in a hierarchical diagram, numbering matches corresponding sections.

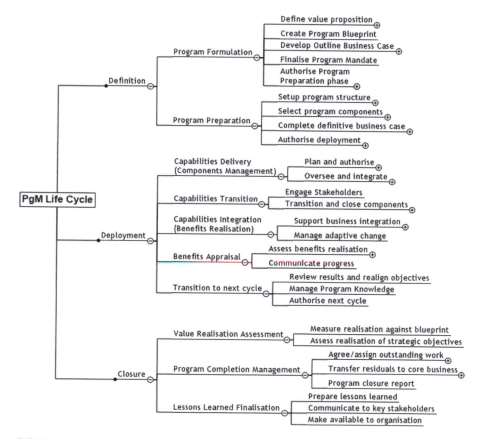

FIGURE 6.2   TAXONOMY OF PROGRAM LIFE CYCLE

CHAPTER 7

Program Definition (Formulation)

Chapter 6 has outlined the program life cycle and demonstrated that it is cyclic and iterative. Definition is essentially a group decision-making process during which all the key stakeholders are able to agree the objectives of the program; set its critical success factors and the measures that will ensure its success. Figure 7.1, on the following page, represents an outline flowchart of the program's definition stage, which is detailed in this chapter.

7.1   Define Value Proposition

The value proposition can be a discrete process, independent of the program, undertaken as part of the portfolio management process or can be part of the program formulation stage. In many organizations, these steps are the responsibility of the Enterprise PMO or the portfolio management team. If this is the case, the program manager and program board will be assigned when the program proposal is approved. But, ideally the program board and program manager should be involved in those steps.

In the flowchart represented in Figure 7.1 the definition of the value proposition is presented as a task preceding the actual start of the program. In a mature organization, a portfolio decision would have to be taken before investing resources in the definition stage of the program. This step is usually a high-level management decision based on an initial assessment of the strategic initiative. This strategic level effort to define strategic objectives in regards of a specific situation results in the definition of a number of value statements that will become the program's value proposition.

A decision is then made at the portfolio level to manage the initiative as a project or a program (see Chapter 3, Table 3.2. p. 71). Following this decision, the program board and program manager are assigned and the definition

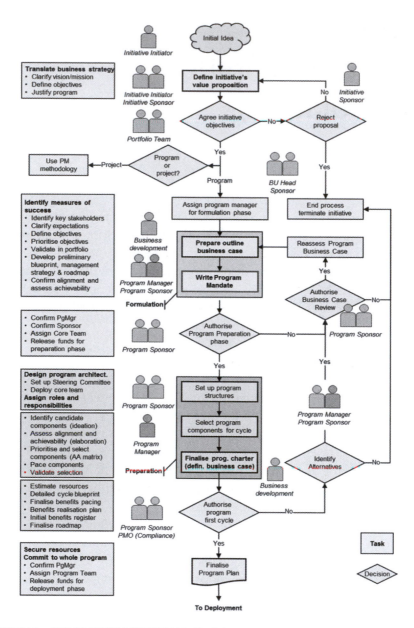

FIGURE 7.1   PROGRAMME DEFINITION FLOWCHART

stage is formally initiated. The "outline business case" is developed during formulation and the "definitive business case" during preparation, as more data becomes available. Figure 4.6 represents this process. In less mature organizations, where control is exercised more centrally, the business case process is developed further by the PMO or portfolio management team before making the decision to launch the program. The value proposition definition comprises two main activities:

1. Translate Business Strategy.
2. Develop Initial Business Case.

7.1.2   TRANSLATE BUSINESS STRATEGY

Programs are generally triggered by an external or internal pressure to change, either because of an unacceptable situation or to seize an opportunity (see Figure 4.2, p. 87). The response to this pressure is typically a strategy development process and uses value management or business analysis methodologies to help clarify the strategy. The process of translating the business strategy into a set of aligned and achievable actions that will lead to tangible and measurable outcomes requires a good understanding of strategic issues and a capability to translate abstract concepts into concrete results. In many organizations, this role is given to the program sponsor or the initiator of the strategic initiative, but program managers need to understand the process and concepts leading to the value proposition in order to fulfil their role.

The first step consists of defining the vision and mission of the program. Most programs are undertaken to increase an organization's competitive advantage; this requires a good understanding of the program's context and of the organization's strategy and capabilities. The vision and mission for the program are defined against portfolio management critical success factors and should align with the corporate strategy; they are translated into strategic objectives. Once a draft strategy and objectives are available, they are validated with key stakeholders to confirm alignment. The final step is to clarify the program justification: why should the organization invest resources into this initiative? Why is it more useful than other competing initiatives? What is the expected value for the organization, both financial and non-financial?

The deliverables of this step are: the program's justification (why?) and mission statement (what?) as well as three to five clear strategic objectives.

Typically, the sponsor is responsible for defining the vision and mission of the program with the initiative's initiator, typically an Executive or Sector Manager.

7.1.1   DEVELOP INITIAL BUSINESS CASE

The initial business case is described in more detail in Section 7.2.6.1. It consists of the formal document that describes the value proposition for the program, translating the strategy into tangible outcomes. Its purpose is to show that the proposed program could create a real opportunity for the organization and allows the executive sponsor to make a decision on the program. Once the program is approved, the program board is formed and the program manager is assigned for the definition stage. At this stage, the person assigned has to have good knowledge of the program process and context and be senior enough to negotiate commitment of senior managers to the program. Typically the initiative sponsor and/or initiative initiator are responsible for recommending the right candidate.

7.2   Program Formulation

In most cases, formulation is associated with the preparation of the outline business case and writing of the program mandate. This process is often funded independently from the rest of the program as its purpose is to gain funding for the program deployment. Because programs often exceed the budget allocation period, formulation is repeated at regular intervals for each of the main cycles of the program. It allows the program team to redefine the program more precisely as results are measured and its ultimate value is better defined. The business case process often overlaps the formulation and preparation stages, going from outline to definitive as more data becomes available.

Commitment to the time and resources necessary for the formulation may require some convincing because sponsors usually want to move things along as quickly as possible, but years of practice of program and change management have demonstrated that sensemaking time is essential to the ultimate success of the program. Because of my background, I use methods derived from value management, which are systematic, relatively easy to use and resource effective; nowadays, business analysis is a method of choice in many organizations. But, alternative methods exist like the Analytic Hierarchy Process (AHP), SWOT (Strength, Weaknesses, Opportunities and Threats) Analysis, Strategy Maps (Kaplan and Norton, 2004), Morphological Analysis, Soft Systems Analysis, Logical Framework or others;[1] the choice will depend on

---

1   All these methods are well referenced on the internet and a quick keyword search will provide the reader with the necessary data to understand their use and effectiveness.

the nature of the situation, the culture of the organization and expertise of the resources available.

The following sections describe the methods and techniques used to develop the outline business case and program mandate. They are divided in eight main activities, each divided in sub-activities:

1. Identify measures of success (Define Expected Benefits).
2. Identify Key Stakeholders.
3. Clarify Expectations.
4. Prioritize Objectives.
5. Create the Program Blueprint.
6. Start Business Case Process.
7. Finalize Program Mandate.
8. Authorize Program Preparation.

7.2.1   IDENTIFY MEASURES OF SUCCESS (DEFINE EXPECTED BENEFITS)

The next step is to identify the benefits that the program must deliver to support the strategic objectives and their measures of success; this is the foundation of the benefits realization plan and benefits register.

Different organizations identify benefits in different ways, but experience and research show that they are not very good at it. In many organizations, expected benefits are defined by a group of executives as ways to resolve concerns they have regarding their own management area. These concerns are then put together to create a list, which is neither prioritized, nor well defined, thereby creating a context for constant challenge and disorganized repositioning. In addition, most organizations still focus on short-term financial benefits when defining the objectives programs thus reinforcing the inevitability of gratuitous readjustment every time these targets are not met or factors change.

In today's increasingly complex and turbulent business environment, organizations need to be agile and adjust quickly to changing circumstances, but haphazard change is not agility. More mature organizations use proven methods like the balanced scorecard or others to define benefits from a wider range of factors. This gives them a broader view of their context and enables them to prioritize the things that are really important to maintain their competitive edge. For many years now, I have relied on value-based stakeholder analysis (see Figure 4.7, p. 97) to define a program's expected benefits and agree on the program purpose and objectives.

The process consists of identifying and mapping stakeholders for the program, clarifying their needs and expectations, agreeing objectives (High-level business benefits – CSFs) and prioritizing these CSFs in regards of their contribution to the program as a whole. The initiative's initiator and/or program manager are responsible for facilitating this step. The next few sections describe in detail the actions required to accomplish this. They consist of:

1. Identify key stakeholders.
2. Clarify their expectations.
3. Define objectives.

7.2.2   IDENTIFY KEY STAKEHOLDERS

It is my experience and implied in all the program management standards that stakeholders play a key role in defining the program objectives. Rather than dealing uniquely with sponsors and clients during the formulation stage, I recommend developing a full stakeholder map and classifying all the stakeholders to be able to identify those that will be key in the success of the program. In addition to rationally expressed needs and expectations, stakeholders may have fears, interests, perceptions, opinions and sometimes hidden political agendas that need to be known to the program manager. After the stakeholders have been identified, using experience, historical data, brainstorming, interviews or other similar means, they are mapped and classified.

The *mapping* of the stakeholders consists of grouping them into categories that will be easier to manage. For example, the board, and C level executives could be grouped into and "executive stakeholder" category; Line managers could be grouped into "support stakeholders" and "demand stakeholders", depending on their role; the contractors, vendors, suppliers and service providers could all be grouped in a "supply stakeholders" category, and so on. Categories will depend on the organization and the program's purpose. The objective is to group in the same category stakeholders that are expected to have similar interest in the program. Within a group some individual stakeholders will be more influential and have specific needs or expectations and those will need to be identified on a case by case basis.

The *classification* of the stakeholders consists of prioritizing them in regards of their potential impact on the program, the objective being to understand how much and what type of effort should be invested in each

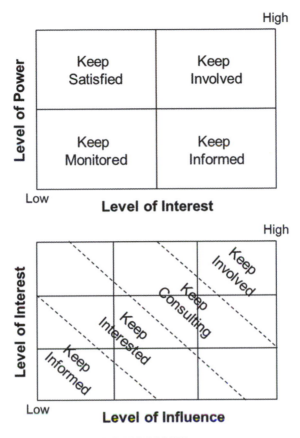

FIGURE 7.2   STAKEHOLDER MAPPING TECHNIQUES

stakeholder. Many methods exist to achieve this: the best known are the Power/Interest Grid (Mendelow, 1991), the Influence/Interest Matrix or the Attitude/Interaction Mapping. Whatever the method used, the purpose is to be able to distinguish the stakeholders that require a constant management or engagement effort throughout the program versus those that only require regular monitoring. Figure 7.2 shows two of these tools. One important point to note when using any of these two matrices is that interest can be positive or negative; a powerful interested stakeholder is key, whether their interest is in the program's success or its failure. It is the old adage of "know your friends, know your enemies better".

Following these two steps, stakeholders are identified and grouped by general interest and the key stakeholders of the program are identified. It is now time to identify their needs and expectations regarding the program.

7.2.3   CLARIFY EXPECTATIONS

The 2nd Edition of the *PMBOK® Guide* (PMI, 2000) mentioned that:

> *Project integration management ... involves making trade-offs among competing objectives and alternatives to meet or exceed stakeholders' needs and expectations. (p. 41)*

But it also said that:

> *Finding appropriate resolution to [stakeholders] differences can be one of the major challenges of project management. (p. 18)*

Although these statements have been omitted in later versions of the Guide, they are still very true. The European Value Management Standard concurs, in saying that:

> *Stakeholders [...] may all hold differing views of what represents value. [...] the aim of VM is to reconcile these differences and enable an organization to achieve the greatest progress towards its stated goals with the use of minimum resources. (BS-EN 12973:2000 VM Standard, p. 6)*

This concept is illustrated in Figure 7.3. The left-hand side represents the alignment with stakeholders' expectations: if offered benefits are greater or equal to the expected benefits stakeholders are satisfied. The right-hand side represents the achievability of the value proposition: if the available capabilities (human and financial resources, expertise, competence, experience, skills,

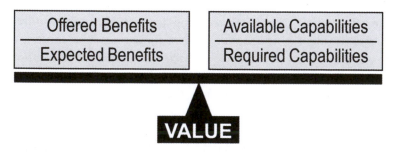

FIGURE 7.3   THE VALUE CONCEPT

knowledge, etc.) are greater or equal to the required capabilities, the value proposition can be achieved.

For many years now I have been very successful in using value management methods to identify and reconcile stakeholders' needs and expectations. This means actively involving the key stakeholders in the decision-making process, an agile concept that will lead to the prioritisation of objectives and the definition of the expected benefits of the program. Value management helps focus the team on finding the alternatives that generate the best value: lowest use of available capabilities for closest alignment with expectations. This can be achieved through creative, open workshops and meetings, which are best facilitated. Similar stakeholder elicitation methods include *Gap Analysis, Scenario Planning, Soft Systems Methodology* or *Logical Framework*.

The output of this process should be a stakeholder's map including both their expected benefits and their contribution to the program (see Figure 4.9). This map will be the basis for the development of the Benefits Map.

7.2.3.1   Define objectives (critical success factors)

Generally the agreement of key stakeholders on program objectives is the main outcome of the value proposition. The program's objectives are its Critical Success Factors. In project management (PM), many synonyms have been used for Critical Success Factors (CSF): success criteria, performance indicators, key requirements, etc. In strategic management, CSFs mean:

> *The limited number of areas in which results, if they are satisfactory, will ensure successful competitive performance for the organization.* (Rockart, 1979)

In this book, I will consider two types of CSFs:

1. *Generic CSFs*: those that should always be present and are usually linked to the business or organization, e.g. communicate effectively; secure top management support, involve users, generate revenue, maintain IT capabilities, maintain competitiveness, etc.
2. *Specific CSFs*: the ones that are determined by a specific strategy and its context or circumstances, e.g. improve communications with clients, involve top management in decisions, consult users on concept, increase client base, improve IT system performance, develop new product, etc.

As you can notice in these examples, the specific CSFs are subsets of the generic ones. CSFs will exist at different levels; project CSFs are a subset of the program's CSFs, which are themselves a subset of the strategy or portfolio's CSFs. One easy way to understand this hierarchy is that lower level CSFs are the "hows" and higher-level CSFs the "whys".

It is mostly the specific CSFs that are determined for each program because they are in direct correlation to the program or project's success. John Rockart (1979) and other strategic writers' define them as: "Areas of activity that should receive constant and careful attention from management". In program management, specific CSFs can be defined as: "The limited number of stakeholders' expected benefits, expressed in measurable terms, which, if realized, will ensure the program's success".

If the initiative requires pre-approval before entering formulation, definition of CSFs is the role of the portfolio team in collaboration with the sponsor. In this case, it is only after approval of the value proposition that the program board or sponsor assign the program manager for formulation. Otherwise, the program manager and program board will be responsible for that task and integrate it with the development of the benefits map.

The following sections describe a number of proven techniques to define the program's objectives that will lead to the development of the program blueprint.

7.2.3.2   Expectations identification workshop

I use value management as a group decision-making process to develop a shared understanding of a situation and an agreement on the options to resolve it. The participants to such workshops must be the key stakeholders, and particularly the people who possess authority over the resources required to implement the decisions.

Sensemaking is the first step of the value management process and typically consists of what value managers call "information phase" and "functional analysis", but in a program would be better termed "understanding of the situation/issues" and "expected benefits elicitation and analysis". This includes the clarification of stakeholder needs and expectations, which will become the requirements, and the agreement on the benefits the program is expected to provide. The objective of the sensemaking process is to clarify the situation or issues that led to the inception of the program and to identify the "values" (needs and expectations) of the different stakeholders in regards of that situation.

In project management, a need is mostly associated with a defined requirement; typically, expectations are considered undefined requirements and therefore not really deemed manageable since project management relies on a clear definition of objectives. In value management, needs are regarded as: "what is necessary for, *or desired* by the user. A need can be declared or *undeclared*; it can be an existing or *potential* one" (italics by author) (VM Vocabulary Standard EN 1325–1, 1997). Because programs are essentially ambiguous, at least to begin with and that ambiguity will rise and fall during the course of the program in a cyclic way, all needs cannot be expected to be clear from the beginning, therefore the value management definition also applies to programs. The program management team will conduct workshops with the key stakeholders and interview those that either cannot or will not attend to record their needs and uncover their expectations. Expectations are often unclear, or even unconscious; it is the role of the program manager, or the manager of the formulation process, to probe and question the stakeholders to expose those expectations that are vague or covert. When the expectations are stated, they become requirements. Expectations left unexposed will lead to emergent changes later in the program or dissatisfaction that may jeopardize the program, mostly if they concern some of the key stakeholders.

Typically, the best way to state requirements is to use an active verb and a measurable noun, for example: increase profit, engage personnel, update system, develop new capabilities, etc. During the workshops or interviews, the team should not necessarily spend too much time on the rhetoric of the statement; it is more important to capture the stakeholders' expectations, but after the gathering process has taken place, it is worth spending the time to clarify these statements. This will ease the next step, which consists of the classification and prioritization of these requirements to identify the benefits that the program should provide.

7.2.3.3   Benefits map and benefits breakdown structure

The first step in the development of the blueprint is to produce a *benefits map* or *benefits breakdown structure*. The benefits map is described in MSP as a means to show how benefits relate to each other and to the projects of the program. The authors of MSP suggest to go from right to left, going from strategic objectives to specific outcomes and to link all the elements of the blueprint in a logical means-to-end process. This intuitive way of doing is useful, but often misses on a number of elements; it is subject to repetitions and open to gaps. The right-to-left approach is also counter-intuitive in Western culture.

Whether benefits are defined prior to the start of the program or imposed, I often use a method where I ask the stakeholders to classify the benefits into four or five columns (from left to right): Strategic Objectives (what will keep the organization competitive), Key Benefit or CSF (direct contribution to strategic objective), Outcome (desired business result), Action or potential project task (means to achieve the outcome) and Capability or Deliverable (expected technical/operational result). I then ask the team to link each capability to an action, each action to benefit, and so on. I then ask them to do the same in the opposite direction and to identify any gaps or duplications and correct them. This process usually enables the team to identify a number of missing links and elements and to classify the expected benefits by order of importance.

The method I use most though is the benefits breakdown structure (BBS). This method is more comprehensive than the above and, although it may be more time consuming, it will save time in the long run in the same way that a good plan saves time in a project. Although it is similar to a work breakdown structure (WBS), it uses different development rules.

The overall objective for the BBS is to model the expected benefits of the stakeholders in a way that represents their collective view of the situation. At the higher, more strategic level, these will be labelled strategic objectives; at the lower, more detailed levels, they will be called benefits, outcomes, outputs/deliverables and capabilities. The fundamental rule is to create a hierarchy of expected benefits that goes from the more abstract, bigger-picture strategic objectives to actual concrete capability improvements using a value management technique called function diagramming. This technique uses a how-why logic to create a classification of the benefits from the more generic-strategic to the more specific-operational. Each expected benefit identified in the previous phase is linked to another using this logic. For example: "*How* do you generate revenue? By increasing your client base"; "*Why* do you increase your client base? To generate revenue". To be valid, the questions have to work both ways. The more you ask the question *why*, the more you go towards the generic and the more you ask the question *how*, the more you get towards the specific (see Thiry, 2013b for a detailed description of the methodology).

To build the BBS, the program team will start with a minimal number of expected benefits and relate them to each other using a how–why logic to develop the basic structure. More expected benefits can then be added in relationship with those already in place. To verify completeness the team can verify the sequence of expected benefits vertically. If all of them are achieved, will their sum fulfil the higher-level expected benefits?

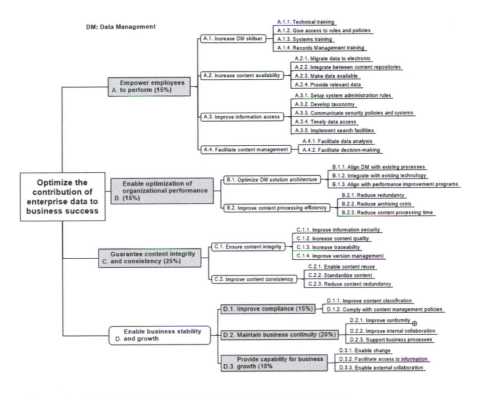

FIGURE 7.4 EXAMPLE OF BENEFITS BREAKDOWN STRUCTURE (BBS)

Figure 7.4 shows an example of a BBS. This example concerns the development of an integrated data management system for a large organization. The grey boxes identify the benefits-outcomes that are agreed critical success factors (see section 7.2.4); the percentage represents their relative weight (see Figure 7.5).

7.2.4 PRIORITIZE OBJECTIVES

Program objectives are expressed as expected benefits and outlined in the benefits breakdown structure. The next step is to identify those benefits that are critical to the success of the program.

Once the BBS is outlined, the team will aim to reach a shared agreement of the value of the program in terms of critical success factors, which are qualitative expected benefits, and key performance indicators, which are the quantitative measures of the program benefits.

7.2.4.1   Select and prioritize critical success factors

The first question now is how to choose the CSFs among all the expected benefits. In most organizations, CSFs are chosen randomly and intuitively; the choice is often political, making sure to please the most powerful. The problem with this approach is that it is then difficult to clearly link the benefits to the strategy and the program's expectations are often unachievable within the given parameters. I experimented with many ways to identify CSFs and have always come back to the BBS as the best way to define CSFs that are both achievable and that are truly a measure of the program's success.

If the BBS is complete and consistent, like a WBS for projects, the sum of each level will represent the full scope of the program. Therefore, achieving all the benefits or outcomes of one level will ensure success. I explained earlier that the number of CSFs should be limited. From experience, the ideal number of CSFs will lie between five and eight, with 12 being an absolute maximum. Do not forget that for each CSF you will need to identify two to four KPIs, which means that you will need to report on a minimum 15 and up to 36 performance indicators. You want to keep that number as small and significant as possible, but also as specific and measurable as possible. I explained earlier that benefits that are too strategic are often also too generic; they could be good corporate or business unit benefits, but the program benefits must be more specific.

So, the method consists of choosing the CSFs within levels 1 and 2 of the BBS, the benefits/outcomes levels, level 0 being the strategic objective of the program. They are high enough in the hierarchy to be significant and specific enough to be measurable. The rules are as follows: start with level 1; select all the benefits of that level. Analyse each one to see if they are specific enough; if yes keep them, if not, go to the next level down. When you go down one level you again select all the "branches" below the benefit that you found too generic, otherwise you will create gaps in the CSFs as their sum should represent the total scope of the program. You can never choose two CSFs on the same branch, because, if your BBS is complete, the lower one is already included in the higher one and that would mean an overlap in terms of measure. In Figure 7.3, for example, the CSFs are on Level 1. "Enable Business Stability and Growth" was considered too generic to be a good CSF for the program, on the other hand, "Empower Employees to Perform" or "Guarantee Content Integrity and Consistency" are specific enough to be representative of the program's success.

Again, CSFs can be on two different levels, but never in the same branch; for example, "Enable Optimisation of Organizational Performance" and "Improve Content Processing Efficiency" could not be chosen together. It is either "Enable Optimisation of Organizational Performance", or "Improve Content Processing Efficiency" *and* "Optimise DM Solution Architecture" together.

In summary, CSFs are an essential means of communication between program managers and their sponsors. They need to be well defined and prioritized as part of the formulation process. Whatever method is chosen to select the CSFs, the key stakeholders of the program should be involved and their backing secured, as the CSFs will help define the scope and clarify objectives of the program, thus enabling more effective decision-making during deployment.

In order to fully achieve these objectives though, CSFs need to be prioritized. The next section presents a few prioritization techniques that I have used effectively over the years.

If CSFs are selected randomly, it is expected that decision-makers will intuitively prioritize the selection, although there is a high risk of having gaps and redundancies. With the methodical CSF selection process I described, *all* the scope of the program is covered and, although all benefits should be realized to ensure success, not all benefits hold the same importance for the achievement of the strategic objectives. The key stakeholders, including the program team, therefore need to clarify their order of importance to assign resources and effort proportionately to this ranking.

The basic principle of prioritization is that you need to obtain a proportional *weight* for each CSF. The total of the weights should be equal to 100. The reason for this is that it makes it easier for these weights to be used with other techniques, it creates consistency to enable comparison with other programs and between projects and, finally, because a percentage is easier to grasp for most people. Many prioritization methods exist.

Simple scoring systems require stakeholders to score each CSF by giving them a number of points. By adding the points you obtain a total score, which is then adjusted on scale of 100. Many methods exist to allocate points and it is not the purpose of this book to discuss them. Again this method is very intuitive and subject to bias, especially if the scoring is done in a workshop where people can influence each other.

The best method I found is the *paired comparison*, also known as *pair-wise comparison*. This method consists of comparing the CSFs in pairs, to score them against each other. Again, there are many techniques available to do a paired comparison, some very elaborate using statistical analysis. The one I

	A	B	C	D.1	D.2	D.3	Score	Weight
A-Empower employees to perform		2	1	3	2	3	11	15
B-Enable optimization of organizational performance	3		1	2	2	3	11	15
C-Guarantee content integrity and consistency	4	4		4	3	4	19	25
D.1-Improve compliance	2	3	1		2	3	11	15
D.2-Maintain business continuity	3	3	2	3		4	15	20
D.3-Provide capability for business growth	2	2	1	2	1		8	10
							75	100

FIGURE 7.5   EXAMPLE OF PAIRED COMPARISON

found most useful, because it has the necessary degree of objectivity without being overly complicated, works as follows:

- A total of five points is shared between each CSF in a pair. There can be no equal score. Possibilities between A and B, for example are 5–0; 4–1; 3–2; 2–3; 1–4 and 0–5.
- The score that each CSF has accumulated against the others is added to give a total score.
- The total score is adjusted to a weight in percentage.

Figure 7.5 shows a comparison between five CSFs. The score of each CSF is added horizontally. For example, A scored 3 against D1 and D3, 2 against B and D2 and 1 against C. B scored 3 against A and D3, 2 against D1 and D2 and 1 against C, and so on. Each score is then divided by 75 (the sum of the scores) and multiplied by 100 to give the weighted score in the right hand side column.

Once the CSFs are weighted they can be used for a number of applications. They are used to justify the program in the business case and will be the basis for reporting and marketing the program. They will also structure the change management and risk management processes.

7.2.4.2   Set key performance indicators

Although CSFs are most often expressed as a qualitative statement, they have to be quantified to be assessed. The agreed term to describe the quantification of CSFs is the Key Performance Indicator (KPI). Each CSF will generate one or more KPIs.

Once the CSFs are selected and agreed upon, the team will identify KPIs for each CSF. These will enable the measurement of the delivery of the program's benefits. Typically, I aim for three KPIs per CSF, but there is no set rule as long as there are enough to truly measure the outcome and not too many to become unmanageable. The KPI is essentially a measure of the CSF. One question that can be asked is, how will we demonstrate that we have achieved the CSF? For example, how will we demonstrate that we have empowered employees to perform? You can use the next lower level of the BBS to find your KPIs; in the case of the example: "Increase DM skillset", "Increase content availability", "Improve information access" and "Facilitate content management" would be good KPIs. But you could also find KPIs independent from the lower levels of the BBS, like "Improve level of autonomous decision".

One easy way to define measures for the KPIs is to identify a criterion of measure, the level that needs to be achieved and the acceptable range. For example, the criteria for these KPIs could be: Number of employees trained in DM; number of access points for data; classification system for data; improved autonomous decision. The expected level would be, for example, 60 per cent of employees trained in first six month or data available from at least three devices, classification system agreed by all concerned line managers. Finally the range, which should be numerical, will set the limits of success or failure for each KPI. In the end there should be between 15 and 25 points of measure (KPIs) for the program.

There are a few basic rules for selecting KPIs. KPIs should be:

- *measurable* in quantitative terms;
- *feasible* in terms of finances, equipment, skills and time;
- *relevant* and *accurate* to reflect what is to be measured in an accurate way;
- *sensitive* to enable identification of changes over time;
- *timely* to inform in time for effective decision-making.

The choice of the right KPIs is as essential as that of the CSFs. If these steps are done well, the rate of success of the program increases significantly because the program team understands on what to focus, the sponsors understand and agree with the measures and these measures provide valuable data for future decision-making and change management.

7.2.5   CREATE THE PROGRAM BLUEPRINT

The development of the blueprint is part of the business analysis or value management processes. It is a narrative of the expected future state of the internal or external client/beneficiary's business unit, organization or context. An initial outline qualitative functional blueprint is produced during the program formulation stage, the more detailed quantitative technical blueprint forms part of the benefits register and is produced during the program preparation stage.

The blueprint details the current state of the organization and how it will need to look like in order to deliver the benefits and capabilities described in the value proposition. It is developed in parallel with the outline business case and can form part of it to ensure continued consistency throughout the duration of the program.

The outcome of the objectives definition and prioritization is what I labelled the *Strategic Blueprint*, which could be seen as the program equivalent of a project's functional specification. The strategic blueprint is typically a descriptive document which outlines the functionalities expected to be delivered by the program (e.g. 1: improve knowledge; 2: expand market). There are different levels of blueprint; in MSP the *blueprint* represents a model of the future desired state of the business or organization, including practices and processes. This more detailed model is what I have labelled the *Operational Blueprint*, it is typically a prescriptive document that details the way new capabilities or deliverables are going to be used to produce the expected results (e.g. A.1.1: Courses delivered to all production personnel; A.1.1: Tests conducted to assess knowledge increase; A.2.1: All significant data available electronically; A.3.2: Comprehensive data classification system distributed). The operational blueprint should also include measures of success. An example of operational blueprint is shown in Figure 8.4.

In program mature organizations that practice organizational project management (OPM), the elements of the blueprint are drawn from the benefits breakdown structure (BBS) and define the requirements necessary to achieve strategy specific objectives.

In organizations that do not use the BBS, the program manager and program sponsor can use corporate level (portfolio) key performance indicators (KPI), often generated through a Balanced Scorecard process, as the elements of the blueprint.

The last option is used when the first two are not available. It consists of focusing on operational results rather than business objectives:

- business models (structures, culture, values);
- work practices (governance, roles, networking);
- internal processes (methodologies, techniques);
- personnel capabilities (knowledge, skills, attitudes);
- social impact (environment, corporate citizenship, ethics);
- data management (business analysis, reporting, scorecards);
- technology (hardware, software, IT/IS, networks);
- facilities and equipment;
- others.

Although these elements need to be addressed in the operational blueprint, using these elements independently from one of the first two can result in a misalignment with strategic objectives.

As can be seen from the examples above there needs to be a clear link between the strategic objectives, the delivered capabilities and the measures of their achievement. In mature organizations, the benefits breakdown structure, Blueprint and benefits register are combined in one single document that emphasizes the program's alignment with the strategy it supports. For simple programs, the blueprint can be produced in a narrative form which is also called the Program Scope Statement.

7.2.5.1   Develop blueprint

The strategic and operational blueprints are compiled by the program manager through a series of workshops, meetings or interviews with the key stakeholders. It is based on the stakeholder needs analysis. The program sponsor and business integrator must review the document before it is issued. Inputs to blueprint are:

- approved value proposition;
- stakeholder needs analysis;
- benefits breakdown structure (BBS).

The Blueprint is updated regularly (at least at each cycle) as data and feedback on results increases the level of understanding of the future state, the purpose being to maintain alignment with the desired outcomes and benefits and adapt to evolving circumstances. The level of detail will depend on the stage of development, internal or external client requirements as well as pace and complexity of the program. The faster the pace and the higher the complexity, the more the blueprint will need to be developed in a progressive and incremental way.

7.2.5.2   Draw benefits management strategy

Once the strategic blueprint is agreed, the program manager can start working on the Benefits Management Strategy by developing the program scope and the program structure in collaboration with Program Board. The formation of the benefits management strategy requires the engagement of the key stakeholders around the program CSFs and the structuring of the program. It is initiated during the formulation, refined in the preparation stage and should be reviewed and updated as necessary at each program cycle.

7.2.5.3   Compose program strategic roadmap

The benefits management strategy will be graphically represented by a strategic roadmap and rolled-out into the outline business case. This roadmap will display the main processes of the deployment stage: Capabilities Delivery; Capabilities Integration and Benefits Appraisal as well as transition between

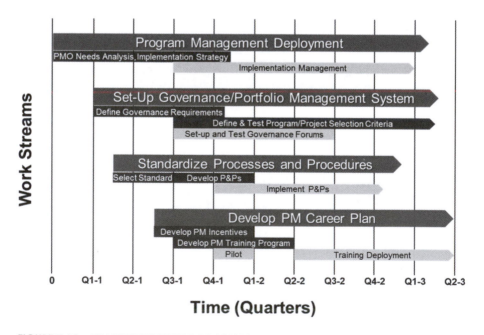

FIGURE 7.6A   EXAMPLE STRATEGIC ROADMAP

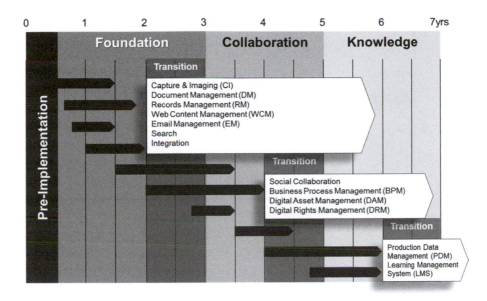

FIGURE 7.6B   EXAMPLE STRATEGIC ROADMAP

the different cycles of the program. I will display the main interfaces between the program's components and key milestones. At preliminary level, the roadmap is usually presented as a high-level Gantt chart (see Figure 7.6a) or a timed list of expected capabilities (see Figure 7.6b).

7.2.6   START BUSINESS CASE PROCESS

The business case is destined to justify the funding of the program. Besides this obvious purpose, it is the core of the program's success because it enables the program team to get buy-in from the organization and is the basis for assessing the program's success. Essentially it aims to clearly demonstrate how the program supports the business' strategic objectives. In most organizations, the business case is based on financial factors. Although financial factors are important, other factors should be taken into consideration when developing the business case as outlined in Section 8.3.2 (p. 195). When financial benefits are used, the method should be consistent with the organization's requirements; for example, one could not use Return on Investment (ROI) for one initiative, Internal Rate of Return (IRR) for the other and Net Present Value (NPV) for a third. Each method measures different aspects of the initiative's financial

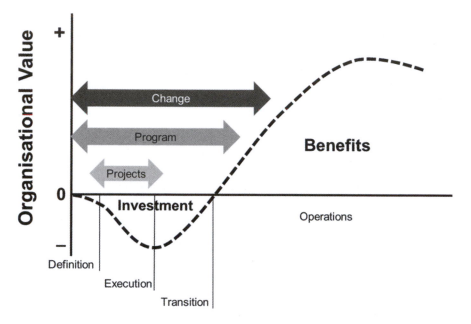

FIGURE 7.7   EVOLUTION OF VALUE THROUGH LIFE CYCLE
Source: Adapted with permission from: Exhibit 1–3.2, p. 19. (PMAJ, 2015) P"M 3rd Edition, *A Guidebook of Program and Project Management for Enterprise Innovation.*

contribution and business initiatives can be compared only if the same method is used throughout and the chosen method represents what the organization really wants to measure. Many good publications are discussing these methods and others and it is not the purpose of this book to detail them. On the other hand, managers have to be careful not to expect short-term program financial benefits. As shown in Figure 7.7 above, the organizational value of a program comes only towards the end. If short-term financial benefits are a key issue, the program will be paced so that the cycles each provide a positive return, which may mean a longer transition period between each cycle.

In this section, I will discuss the tiered process approach described in Figure 4.6 (p. 95). In architecture, design is divided into three steps: concept, preliminary design and detailed design. These steps are usually preceded by the Architectural Program, which describes the intended building in terms of the users' requirements. The stakeholder analysis process corresponds to the architectural programming; the development of the benefits map and CSFs corresponds to the conceptual design phase. These two steps constitute the basis for the *Initial Business Case.* When the concept is approved, the design team is authorized to develop a preliminary design, which consists of developing alternative options for construction, including engineering requirements, and a functional level specification. This phase includes the testing of different alternatives in terms of their technical achievability. Although it is still high level, it is precise enough to estimate the resourcing impact and get approval for the detailed design. In the program, this corresponds to the *Outline Business Case*; an evaluation of different alternatives against the CSFs and a measure of their achievability to finalize the options. Finally, when the preliminary design is approved the design team (architect and engineers) is authorized to proceed with the detailed design, which includes full estimates and technical specifications of each building component. This is the *Definitive Business Case* that will warrant approval of the budget for the program's first cycle and overall approval of the program funding.

7.2.6.1   Initial business case

The *initial business case*, or opportunity case, is a demonstration that the proposed program could create a real opportunity for the the organization or its stakeholders. Programs typically start in two ways: they are defined by a strategic intent (deliberate program) or they stem from a need to regroup existing discrete business initiatives (projects and other actions) at the strategic level (Ad Hoc Program) (see Figure 3.1, p. 51). In each case, the incentive, for the organization, to invest in a program to manage them needs to be justified. Typically, the potential sponsor or business manager nominates someone to spend a minimal time (a few hours to a few days) to develop a program concept, which is then evaluated by the sponsor or a sponsor group. At this stage the assessment is rough because detailed data is not available.

The initial business case is part of the definition of the value proposition; following its approval, the commitment of the sponsoring group is limited to the launch of the formulation cycle of the program; a minimal investment compared to the overall cost of the program, as formulation can usually be achieved with a small core team of key stakeholders.

7.2.6.2   Outline business case

The outline business case is developed during formulation and submitted to the program board (see Tables 5.1 and 5.2) for approval. The outline business case will enable the organization to commit to the launch of the preparation cycle and, potentially, to the first deployment cycle of the program. The Program Board evaluates the potential of the concept to support the strategy and, if it is acceptable, they ask the team to prepare a definitive business case as part of the preparation, drawing on all the required organizational resources. This document is called Programme Brief in MSP and Program Charter in the PMI Standard.

The process consists of the following actions:

1. Consult with the key stakeholders, subject matter experts (SMEs) and collect data to complete the analysis.
2. Confirm alignment and assess achievability, based on approved business case factors.
3. Clarify outcomes: Time frame (Short-Medium-Long); Expected Return (Financial and others); Outputs (New Capabilities).
4. Prioritize objectives, develop outline blueprint.

The outline business case will demonstrate alignment with business strategy and establish comparative value of program against other initiatives, based on opportunity vs. investment. It will contain the following elements:

1. Program Outline Proposal:
    1.1. *Program justification/drivers*: Reasons why this program/ project needs to be undertaken. This is to include the opportunity or problem being addressed.
    1.2. *Program purpose/objectives*: Overall objective(s) of the program. This is to include the high-level scope and time frames of the program, including major expected benefits. Agreement on PgM objectives from key stakeholders.
    1.3. *Program classification*: A program can cover more than one class of activities. Typical classes are: Transformation, Continuous Improvement, Maintenance and Compliance. They need to be defined to assess the impact of the program on the business.
    1.4. *Alignment assessment*: How the program will contribute to each of the weighted CSFs. Where relevant, specific contributions to the CSFs are included.
    1.5. *Achievability assessment*: Achievability of program/project, based on pre-set factors. At this level, the assessment is subjective but needs to be documented.
    1.6. *Program key deliverables and milestones*: Key program/project deliverables and the CSF/KPI they contribute most to. Expected

delivery date (milestone) for each of these deliverables assuming this program/project is approved. Typically an outline blueprint, management strategy and roadmap and executive level benefits register.

1.7. *Major risks identification*: Most significant risks (threats and opportunities) of the program/project and their impact on strategic objectives.

1.8. *Human resource requirements*: Estimated resource FTE (Full Time Equivalent) and other resource requirements. List specialist expertise resources required and identify source.

1.9. *Impact on organization*: The impact of the proposed program on other business initiatives, specifically in terms of resources and outcomes. Identify any possible synergy or source of conflict.

2. Cost/Benefits Identification:

2.1. *Costs*: Estimated "Order of Magnitude" program cost requirements. This should include all fixed and variable costs that can be incurred by and/or assigned to the program, except FTE.

2.2. *Financial benefits realization plan*: Outline of expected financial benefits, when they are expected to be realized, and who is responsible for their realization. A financial benefit is a tangible economic benefit that has a traceable cause-effect relationship and can be measured.

2.3. *Non-financial benefits realization plan*: Outline of expected non-financial benefits, when they are expected to be realized, and who is responsible for their realization. A non-financial benefit is any benefit that cannot be explicitly expressed in monetary value but can be measured. If non-financial benefits are intangible; if so they should be identified as such.

The typical level of detail of the preliminary business case is shown in Figures 7.8 and 7.9 on the following page. Figure 7.8 uses the weighted CSFs to assess the alignment of the program with the strategic objectives. Typically I find that defining specific contributions helps justify the score and clarifies the scope of the program and its component actions. In the example below, the total weighted score is 660 on 1,000, which, in the Alignment-Achievability Assessment (AAA) matrix (Thiry, various publications 2003 to 2015) selection tool (see Figure 7.10, p. 172) equates to a high contribution to benefits. Even in the case of a high

Critical Success Factor	Contribution Description (How does this program/project contribute to this CSF?)	Score (0-10)	Weigh Score
Increase alignment with strategy (30%)	The corporate PMO will play a portfolio management role and select projects. A governance system will be put in place	7	210
Develop strong PM Culture (10%)	The corporate PMO will develop a PM training program in collaboration with HR departments	5	50
Develop formal unified practice (15%)	The Corporate PMO is set to standardize PgM and PM practice	8	120
Refine portfolio management processes (20%)	The program will clarify PfM aligning and monitoring processes and criteria (selection and data collection and analysis to be implemented	6	120
Coordinate HR functions (10%)	The corporate PMO will arbitrate resource issues between entities	3	30
Create administrative support role (5%)	The Corporate PMO will develop templates for PM	4	20
Assist PMs with data & time intensive tasks (10%)	The Corporate PMO will hire/provide specialist resources to each entity	9	90
Total score / 1000	(Multiply score by weight, for each CSF)		660

FIGURE 7.8   ASSESS ALIGNMENT (CONTRIBUTION TO CSFS)

Achievability Assessment Factors	High/10	Medium/5	Low/2	Score	
A. Financial Factors				Co1	Co2
1 Project cost /total Portfolio budget*	≤ 5%	5-20%	≥ 20%	5	10
2 Expected Return/Benefits	Very short-term	Short-term	Medium-term	2	5
3 Funding (Financial Authority)	Internal to BU	Other business unit	Outside Org.	5	5
B. Parameters & Constraints					
1 Resource Availability (FTE Capacity)	≥ 2:1 (200%)	2:1-1:1 (200-100%)	≤ 1:1 (100%)	5	10
2 Type of project (Authority)	BU initiated	Org. initiated	External/Regulatory	5	2
3 Schedule	Acceptable/estimated	Tight/negotiated	Inadequate/imposed	10	2
C. Human Resources and People Factors					
1 Spread of Resources	All internal	Internal + External	PM + External	5	5
2 Dedicated workforce (Fulltime)	All	most	Few	2	10
3 Staff Expertise/ experience	↗ Requirements	Sufficient	↘ Requirements	5	5
D. Complexity Factors					
1 Type of Work/Innovativeness	Known	New	Breakthrough	10	10
2 Interdependency of projects	Negligible	Significant	Essential	2	2
3 Objectives & Scope	Well Defined	Unclear	Undefined	10	10
Score Total /120				66	76
Achievability Score (Total score/120x1000)				550	633

A1 Budget includes actual and committed (pipeline)

B1 Available resources/required resources for program/project in regards of the workload (actual and committed)

C2 Multi tasking generally leads to a lower achievability

Co1-Co2 Component 1 and Component 2

FIGURE 7.9   ASSESS ACHIEVABILITY (OUTLINE LEVEL)

alignment, the program has to be evaluated in terms of its achievability before it can be approved.

In Figure 7.9, pre-set factors are used to assess the achievability of the program. It is in fact an assessment of the supply against the demand; all these factors assess the capability of the organization to respond to the demand generated by the program on its resources.

Based experience and research, specifically in the domain of organizational effectiveness, I have used four achievability factors major areas (Thiry, 2003).

Financial factors
These factors are all related to the difficulty to achieve the program in regards of the overall availability of funds. They include: total estimated capital cost, impact on company cash flow; source of funding, delay in expected return/ benefits and life cycle-cost, if the organization is committed to the operation of the deliverable.

Parameters and constraints
This set of factors includes all the criteria imposed by the client, the organization's structure or the program itself; they are the number of members in team, level of familiarity with contract type, geographical spread of work, as well as acceptability of schedule and budget.

Human resources and people factors
The quality of human resources is crucial to the achievability of a project within a program; the factors listed here all have to do with the capability of resources to deliver the product. They are the spread of resources, familiarity with resources; other critical work being undertaken by the organization at the same time, customer perception of resources allocated, and staff expertise.

Complexity
The last point concerns the degree of difficulty to achieve the program, based on its complexity. Complexity factors include familiarity with type of work/ innovativeness, interdependency of deliverables, number of stakeholders, stakeholders spread, clarity of objectives, benefits and CSFs and clarity of scope statement.

These factors should be validated for each organization as their culture, capabilities and requirements may differ. The factors shown in Figures 7.9 and are typical of most organizations.

The program achievability matrix is used to assess the program's likelihood of success, but also to define its parameters and constraints. All the factors on the basis of which the program has been chosen become its parameters. For example, in the case shown, Component 2 will use less than 5 per cent of the portfolio budget; it will provide short-term benefits and its budget will come from another business unit, etc. If any of these factors changed, the component would need to be re-evaluated.

Finally the combination of the contribution to benefits and achievability scores are mapped on the AAA (Alignment-Achievability Assessment) matrix to get the Combined Alignment/Achievability Score of the program. Because alignment is considered more important than achievability (e.g. an option having a high contribution to benefits and a medium achievability will be favoured over a highly achievable option with medium contribution to benefits), the scoring factors of benefits grow exponentially whereas the scoring factors of achievability grow linearly (see Figure 7.10).

This system does not make the decision for you, but will both help make the decision and justify it. It can be used for both a selection between two or more mutually exclusive options or to select a limited number of components among many alternatives (see Figure 7.11). Other factors, explicit or implicit, may need to be considered when making the final selection. When finalizing

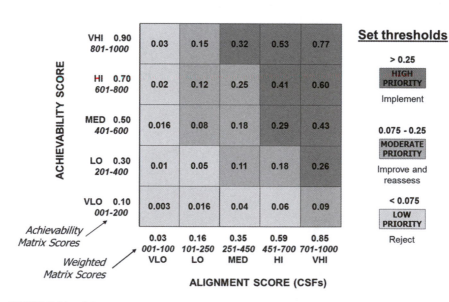

FIGURE 7.10   COMBINED ALIGNMENT/ACHIEVABILITY ASSESSMENT

Source: Adapted from Thiry (2003).

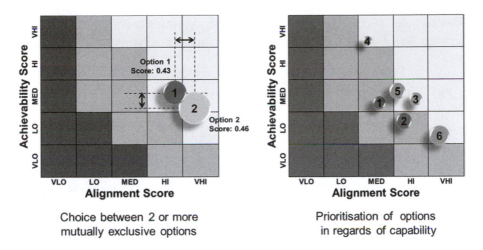

Choice between 2 or more
mutually exclusive options

Prioritisation of options
in regards of capability

FIGURE 7.11   TWO OPTIONS FOR USE OF ALIGNMENT/ACHIEVABILITY MATRIX

Note: Size represents cost.

the selection process, decision-makers should always take a wide view of organizational issues that includes the whole program, interdependencies between actions, interface with other programs and the organizational context, including competitiveness. Stakeholder engagement is essential to the program's success and it is therefore imperative that the key stakeholders approve the final decision.

The same outline business case will be used to assess potential program components. Once components are selected, they can be added to the program scope and used to refine the evaluation.

Business development is responsible for preparing the business case with the program manager and the sponsor is responsible for validating it. If a business integrator is involved, they should endorse it. The PMO typically validates the format.

7.2.7   FINALISE PROGRAM MANDATE

The program mandate is an executive summary of the outline business case. It is often called program(me) brief or program charter. I have decided to use the term mandate to clearly distinguish it from project-specific terms. From the business case, the program manager will extract the program mandate, which will be the basis for the authorization of the preparation phase. The program sponsor validates the mandate in regards of the business portfolio and business strategy. In most cases, the business case can act as the mandate.

7.2.8   AUTHORIZE PROGRAM PREPARATION

Following examination of the Business Case and Mandate, the sponsor authorises the program's preparation. This consists of: confirming the program manager, assigning the core team, releasing funds and resources for preparation and committing to the overall program. The sponsor is responsible for this approval and has basically three options:

1. Validate PgM strategy and approve program.
2. Realign program and reassess program business case.
3. Realign overall strategy in regard of findings.

CHAPTER 8

Program Definition (Preparation)

In Chapter 7, we have examined how the program objectives are defined by its stakeholders, how the purpose and objectives of the program are defined and how the program is evaluated. In Chapter 8 we will see how to set it up to be able to deliver value to the business. Preparation consists of setting up the governance system, defining the program architecture, deploying the initial team and developing the detailed business case and program plan. It is also during this process that proposals are made for candidate components (projects and other actions). The ultimate purpose of program preparation is to get approval for the program deployment.

Preparation is iterative with formulation; it will enable the team to plan and pace benefits realization and finalize the program scope for the next deployment cycle. This process requires the engagement of the key stakeholders around the program CSFs and the structuring of the program.

The scope of the program and benefits realization strategy are initiated during the formulation stage, refined in the preparation stage and reviewed and updated as necessary at each program cycle.

The second part of the chapter discusses how to organize the program to achieve these objectives: what framework and structure to put in place to manage and realize benefits; what needs to be managed and how to do it and who should do what. It also outlines the development of the definitive business case that will secure the funding and resources for the program. There is clearly a lot of iteration between the formulation and preparation and they are often funded and undertaken as a single definition stage.

The chapter is divided into four sections:

- 8.1   Set-up Program Structure
- 8.2   Select Program Components for Cycle
- 8.3   Prepare Definitive Business Case (Benefits Realization Plan)
- 8.4   Authorize Next Cycle Deployment

8.1   Set-up Program Structure

This process consists of setting up the program organization, governance processes and assigning roles and responsibilities for the different program requirements. It is the first step of the program preparation stage as will define its next steps. It comprises four main activities:

1.   Design Program Architecture.
2.   Develop Governance Systems.
3.   Engage Stakeholders.
4.   Assign Roles and Responsibilities.

8.1.1   DESIGN PROGRAM ARCHITECTURE

I have explained three major program governance architectures (see Sections 4.3.2 to 4.3.4, pp. 90–92). The networked approach, requires an in-depth cultural change for which most organizations are not ready. So there are basically two choices:

1.   If the program is well defined and the scope clear, the structure will be more controlled and resemble that of a complex waterfall project with a sponsor making decisions and the program manager managing the execution.
2.   If the program still requires negotiation of objectives and the predictability of its outcomes is unlikely, the organization should be integrated, with the sponsor, key stakeholders and business integrator working in collaboration with the program manager, very much like an agile approach.

Our experience is that, if the program scores 3 in any of factors 1, 3 or 4 of Table 3.2 (see p. 71), Option 2 applies.

The first approach has been discussed extensively in project management books. I will therefore focus on the integrated approach, which is becoming the norm for organizations that need to be dynamic and responsive. The integrated approach requires that the organization views the program as a value chain where all the actors participate to the achievement of the program objectives (see Figure 3.2, p. 68).

The program architecture, as any organizational structure, is not defined by the physical decision and communication channels or their material configuration, but by the relationships it enables its actors to develop through it. Initially, the program team will establish what I would call the "bricks and mortar" structure, but it is only when it starts enabling interactions between the different actors that it will form the program architecture. In my experience, the best approach to structuring the program is to view it as a value chain (Porter, 1985) where the relationship between the program itself and the business is defined by needs definition as the inbound process and integration of capabilities as the outbound process. The key to a successful value chain is that all actors contribute to the common business goal across boundaries and personal interest.

Michael Porter (1985) identifies two major types of activities in the value chain: the primary activities, those that directly contribute to the product being delivered; and the support activities, those that enable the primary. A program is very similar in that it has a series of processes and activities that directly contribute to the delivery of the benefits; those that were identified in the BBS and blueprint and the enabling activities delivered by structures external to the program like IT (support systems), line activities (human resources, procurement, finance, etc.), the Program Management Office (tools and techniques, standards, expertise, etc.).

My experience has shown that there are essentially four steps to build a successful value chain:

1. *Identify the activities/functions required*: In an integrated value chain structure, the designer focuses first on the main process; in the program: "deliver benefits to realize value for the stakeholders". Only then does the team identify all the activities, primary and support, required to ensure that the vision is maintained and that the objectives and benefits are achieved. These include both the performance and learning activities (production and control).

2. *Define the interactions required between the functions*: The second step is to define, first the mandatory, and then the discretionary interdependencies between activities or groups of activities: i.e. needs must be identified before scope is defined; training must be delivered before product is delivered to operations, etc.

3. *Develop management teams*: Once activities and interactions have been defined, roles and responsibilities are assigned, not in terms of business hierarchical structures but in terms of the functional

requirements, and management teams are formed for each group of activity; i.e. stakeholder analysis, business case, project management, operational integration, etc.

4. *Set governance systems*: The governance systems concern mainly the processes through which the teams will report to the Program Board or Steering Group, coordinate and integrate their work, perform together and interact to create value for the business. A good program governance system will hinge on the creation, and effective management of, team overlaps to foster full integration of the processes and create synergy between the teams.

As you notice in this process, the governance structure is defined from the functions required, not the opposite. Many organizations still try to force fit functions into a pre-determined structure; this does not create value, but merely reassures control-focused managers. The success of a value chain for programs requires a cultural reframing from the traditional model of organizations; more specifically it requires moving from:

- control-focused approach to *empowerment focused approach*;
- individual accountability to *both individual and team accountability*;
- task-oriented focus to *both task and results-oriented focus*;
- shareholder-only perspective to *stakeholder perspective*;
- bottom-up only to *top-down and bottom-up integrated vision of governance*.

Because it is not possible at the beginning to predict the program in detail, a program is generally constructed around a series of sequential or concurrent cycles. These cycles are generally associated with a group of projects and other actions that deliver a specific objective or CSF, or, more classically, with phases leading to go/no-go decisions. MSP defines a "tranche" as "a group of projects structured around distinct step changes in capability or benefits delivery" (OCG, 2011, p. 287). In each cycle, the three stages of the program life cycle are repeated. Sometimes, large complex projects that are part of a program can be considered as an independent cycle.

This means that the program architecture is built around a core group of key stakeholders who are typically the main decision-makers, and can evolve throughout the duration of the program. It is now time to confirm and set up the Steering committee of the program.

8.1.2   DEVELOP GOVERNANCE SYSTEMS

Program governance is a subset of organizational governance, which is the way significant components of the firm are organized to achieve the mission and how they are coordinated to deliver strategies (see Section 4.3, p. 88). In this section, I will discuss the integrated governance approach (see Section 4.3.3, p. 91), which is composed of three processes:

1.   *Maintain direction* (clarify and adjust vision, mission and strategy).
2.   *Put in place the structures* necessary to ensure success (secure resources, define and support policies, processes, roles and responsibilities, arbitrate conflicts, etc.).
3.   Make sure the *objectives/benefits are achieved* (setting up and managing the monitoring and reporting process, including the program and project review and approval process, evaluate and approve change, read and feedback on reports, etc.).

The first step is to assign roles and responsibilities for program governance. They will be shared between:

- The *program board* for leadership and maintaining direction.
- The *sponsor and program manager* for putting in place the structures necessary to ensure success, including the deployment of the core team.
- The *sponsor* will also make sure the objectives/benefits are achieved.

The appraisal system is a subset of the program's governance system. It includes the development of the project review processes and program appraisal system – milestones, gates and evaluation criteria – but is not restricted to it as the complete governance system will also comprise the integration and coordination of all the benefits realization processes to achieve the program objectives.

8.1.3   ENGAGE STAKEHOLDERS

At this point, the program team should be able to rely on a complete list of stakeholders classified (see Section 7.2.2, p. 150) and agreed expected benefits of the key stakeholders (see Section 7.2.3, p. 152). These elements should be re-confirmed with all the stakeholders that will actively be involved in the program. The team will then establish the expected contribution from those key stakeholders to the program (see Figure 4.8). For example, if a customer expects a good quality product to be delivered in time, they should define their requirements clearly and approve deliverables in a timely fashion. The expected benefits and quid pro quo contribution is the basis of the stakeholder engagement plan. Too often, programs focus only on the benefits side of it and neglect the other side of the engagement deal.

As I stated earlier, engagement requires a good marketing strategy to maintain the key stakeholders' motivation throughout the program. The team should develop an interactive communication system aimed at gaining stakeholders' support in terms of the strategy and delivery of the program benefits.

A preliminary marketing plan should be part of the detailed business case. This marketing plan is based on milestones corresponding to key deliverables, those that directly contribute to the realization of a benefit, and even more specifically a CSF. If the deliverables that contribute to benefits are clearly identified, as in the preliminary business case for example (see Figure 7.8), milestones for their delivery and measures of success (KPIs) will be key aspects of the marketing of the program. If contributing stakeholders see that their expected benefits are realized, or probably to be, they will continue to support the program. The marketing plan should focus on measurable outcomes and spread their delivery between short, medium- and long-term (see Pace Components and Benefits, Section 8.3.1).

Goal setting theories state that there are three important factors that come into play when trying to motivate people to achieve a goal:

a) the meaningfulness of the goal;
b) its achievability; and
c) the pace at which one is progressing towards the goal.

In the formulation stage, stakeholders expressed their needs and expectations and the benefits that the program will help realize stems from these, so they are meaningful. At the preliminary business case and later in the organization stage, the achievability of the options has been analysed and demonstrated. It is during the preparation stage that the pace for benefits realization will be set and it needs to be done in a way that will maintain the motivation of the key stakeholders by allowing them to measure that they are effectively on the way to achieving their objectives. I will discuss pacing in detail further in this section.

8.1.4 ASSIGN ROLES AND RESPONSIBILITIES

Roles are dependent on the governance approach used in the program; the governance approach is usually predetermined, or determined during the formulation stage of the program and key roles are assigned early on (see Tables 5.1 and 5.2, p. 118 and p. 120). Responsibilities for deployment are often assigned before all the elements, or components, of the program are identified and coordinated; this is a mistake as responsibilities for deployment should derive from the benefits realization plan and not the opposite. In an integrated approach, authority is given in accordance with responsibility; procedures and rules are limited and simple since empowerment is privileged over excessive control. This enables teams to be creative in ambiguous, complex and turbulent situations where quick and decisive decision-making is essential for success.

Roles and responsibilities can be assigned for the key stakeholders and the core program team early on, although they should be revisited when the program plan is completed and at the beginning of each new cycle. In some organizations, these roles are temporarily assigned as part-time roles for the definition stages; once deployment is approved, the sponsor and program manager will agree to delegate responsibilities to different people in the organization, they will deploy the full program team of the program to deliver the program benefits.

CSFs	Board	CEO	Program Manager	Marketing Dep't Head	Quality Dep't Head	HR Dep't Head	Experienced PMs	Others...
Increase credibility with customers	I	A	R	R	C	C	C	
Deliver to agreed parameters (Short term)	I	I	R	I	C	I	A	
Demonstrate control of projects	C	R	A	I	C	C	R	
Maintain/improve delivery efficiency	I	C	A	C	R	I	R	
Improve knowledge & skills of new PMs	I	I	R	I	C	A	R	
Normalize practice of experienced PMs	I	C	R	I	R	R	A	
Standardize PM processes	I	I	R	I	A	C	R	

Key stakeholders

Use RACI or other system

FIGURE 8.1 RACI MATRIX BASED ON ACCOUNTABILITY FOR CSFS

Over the years, I have discovered that the best way to ensure a program's success is to align the core team responsibilities with the realization of the CSFs, as they are warranting the program's success. Figure 8.1, on the previous page, is an example of the responsibility assignment based on the CSFs. It is based on an organization that has had complaints from clients concerning the management of their projects and has launched an organization-wide program to address this issue. It uses the RACI model: R: Responsibility for delivery; A: Accountability for deliverable; C: Consult to make decisions; I: Inform of decisions.

Accountability is established for all CSFs, with only one party accountable, so as not to create confusion. Responsibility can be shared among many parties. A party could be both accountable and responsible. When establishing responsibilities for the rest of the team and other stakeholders, I typically use the BBS and blueprint. This is the best way to ensure that each outcome and output has a person or party accountable and that there are no overlaps of responsibility, although most transition and governance tasks, as well as dependencies, will require close collaboration and overlap of responsibilities to ensure a smooth transition.

8.2   Select Program Components for Cycle

This process consists of identifying the projects and other actions that will form the program scope for the next cycle and clarifying the pace and mode of benefits realization. It comprises five main activities:

1.   Identify Candidate Components.
2.   Assess Alignment and achievability.
3.   Define Interdependencies.
4.   Select Program Components for Cycle.
5.   Finalize Program Scope.

8.2.1   IDENTIFY CANDIDATE COMPONENTS (IDEATION)

Once the CSFs are identified, the program team will start to identify the program components (projects, transition and integration activities, operations and other support actions) that will enable the program to realize its expected benefits. This process is generally performed in two steps: a first preliminary step during formulation and a more detailed step during preparation. During the first step, concept level ideas are developed, usually for the whole program, with a rough level estimate of resources required. The second step consists of developing some of these ideas for the first, or next, cycle to a level where they can be estimated for budgeting.

In organizations where programs are ad hoc (see Figure 3.1, p. 51), the actions, especially projects, already exist and therefore the component generation process consists more of "testing their fit", typically by linking them to the appropriate CSFs and ensuring that they should be part of the program. In a recent ad hoc program, this process enabled me to identify a project that did not belong with the program; it was reassigned to another initiative, and having identified that one of the CSFs was not covered by any project, a new project was initiated to fill that gap.

If the program is deliberate (see Figure 3.1, p. 51), component initiatives and actions should be derived from the CSFs, which represent the expected benefits and outcomes of the program. If all the CSFs are covered by at least one component initiative or action, the program should be successful. Again, this process can be done intuitively in meetings or workshops, but I strongly suggest using a more objective method that will enable the program team to control the level of politics that will influence the process. The ideation-elaboration method described below is such a method.

Ideation consists of a creative generation of alternative ideas that will enable a high-quality and innovative decision process. Ideation is usually run as a workshop; it should feature a good mix of people with no major power relationships and, ideally, a facilitator should lead the process. All the ideas that are generated through ideation will be evaluated and reduced to a few workable alternatives in the next stage: *elaboration*. It is therefore important to allow freethinking and creativity to flow in order to generate as many innovative and potentially valuable ideas as possible. Ideation is based on the principles of creative thinking developed by Edward de Bono who advocated the separation of *vertical* and *lateral* thinking. Vertical thinking is rational thought, analytical and logical; lateral thinking is creative thought, open and innovative. The principle of creative thinking is to first gain as many ideas as possible though a lateral thinking process, typically a facilitated workshop using creativity techniques and, only after this first step is completed, to analyse these ideas for feasibility.

In programs this technique is very efficient to identify the actions and deliverables that will support the strategic objectives and the CSFs. Typically, the stakeholder group will generate as many potential actions and deliverables as possible, in a limited time, for each of the CSFs in turn, starting with those that have the highest priority. Popular ideation techniques are Brainstorming and Nominal Group Technique or Stepladder technique. The recommendation is, again, to use verb-noun statements, the verb being the action and the noun the deliverable. Once the group has a reasonable number of ideas for each CSF, typically between 10 and 20, they are analysed to verify that they are achievable within the agreed parameters.

8.2.2   ASSESS ALIGNMENT AND ACHIEVABILITY (ELABORATION)

The *elaboration* process consists of evaluating the alternatives generated during ideation. The first step is to eliminate all non-viable ideas; the remaining ideas are then combined and/or modified to generate viable options that will become projects or other program components. The grouping is done according to the favoured management approach (i.e. grouping by department, grouping by management area, or technical area, grouping by CSF/KPI, etc.). Once the team has generated the options required for the first, or next, cycle, they are analysed in terms of their contribution to expected benefits and their achievability.

As explained for the Outline Business Case (Section 7.2.6.2, p. 167), the team should first assess component alignment with objectives, and then achievability. At this stage, I recommend that a first assessment be made against the CSFs; all the acceptable components are then improved. The team can combine components, streamline them and use value analysis and risk analysis to improve them. Value proposals and risk responses are then integrated into a new proposal which is re-evaluated and only then is the achievability evaluated. This will make effective use of resources as proposals are evaluated for achievability only when they have demonstrated their full alignment. Figures 8.2 and 8.3 demonstrate the level of detail expected at that level.

Figure 8.2 demonstrates the use of a weighted matrix to select the components that will form the program. There are many other techniques, like a simple scoring system, that can be used to create a list of prioritized actions, but the weighted matrix has demonstrated that it is both reliable and relatively objective. It is a good group process and allows a better buy-in from all the stakeholders. In Figure 7.5, I described the use of paired comparison to weigh the CSFs, other techniques can be used, like: 5 = Mandatory; 2 = Desirable; 0 = Optional. It is for the organization to choose its own system; the important thing being to keep consistency across.

With the weighted matrix, the contribution of each action is assessed against each CSF with a score varying from 0 to 10. In order to get consistency among the team who make the evaluation, I suggest using the following scale: 0 = Useless; 2 = Desirable; 4 = Useful; 6 = Important; 8 = Necessary; 10 = Essential, in which each score represents the contribution of the component to that particular CSF. The reason the scoring is done on 10 is that the total score is then on a basis on 1,000, which can easily be understood and transferred across other programs. Another type of scoring can be: 3 = Fully satisfies; 2 = Reasonably satisfies; 1 = Partially satisfies and 0 = Does not satisfy. Again, each organization can choose its own system. In the example from Figure 8.2, Action 3 scores highest and Action 1 scores lowest. Although the scores may seem low, do not forget that a score between 250 and 450 indicates medium alignment to overall objectives and a score over 450 a high alignment to overall objectives (see Figure 7.10, p. 172). Figure 8.2 also outlines the value equation displayed in Figure 7.3 (p. 152) where value is dependent on the positive ratio between offered benefits (the sum of program components) and expected benefits (the sum of critical success factors).

Figure 8.3 shows a detailed achievability analysis, which is an extension of the one used for the outline business case (Figure 7.9, p. 170). In terms of

Expected Benefits

Σ = Offered Benefits / Option	CSF A	CSF B	CSF C	CSF D	CSF E	Total
Weight	40	30	15	10	5	100
Comp. 1	4 / 160	4 / 120	6 / 90	3 / 30	8 / 40	440
Comp. 2	7 / 280	4 / 120	2 / 30	5 / 50	8 / 40	520
Comp. 3	6 / 240	7 / 210	3 / 45	5 / 50	1 / 5	550
Comp. 4	4 / 160	4 / 120	3 / 45	9 / 90	2 / 10	425
Comp. 5	2 / 80	7 / 210	4 / 60	6 / 60	9 / 45	455

FIGURE 8.2 EXAMPLE OF ALIGNMENT SCORING WITH WEIGHTED MATRIX

Project Achievability Assessment Form							
Project Name/Ref No.							
Impact Criteria / Specific Factors	10	5	2.5	1.25	0.625		
Financial Factors							
Total estimated capital cost	<5% of all projects	5-10%	10-15%	15-20%	>20% of all projects	7	70
Impact on company cash flow	<5%	5-10%	10-15%	15-20%	>20%	7	70
Funding	100% internal availability	25% external	50% external	75% external	100% external	4	40
Expected Return/Benefits	Short term (<3 months)	3-12 months	Medium term (1-2 yrs)	2-5 years	Long term (>5 years)	5	12.5
Life-Cycle-Cost (optional)						0	0
Parameters & Constraints							
No. members in team	01-02	03-05	06-10	11-50	>50	4	20
Type of contracts	Standard contracts	<-->	Some customized	<-->	All customized	3	7.5
Spread of work	Single location	2 – 3 sites	+3 sites	Base team + virtual	Fully virtual team	6	30
Schedule	Acceptable timeframe	<-->	Tight timeframe	<-->	Inadequate timeframe	5	12.5
Budget	Acceptable budget	<-->	Tight budget	<-->	Inadequate budget	3	30
Human Resources / People Factors							
Spread of resources	Team (same division)	Internal (2 areas)	Team + outsourced	All outsourced	Internal + outsourced	5	25
Familiarity with resources	All known	<-->	Some new	<-->	All unknown	3	7.5
Other critical work	None	Little	Little but significant	Major	Major and significant	6	30
Customer perception	Above expectations	<-->	As expected	<-->	Below expectations	2	5
Staff expertise	Good skills/ expertise	<-->	Half with necess. expertise	<-->	Expert staff not available	7	70
Complexity							
Type of work / Innovativeness	Known technique	Variation from known	Some new development	Significant new development	Breakthrough	7	17.5
Interdependency of deliverables	Negligible	Minor	Significant	Major	Essential	6	30
No. of stakeholders	one or two	Few at project level	Multiple at project level	Multiple project / program	Multiple internal & external	5	25
Stakeholders spread	Similar business area	<-->	Multiple bus areas	<-->	Large spread across environ.	6	15
Objectives, benefits & CSF's	Very clear	Unclear	unspecified	undefined	Unknown	6	15
Scope statement	Very well defined	Minor clarification required	Some elements undefined	Major elements undefined	Undefined	3	7.5
* Considering programme / business level						100	
** Impact x Weighting					**Total Score/1000**		**540**
Chosen levels become parameters of project/program	Level X						

FIGURE 8.3   EXAMPLE OF PROJECT ACHIEVABILITY ASSESSMENT

achievability, a first pass can be made at the same level as that of the outline business case for all the viable options and at the level of detail shown in Figure 8.3 for the components that, following this first pass, have been selected for the first, or next, cycle.

The deliverable for this process is a list of candidate components scored against weighted CSFs and agreed achievability factors and mapped on the AAA Matrix (see Figure 7.10, p. 172). This process is facilitated by the program manager with the collaboration of the sponsor and business integrator, and involves the program team and key stakeholders.

8.2.3   DEFINE INTERDEPENDENCIES

During the preparation stage, all the interdependencies between projects and other actions within a program, as well as interdependencies with other programs and business activities, including transitional activities must be defined, at least for the next cycle. Interdependencies often require an overlap of responsibilities to ensure a smooth transition between activities of two different components or entities. Most of the interdependencies between the program and other programs or business activities were identified at during formulation and outlined in the preliminary business case; they need to be reviewed to identify any changes. Interdependencies between components can be of three types:

a) an output of one component is a required input of another;
b) key resources are shared between two or more components; and finally
c) one component creates synergy for another.

The output–input relationship will very much depend on the respective scope of each component; as its scope is defined and refined, relationships will appear or be modified to ensure a smooth flow for the delivery of benefits. This type of dependency is defined first at the program manager's level during preparation and refined with the help of project managers during deployment as projects are planned. As with project activities, dependencies can be mandatory, and therefore non-negotiable, or discretionary, and therefore subject to negotiation as the program develops.

   When resources (people, equipment or facilities) are shared between projects, or with the rest of the business, this creates a dependency that needs to be managed at program level. Plentiful resources require less coordination, but scarce or specialized resources need to be managed closely. This is an area where critical chain (Goldratt, 1997) principles can be applied successfully, more specifically staggered project pacing and the use of buffers to reduce risks of conflict between different project activities using the same critical resources. By pacing the project activities around the use of these key resources, the program team will greatly reduce the risk of time slip.

In the case of resources shared with other business areas, typically in a matrix environment, the program manager needs to supervise the negotiation of the resource availability between line and projects. They need to secure firm commitment from the business to make resources available at the required time and commitment from the project managers to alert resource owners of any change in requirements (timing or other) so that the business manager can readjust their resource usage as soon as possible.

Finally, some projects, although not essential to the success of the program, can create important synergy so that the success of another project is more likely. A typical example is a mandate in which I was asked to formulate a program for the improvement of the security of a large pharmaceutical facility. We identified a number of elements regarding security, from physical site security to data security and personnel security, all with obvious interdependencies. The interesting synergetic project consisted of the identification of the need to communicate security measures and requirements to all the personnel. Although this was not directly part of the program, we identified that the lack of clear and explicit communication of security measures, and their reason for being, would be detrimental to the success of the whole program because people would not understand the need to follow the procedures and the consequences it could have on the whole business. The communication project, although managed outside the program by the communications department, was closely monitored by the program team and its scope and contents were developed with the program sponsors as the customer.

A program cannot be successful if these three types of interdependencies are not identified and managed. This is also the stage where any other supporting actions required to complete the program are defined.

8.2.4   SELECT PROGRAM COMPONENTS FOR CYCLE

I clarified in the previous section how to generate projects and other actions that will fit within the program objectives. Once the program team has a list of prioritized actions available, they need to select the best mix of actions to realize the expected benefits. Some actions may be synergetic and others sequential, one producing outputs that help, or are necessary to, achieve the other.

Based on the results of the different analyses discussed above, the program team will finalize the choice of components and their relative pacing. The program's marketing and communications management plan will then be linked to this pacing. It must be clear though that the tools described above only help make the decision, and it is for the program team to take into consideration other factors like synergy between projects, the need to deliver short-term results or the need for specific benefits over others in order to finalize the selection of the components for the program. This is an iterative process that will be re-evaluated during the preparation of the definitive business case.

For example, in Figure 8.3, the areas shown in grey represent the factors on which a specific component has been chosen. As such, they become the parameters of this component, defining its cost, funding source, expected return, number of members in team, spread of resources, type of work, etc. If these factors change between the component assessment and its initiation, its priority will be revised accordingly.

The final deliverable of this process is a list of components that will be recommended as part of the definitive business case or benefits realization plan for the next cycle. The scoring and mapping are an aid to decision; the program team and key stakeholders should discuss the scoring and agree the final selection.

8.2.5   FINALIZE PROGRAM SCOPE

Following the description of components and identification of the key component parameters and constraints through the above process, the program team is ready to finalize the scope of the program that will be the basis for the definitive business case.

The PMI Standard recommends that each component should be integrated so that their outputs contribute to the program as a whole (PMI, 2013b, p. 40). MSP insists on the fact that each benefit represents some aspect of the program's outcomes and be validated through a business case (OGC, 2011, p. 194). The team will use the preliminary benefits map and strategic blueprint to develop a detailed and integrated BBS and operational blueprint which will represent the program scope. These two processes are iterative and will be progressively refined as the organization stage is completed.

Figure 8.4 shows a partial BBS and blueprint, including the current situation and new expected business capability. This mapping outlines the link between the expected benefits and the deliverables. When KPIs are set for

← WHY				Blueprint		HOW ➔
Benefit (Level 1)	Outcome (Level. 2)	Output (Level 3)	Current Situation	Future Capability	Deliverable (Capability)	Deadline
1 Increase alignment with strategy	1.1 Select Pj/Pg based on strategic objectives	1.1.1 Define selection criteria based on strategic objectives	No formal alignment with strategy (only after the fact)	All Pj and Pg will be selected on the basis of their alignment with the strategic objectives and achievability	Implement Pj/Pg selection process (based on SOs)	6 months
		1.1.2 Define achievability criteria	No concept of achievability beyond ROI		All Pg/Pj selected based on achievability criteria	12 months
	1.2 Govern projects and programs in alignment with strategy	1.2.1 Put in place governance forums (decision-making)	Governance is only based on basic (T/C/Q) control	Governance forums will focus on strategic decision-making and organization-wide approach	Governance System in place and agreed	6 months
		1.2.2 Monitor strategy alignment	No formal monitoring against strategic objectives		Governance decision forums regularly attended	9 months
2 Develop strong PM Culture	2.1 Harmonize practice based on existing	2.1.1 Develop unified practice from existing	PMs (mostly experienced) use own methods	Recognized framework will be adopted throughout the organization. Practice will be monitored against standard	Framework developed with input from experienced PMs	3 months
		2.1.2 Align practice across organization	No known standard is being promoted across organization		Standard practice agreed and implemented throughout	6 months
	2.2 Standardize PgM and PM knowledge	2.2.1 Develop common language among existing resources	Each PM uses own terms, no uniformity of reporting	Standards will be promoted, taking into account existing	Launch standardized multi-level PM training program	6 months
		2.2.2 Induct new resources uniformly across organization	New PMs are mentored by "old hands"	Standardized induction will allow uniform PM culture	Run induction program for new resources	6 months
3 Develop formal unified practice	3.1 Standardize PgM and PM practice	3.1.1 Select accepted worldwide standard	Practice standards are internal	Practice will be standardized across all organization, current good practices will be taken into account	Recognized standard selected and accepted	3 months
		3.1.2 Develop standardized PgM and PM methodology	No standardized methodology except within some entities		Standardized PgM and PM method agreed (see 2.1.2)	6 months
	3.2 Harmonize practice with recognized methodologies	3.2.1 Accept standardized practice across organization	Project managers are resistant to change methods	"Old" PMs will be involved in and mentor development	Standardized practice used across organization	6–18 months
		3.2.2 Align practice with known standards	No one standard is universally accepted	Chosen standard to recognize existing best practice	Practice aligned with accepted standard	12–24 months

FIGURE 8.4   EXAMPLE OF PARTIAL BLUEPRINT BASED ON BBS

each of the deliverables, the program team can regularly report on the progress towards that stated objectives in a realistic and tangible way.

Obviously some programs will require much more detail than what is shown in Figure 8.4, but the program team must be careful not to go into too much detail for the reporting process as good marketing requires a clear focus on the main message. In my experience a regular executive report covering 20 to 30 key deliverables for the program is sufficient. In very large complex organizational change programs one could go up to 40, but not more. Obviously, some stakeholders will be more interested in one project or the other; they should then be allowed to access more detailed reports on these project deliverables.

8.3   Prepare Definitive Business Case (Benefits Realization Plan)

The definitive business case is intimately linked to the development of the benefits realization plan. Both the PMI Standard and MSP mention the benefits realization plan as a key element of the successful realization of the strategic objectives. MSP defines it as the "a complete view of all the benefits, their dependencies and the expected realization timescales and is derived from the benefits map" (OGC, 2011, p. 86). For the PMI it:

> *formally documents the activities necessary for achieving the program's planned benefits. It identifies how and when benefits are expected to be delivered to the organization and specifies mechanisms that should be in place to ensure that the benefits are fully realized over time (PMI, 2013b, p. 38).*

In both cases the benefits realization plan defines how the program team intends to realize the program's stated benefits.

This is also the step that requires comprehensive identification and planning of resource requirements for the delivery, transition and integration of capabilities for the first or next cycle and as detailed as possible estimate for the whole program. It comprises seven main activities:

1. Pace Components and Benefits (Master Schedule).
2. Plan Transition.
3. Draw Detailed Cycle Roadmap.

4.   Plan for Risks.
5.   Develop Appraisal System.
6.   Budget Program.
7.   Finalize Operational Blueprint and Benefits Register for Cycle.

8.3.1   PACE COMPONENTS AND BENEFITS (MASTER SCHEDULE)

Following the selection of the program's components, and clarification of their interdependencies, it is possible to identify the key activities of the program. These activities are those that will help achieve the program objectives and its key benefits (Level 1 and 2 of the BBS).

The resources necessary to accomplish these critical activities, as well as any shared resources and resources that are critical because of their scarcity, specialization or high demand, should be identified and managed at the program level, even if they only accomplish project level work. Their usage is coordinated and prioritized by the program manager and, for the transition, with or by the business integrator and operational or line managers. The usage of these key resources is one of the factors that will be taken into consideration when pacing the projects and other actions.

Cash flow is another important factor that will set the pace of the program's actions. The cash necessary to run the program can be generated through revenues or funding. In the first case, revenue generating actions will be prioritized to fund the program, therefore short payback period will be privileged over other financial measures, at least for the first cycle. ROI (Return on Investment), NPV (Net Present Value) or IRR (Internal Rate of Return) can be the main financial factor for the next cycles, depending on the company's priorities. If cash flow is generated through funding, external or internal, it will be important to focus resources on the actions that will produce benefits that are significant for the stakeholders who actively participate in the funding of the program. These need to be fairly short-term to maintain their motivation to finance the program and should demonstrate the value of the program to them and taken into consideration in the engagement plan (see Section 9.2.1, Engage Stakeholders, p. 227). When benefits are too remote, it is difficult to maintain the motivation of the sponsors, therefore it is important to find the right mix of short-term benefits as well as medium- and long-term ones and to be able to demonstrate the tangible achievements of the program through a sound marketing plan.

Finally, readiness for change (resistance and/or acceptance of change) and urgency of the change are also factors to be taken into consideration when pacing the program. It is well known that if change is introduced at too fast a pace and too much at a time, resistance to change will grow. Karl Weick (1995) has studied the concept of resistance to change in depth and has concluded that individuals and groups need sensemaking time to increase acceptance of change. The greater the change, the more sensemaking time is required. MSP, in its 1996 edition, recommended that the program should exhibit periods of stability during which benefits are delivered in increments; the PMI Standard recommends that benefits be delivered in an incremental, iterative way so that the ultimate benefits are achieved in a "cumulative manner". The current version

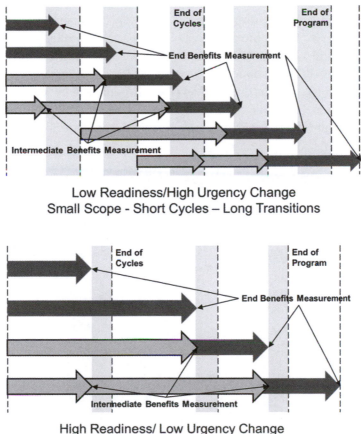

Low Readiness/High Urgency Change
Small Scope - Short Cycles – Long Transitions

High Readiness/ Low Urgency Change
Larger Scope - Longer Cycles – Shorter Transitions

FIGURE 8.5 PACING THE CHANGE

of MSP recommends the partition of the program in "tranches" (which I have labelled "cycles" in this book), groups of projects that each deliver benefits in a controlled manner, consistent with the need to maintain operational stability of the business during the transition process. Figure 8.5 represents the impact of those factors on the program's pacing and benefits release.

My own experience is that the successful delivery of benefits, at business and operational level, is highly dependent on the pacing of the benefits delivery in a series of cycles in accordance with the organization's receptiveness or resistance to change. Sensemaking time and preparedness of the organization are important aspects of the benefits realization and should be taken into consideration in the pacing of the program. Figure 8.6 below is a graphical representation of the concept described above; it shows that without the controlled release of benefits into the business resistance to change is likely to trigger an unacceptable drop in performance that can jeopardize the whole program or cycle. If the introduction of change is controlled, the drop of performance will stay at an acceptable level. Given time, the people affected by the change will understand the positive aspects of the change and their performance will rise to the expected level and benefits will be realized.

The program schedule is a milestone schedule and identifies only component high-level activities or groups of activities and interfacing activities.

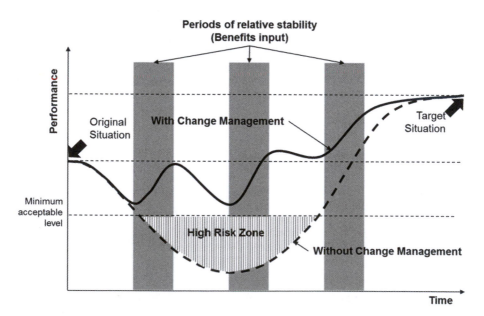

FIGURE 8.6   PACING FOR ULTIMATE ACHIEVEMENT OF BENEFITS

It should clearly identify component reviews (at delivery of key deliverable) and transition activities, as well as expected benefits delivery. The program manager is responsible for developing and updating the master schedule. It must be coordinated with the component managers and business integrator.

In summary, program pacing is dependent on interdependencies between components and with other business activities, key resource usage, cash flow and finally readiness and urgency of change. The pacing of benefits delivery and actions will define the program's major milestones and review gateways; more importantly, the transition of project deliverables to operational capabilities and business benefits. This process may require a reassessment of component selection.

8.3.2   PLAN TRANSITION

The transition from project deliverables to organizational capabilities and, ultimately, realised benefits is the crux of the success of the program. The program team should clearly define all the activities necessary for the integration of project outputs and implementation of new capabilities into the business. This process should be closely coordinated with interdependencies, roles and responsibilities and reflected in the program roadmap.

The transition process is initiated at the Program Board level where the sponsor, program manager and business integrator can define and coordinate all the activities necessary to ensure a smooth transition. Once the program team has paced the components' key deliverables, those contributing to benefits, the management team can start planning for integration of these deliverables into business-as-usual. It is ideally the role of the business integrator to prepare the organization for the change and to identify any supporting activities like training, testing or other required to ensure a smooth transition process and minimize resistance to change.

The business integrator is the person best placed to understand the culture of their business area and consider the receptivity of the people concerned by the change. The program manager should understand the need for sensemaking and how to improve the acceptance of change. Together, the program manager and the business integrator will organize workshops, information sessions, or meetings with the change recipients to inform them, try and understand their concerns and address those as much as is feasible. It is not the purpose of this book to discuss change management in detail, but a program usually involves a number of changes in the way an organization functions and therefore requires change management competencies. All these change management steps should be identified clearly and be part of the program's benefits realization plan.

Once the transition plan is completed with all the necessary activities identified and milestones agreed, both by the program manager and the business integrator, the transition process is approved by the program board and the sponsor.

8.3.3 DRAW DETAILED CYCLE ROADMAP

The roadmap is to the program what the schedule is to the project. At program level it is not possible to develop a detailed activity-based schedule; this is the job of the project managers that will be part of the program. Although there are specific program tasks, they are generally of a more strategic level and do not need to be developed to the level of detail required at project level. The program roadmap is built on milestones, which are result-based, rather than on tasks and activities, which are process-based. This is also the view promoted by the PMI in the third edition of the program management standard. For each benefit or key deliverable, the team sets the delivery or realization date and clarifies expected output or outcome. The program team also needs to identify interdependency activities, transition activities and any review, appraisal or reporting activities which are all managed at program level. The roadmap

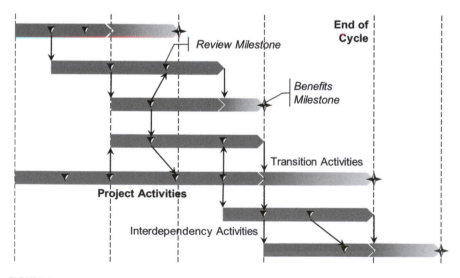

FIGURE 8.7   PROGRAM STRATEGIC ROADMAP

is built from the benefits realization plan and therefore takes into account resource availability and project achievability factors.

Figure 8.7 shows a program roadmap where project activities, transition activities and interdependency activities are identified, as well as review milestones (project key deliverables) and benefits milestones. This is the type of representation that is used to communicate with key stakeholders and sponsors. For the actual planning of activities the program team can use the activity-on-arrow (AOA) networking method, which is probably more appropriate at program level than the traditional activity-on-node (AON). Figure 8.8 displays a simplified program network diagram using the AOA method. Not all activities have been identified for clarity reasons. In this diagram, each node corresponds to a key deliverable of benefit milestone and each arrow corresponds to a high-level project, interface or transition activity. In order to simplify understanding, each type of activity or milestone can be made distinct by using colour of texture. In Figure 8.8, for example, bold arrows represent project activities, slim arrows represent interfacing activities and dotted arrows represent transition activities.

The final roadmap can only be established at the end of preparation, when all activities are identified. But the team will start building the roadmap during formulation; it will be detailed progressively as more data becomes available

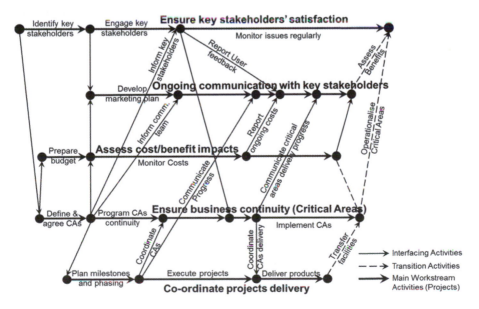

FIGURE 8.8   PROGRAM DETAILED CYCLE ROADMAP

and as better agreement is reached among the key stakeholders. The program roadmap is an essential tool for developing the program plan and the business case.

8.3.4   PLAN FOR RISKS

Risk management and program risk management have been addressed in many recent publications; it is not the purpose of this book to address it in detail, but I find it important to clarify a few points about program risk management.

Risks are directly related to uncertainty, which is typically due to a lack of information that forces the project team to make assumptions. If these assumptions hold true, the risk will not materialize; if the assumption proves false things will not go as planned and the potential risk will materialize. The more accurate the data available, the lesser the risk. Projects are typically subject to higher uncertainty at the beginning and uncertainty lowers as the project progresses. Project planning, the breaking down of the project work in smaller components, estimating and risk management all help to reduce uncertainty.

Programs are subjected not only to uncertainty, but also to ambiguity. Whereas uncertainty can be managed using methods and techniques that generate better and more accurate data, ambiguity is caused by the ratio of expectations vs defined requirements, conflicting aims and continuous readjustments and can only be managed through softer methods like identification of needs and expectations, negotiation and decision-making. Traditional risk management methods cannot be used in this case and the program team has to rely on methods like value management to reduce ambiguity (see Section 1.3, p. 20). Complexity also adds another dimension to programs. Risk management is well honed to deal with what complexity authors labelled the "known-unknowns" or "knowable"; those elements that can be identified through data gathering and fact finding. It is not suitable to deal with the "unknown-unknowns", those elements that are emergent and cannot be predicted because they are due to the interaction of a large number of related factors; this is where agile methods are best suited.

In a program there are essentially three types of risks: the program risks, those that concern the uncertainty of the program and affect the whole program; the project risks, those that affect single projects within the program; and finally the aggregated risks which are similar risks that affect more than one project within the program and are best managed at program level. Program and project risks are managed with traditional risk management methods, albeit program risk responses will be more strategic in essence and require a higher level of authority. A typical aggregated risk would be the unavailability of critical or shared resources. Aggregated risks are also managed at a more strategic level but the key is to identify them as aggregated risks. They are often identified at the project level and it is only through coordination of the risk effort at program level that they can be identified as aggregated. It is therefore important to plan for sharing of project planning data at regular intervals of the program and project life cycles. Interdependencies are also typically an area of aggregated risks and should be managed in multi-project teams.

Finally, risk impact is typically assessed against project targets, namely time, cost and quality. This is definitely not appropriate at program level. A program's aim is to realize benefits, therefore all program risks and aggregated risks must be assessed against their likelihood to impair or help the achievement of the program's stated expected benefits. For many years now, I have also assessed project risks against the achievement of benefits, making their likelihood of success and contribution to the program greater. Using the BBS and blueprint, program and aggregated risks are typically assessed against the weighted CSFs as shown in Figure 8.9.

Risk #	Risk Description	Prob	CSF1 0.30		CSF 2 0.25		CSF 3 0.20		CSF 4 0.15		CSF 5 0.10		Impact Score	Comb Score
			I.S.	W.S.	I.S.	W.S.	I.S.	W.S.	I.S.	W.S.	I.S.	W.S.		
1	Loss of key resources	0.70	0.05	0.015	0.40	0.100	0.40	0.080	0.40	0.060	0.40	0.040	0.30	0.21
2	Insufficient budget and resources	0.50	0.05	0.015	0.40	0.100	0.80	0.160	0.20	0.030	0.80	0.080	0.39	0.19
3	Slow uptake of recommendations	0.50	0.10	0.030	0.40	0.100	0.80	0.160	0.05	0.008	0.10	0.010	0.31	0.15
4	Lack of coherence with client	0.70	0.05	0.015	0.40	0.100	0.40	0.080	0.10	0.015	0.40	0.040	0.25	0.18
5	Difficulty to communicate with stakeholders on ongoing basis	0.50	0.05	0.015	0.80	0.200	0.10	0.020	0.40	0.060	0.40	0.040	0.34	0.17
6	Difficulty to secure additional resources/funding	0.70	0.10	0.030	0.40	0.100	0.10	0.020	0.20	0.030	0.40	0.040	0.22	0.15
7	Resistance to change (Combine with other risks)	0.70	0.05	0.015	0.20	0.050	0.40	0.080	0.20	0.030	0.20	0.020	0.20	0.14
8	Company policy (combine with 0.13)	0.30	0.05	0.015	0.80	0.200	0.80	0.160	0.40	0.060	0.20	0.020	0.46	0.14
9	Lack of coherence between external interests	0.30	0.05	0.015	0.20	0.050	0.80	0.160	0.40	0.060	0.80	0.080	0.37	0.11
10	Lack of co-operation between client & organization	0.30	0.05	0.015	0.20	0.050	0.20	0.040	0.20	0.030	0.20	0.020	0.16	0.05
11	Lack of coherence between projects in programme	0.10	0.05	0.015	0.40	0.100	0.40	0.080	0.40	0.060	0.40	0.040	0.30	0.03
12	Lack of mature data to support business case	0.10	0.05	0.015	0.10	0.025	0.20	0.040	0.20	0.030	0.40	0.040	0.15	0.02

WS: Weighted Score = Impact Score (I.S.) x CSF Weight
Impact Score: Sum of Weighted Scores (W.S.).
Comb. Score: Impact Score x Probability

FIGURE 8.9 EXAMPLE OF PROGRAM LEVEL QUALITATIVE RISK ANALYSIS

Figure 8.9 is an example of this method. The impact (IS) on the CSF is scored in the same way as that stated in the *PMBOK Guide®*: 0.05 = Very Low risk; 0.1 = Low; 0.2 = Medium; 0.4 = High and 0.8 = Very High. Each score is then multiplied by the weight of that CSF (WS). All the weighted scores are added to create the total impact score, which is then multiplied by the probability to give the combined probability-impact score of that risk in regards of the program benefits.

Project risks and less strategic aggregated risks can be assessed against the relevant outcomes (Level 2) or outputs (Level 3) (see Figure 8.4, p. 190), depending on the size and impact of the project. Ideally these benefits should also be weighted to give an accurate assessment of the importance of the risk.

8.3.5   DEVELOP APPRAISAL SYSTEM

The appraisal system is a subset of the program's governance system; it is the third part of the system – making sure the *objectives/benefits are achieved* (see Section 8.1.2). The processes that need to be put in place are the controlling and monitoring of project key deliverables, the deliverables linked to benefits realization, the evaluation and approval of program level changes, including project changes that may affect the program (see Figure 8.10), the assessment of the implementation of new capabilities and of further benefits and finally, the distribution and feedback process of program reports. Roles and responsibilities must be set for each of these processes (see Section 8.1.4). The program appraisal and project review system is developed incrementally during preparation, but it will be completed only after all the elements of the plan are coordinated. This is when the gates can be established.

The project review, benefits appraisal and change management systems will be based on the CSFs and KPIs that were established for the program and projects; they are the measure of the program's success and represent the program's ultimate objectives. Capabilities will be measured against the blueprint elements. As soon as possible, the program team will define the project's key deliverables, using the BBS to identify those deliverables that lead to benefits and set their measures (KPIs). These are the only ones that should be monitored at program level; the rest of the project activities are monitored at project level.

As part of the program roadmap the program team will define review points that are significant. Significance is again established on the basis of benefits

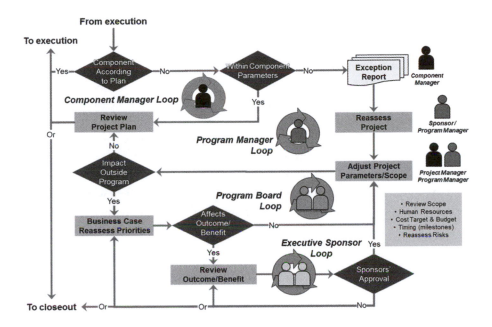

FIGURE 8.10 PROGRAM CHANGE DECISION LOOPS

delivery, so should be focused on key project deliverables, new capabilities and benefits realization. Once set, these milestones will be gates that will warrant the projects' and program advancement and enable decision-makers to assess the continued progress towards the stated objectives.

Finally, the system should take into account the handling of program changes. A consistent change process is established to account for different levels of change with authority in accordance to the importance of the change. Figure 8.10 shows such a system where the change decision authority (loop) is in accordance with the importance of the change and the delegated authority rather than with set financial boundaries.

In summary, the program appraisal system should:

- Combine change management and benefits appraisal around project gates.
- Be based on key project deliverables and expected benefits delivery.
- Be linked to CSFs and KPIs measurement.
- Clearly establish roles and responsibilities for approvals.
- Establish suitable communication/reporting system with sponsors.

8.3.6   BUDGET PROGRAM

Whereas it is difficult to establish a detailed budget for the whole program at the beginning, the program team should be able, at the end of the preparation stage, to establish the budget for the next cycle. Typically, at each cycle the program team should readjust the overall program funding requirements and give the sponsors detailed financial requirements for the next cycle.

This financial plan should be adjusted in regards of the evolving circumstances of the program and of any changes in the stakeholders' needs and requirements and approved at the beginning of each new cycle of the program; approval will be dependent on results obtained in the previous cycle.

8.3.7   FINALIZE OPERATIONAL BLUEPRINT AND BENEFITS REGISTER FOR CYCLE

The operational blueprint is developed in accordance with the process described in Section 7.2.5. The elements of the operational blueprint are drawn from the benefits breakdown structure (BBS) levels 3 and 4 and define the requirements necessary to achieve specific objectives. At this point, workshops, meetings or interviews have been conducted with the key stakeholders and will enable the program core team to finalize the operational blueprint. The operational blueprint is updated regularly (at least at each cycle) as data and feedback on results increases the level of understanding of the future state.

8.3.8   CONSOLIDATE DEFINITIVE BUSINESS CASE

The definitive business case is one of the outputs of the preparation stage that consolidates all the program's elements for approval of the deployment of the program. In many organizations, the business case is a financially oriented document, the only purpose of which is to get funds released. With such an approach, executive sponsors focus on return on investment and do not take the time to understand the program. Recently, the PMI and Boston Consulting Group have conducted a "research into executive sponsorship [that] shows that one in three unsuccessful projects fail to meet goals due to poorly engaged executive sponsors" (PMI, 2014, p. 14). I have always preferred to build business cases addressing the broader justification and strategy of the program where I can get a strong commitment of executive sponsors to the program strategy and engage them in the process.

Typically this type of document will contain the following elements which will lead to the program plan.

Outline of Program Strategy (Executive Summary)

Elaborated from the Outline Business Case Sections 1.1 and 1.2 (see Section 7.2.6.2, p. 167). It states the reasons why the program needs to be undertaken and includes the opportunity or problem being addressed as well as the overall objective(s) of the program/project.

It should clarify the overall purpose and benefits of program (from CSFs and KPIs) and include the high-level scope and time frames of its expected benefits realization.

Program Governance

PROGRAM ARCHITECTURE (SEE SECTION 8.1.1)

Program structure and value chain, relationships and decision/communication channels. List of classified stakeholders, agreed expected benefits for and expected contribution from the key stakeholders to the program. Develop program marketing strategy and preliminary marketing plan.

STAKEHOLDER ENGAGEMENT PLAN (SEE SECTION 8.3.3)

This section contains the detailed stakeholder analysis, including list of key stakeholders, roles and expected impact on program as well as a marketing and communication management plan (focused on significant stakeholders and key deliverables).

ROLES AND RESPONSIBILITIES (SEE SECTION 8.3.4)

Roles and responsibilities assigned for all the key stakeholders and core program team. Accountability established for all CSFs. Remember to use the

BBS and blueprint to assign detailed roles and responsibilities. This is the best way to ensure that each outcome and output has a person or party accountable and that there are no overlaps of responsibility. Most transition and governance tasks, as well as interdependencies, will require close collaboration and overlap of responsibilities to ensure a smooth transition.

GOVERNANCE SYSTEMS (SEE SECTION 8.1.2)

Clarify role and composition of the Program Board.

Define project review processes and program appraisal system: milestones, gates and evaluation criteria in accordance with the chosen governance approach. Confirm change management processes. Clarify reporting process and documents.

Program Scope

DETAILED BENEFITS BREAKDOWN STRUCTURE (SEE SECTION 8.2.3)

Produce the detailed benefits breakdown structure for this cycle, including component key deliverables.

LIST AND PRIORITIZATION OF COMPONENTS (SEE SECTION 8.2.4)

Produce a list of all program components for next cycle, prioritized. For each component, define major deliverables (from alignment analysis) and parameters (from achievability analysis).

Define interdependencies, all project major interdependencies within program and with other programs and business activities, including transitional activities.

DETAILED BLUEPRINT AND BENEFITS REGISTER (SEE SECTIONS 7.2.5.1 AND 8.3.7)

Produce a detailed strategic and operational blueprint and benefits register for the next cycle.

Program Deployment Plan

PROGRAM RISK REGISTER (SEE SECTION 8.3.4)

List of prioritized program and aggregated risks, including opportunities.

List of risk responses and confirmation of their inclusion in the schedule and budget.

PROGRAM ROADMAP (SEE SECTION 8.3.3)

The roadmap is to the program what the schedule is to the project. At program level it is not possible to develop a detailed activity-based schedule; this is the job of the project managers that will be part of the program. The program roadmap is built on milestones, which are result-based, rather than on tasks and activities, which are process-based.

For each benefit or key deliverable, the team sets the delivery or realization date and clarifies expected output or outcome. The program team also needs to identify interfaces, interdependency activities, transition activities and any review, appraisal or reporting activities which are all managed at program level.

The pace of each component within the cycle is based on resource availability and project achievability factors as well as urgency and readiness of the organization.

TRANSITION PLAN (SEE SECTION 8.3.2)

Define activities necessary for integration of project outcomes and new capabilities into the business (coordinate with interdependencies, roles and responsibilities and roadmap).

CAPABILITY REQUIREMENTS (SEE SECTIONS 8.2.5, 8.3.1 AND 7.3.4.1)

Based on achievability and risk analysis, define capability requirements (pipeline) for the program, including availability analysis and pacing for any shared resources between program components.

Program Financial Analysis

FUNDING AND BUDGET (SEE SECTIONS 8.2.5, 8.3.1 AND 8.3.6)

Establish whole program funding requirements (financial plan) and detailed financial requirements for first/next cycle.

COSTS (SEE SECTIONS 8.2.5, 8.3.1 AND 8.3.6)

Include direct one-time costs such for purchase or installation of capabilities (facilities, equipment, processes and services) as well as transition and support costs. Also include one-time and recurring hard and soft costs to a business unit from implementing the new capabilities.

BENEFITS (SEE SECTIONS 7.2.3, 7.2.4 AND 7.2.5)

Calculate specific financial benefits that stem from the program, including revenues, increased efficiency savings or cost avoidance that are expected to be realized after delivery of capabilities (see Figure 7.7, p. 166).

FINANCIAL RISKS

Analyse and highlight any financial risks related to the process and completion of the program and its objectives.

8.4   Authorize Next Cycle of Program Deployment

The sponsor and/or Program Board are responsible for the authorization of the program deployment; the PMO usually has authority over the compliance of the process and documents. If this is the first cycle of the program, the authorization also includes commitment to the program as a whole. If approved, the program goes to the next deployment cycle; if rejected, the program is either stopped or alternatives are identified.

The authorization process comprises three main activities:

1.   Secure resources for Cycle.
2.   Commit to Whole Program.
3.   Finalize Program Plan.

8.4.1 SECURE RESOURCES FOR CYCLE

If the definition stage program manager is not the person who will manage the deployment stage, the deployment program manager is confirmed and the authorization process constitutes the overlap between the two. Once the business case is approved and the deployment phase is authorized, the program sponsor and program manager will negotiate resource commitment with functional managers and assign the program team for deployment. The program sponsor and/or program manager needs to have the necessary authority to negotiate these commitments. If this is not the case, the executive sponsor must delegate the necessary authority to do so.

Resource owners should commit the resources to the authority of the program manager for the time agreed. I always recommend securing written commitments from resource owners in line with program plan requirements. This will enable better planning and clarification of resource availability for both the resource owners and component managers.

8.4.2 COMMIT TO WHOLE PROGRAM

On the basis of the definitive business case, the program board and executive sponsor will commit to the whole program. The commitment is the same as for a budget and should be reconfirmed at every cycle, based on re-estimation. The program manager will seek a recorded approval of program funding plan subject to reviews at every cycle gate.

The program manager and sponsor prepare the necessary documents for the program board, which is responsible for approval. The executive sponsor authorizes the release of funds for the deployment stage of the next cycle.

8.4.3 FINALIZE PROGRAM PLAN

The program plan is the output of the preparation stage that consolidates all its elements for launch of the deployment stage of the program. The program plan is elaborated from the approved definitive business case. Whereas the business case was aimed at getting commitment of the sponsors for the program, the program plan's purpose is to outline the work of the program team for the deployment phase. Typically it will contain the following elements which are also part of the benefits realization plan:

1. *Detailed Stakeholder Analysis and Stakeholder Engagement Plan*: List of classified stakeholders, agreed expected benefits for and expected contribution from the key stakeholders to the program. Develop program marketing strategy and preliminary marketing plan.
2. *Finalized Scope*: Detailed BBS and operational blueprint, including KPIs.
3. *Program Budget*: Whole program baseline budget and program funding requirements (financial plan). Detailed financial requirements for first/next cycle.
4. *Organizational Structure*: Program structure and value chain, relationships and decision/communication channels.
5. *Assigned Roles and Responsibilities*: Roles and responsibilities assigned for all the key stakeholders and core program team. Accountability established for all CSFs.
6. *Interdependencies Defined*: All project interdependencies defined within program and with other programs and business activities, including transitional activities.
7. *Transition Plan*: Define activities necessary for integration of project outcomes and new capabilities into the business (coordinate with interdependencies, roles and responsibilities and roadmap).
8. *Projects/Benefits Pacing*: Develop a program roadmap from the benefits realization plan. Take into account resource availability and project achievability factors.
9. *Governance Systems*: Develop project review processes and program appraisal system: milestones, gates and evaluation criteria in accordance with the chosen governance approach (see Program Governance, p. 88). Develop change management plan.
10. *Projects/Activities for Next Cycle*: Prepare project charters for the projects selected for the next cycle and clarify any specific program activities required for interfacing and transition.

8.5   From the Decision to Its Implementation

The definition stage has enabled us to develop the program to the point where a decision can be made to deploy the first, or next, cycle of the program. In the next chapter, we will examine the steps necessary to deploy the program, launching projects and other activities that will deliver outputs, outcomes and benefits for the business.

CHAPTER 9

Program Deployment (Capabilities Delivery and Transition)

In Chapter 8, we have examined how the program is organised to be able to deliver value to the business and gain support for its deployment. In Chapter 9, I will describe in detail how to manage projects and other actions from a program point of view, including how to create synergy in the program and manage the program's different stakeholders and how to transition and close components.

In the PMI Standard, "Program Benefits Delivery" is divided into "Components Planning and Authorisation", "Component Oversight and Integration" and "Component Transition and Closure" (PMI, 2013b, p. 13). In MSP, "Managing the Tranches" is divided into "Delivering the Capability" and "Realizing the Benefits" (OGC, 2011, p. 175). I have decided to keep the label "Deployment" for this stage of the program, but to include in it what I had labelled "Appraisal" in the first edition of the book. Appraisal of the benefits is an integral part of the program deployment and, as much as I wanted to emphasize the need for appraisal in the first edition, it does not truly represent the program management process.

I believe the projects and other program components deliver capabilities, not benefits. This is why I have labelled the first section Capabilities Delivery, which consists in managing the components, but also managing the program as a whole; this combines both MSP and PMI's labels. It is only when the capabilities are integrated into the business that benefits can be realized; the role of the program manager is to manage the integration of the capabilities in order to realize the benefits. The "Capabilities Integration" section includes the transition of component deliverables, but also support for their integration into the business operations. Benefits realization is an outcome that needs to be appraised, not a process that can be managed. All these processes are concurrent and cyclic during the deployment stage of the program.

Capabilities Integration and Benefits Appraisal are covered in Chapter 10. This chapter is divided into two sections:

- 9.1 Capabilities Delivery (Components Management)
- 9.2 Capabilities Transition

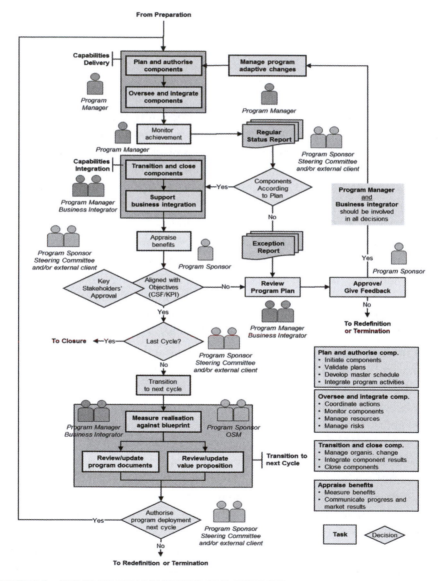

FIGURE 9.1 PROGRAM DEPLOYMENT STAGE FLOWCHART

In summary, deployment consists of the harmonized governance of the initiation, planning, execution and closing of a number of aligned components. It includes the management of the interdependencies between components as well as capabilities transition and integration activities. The purpose of this cyclic phase is to realize benefits in a controlled sequence. The key to successful deployment is the harmonization of all the resources and constituents of the program to realize benefits consistently through the delivery of usable capabilities and sustainable change (what I had labelled "Manage the Value Chain" in the first edition of this book).

9.1   Capabilities Delivery (Components Management)

A successful program is dependent on the fact that projects and other activities are coordinated and monitored to ensure the consistent delivery of capabilities that will produce benefits. Component planning includes the activities necessary to integrate any new component into the program as well as the re-planning of existing components. Authorization requires a clear scope and set of deliverables for each component as well as resources required. Overseeing and integrating components involves the monitoring and coordination of program components in order to produce expected benefits. This may require integration and transition activities at program level.

9.1.1   PLAN AND AUTHORIZE COMPONENTS

There are many excellent books on project management, so it is not my intention to describe project management processes in detail; rather, I want to identify the elements of the project management process that specifically concern the program manager and apply them to all program components whether they are projects or not. The program manager should have the role of component sponsor. As such they will initiate the components and issue component (project) charters, monitor and review the component planning processes, oversee component execution and the delivery of outputs as well as monitor component interfaces, implement the review and approval process and finally supervise component closing. The program manager should be given the authority and responsibility to allocate and reallocate resources to all the projects and other actions within the program.

The key is for the program team and board to keep a precise but high-level view of the program's components in order to be able to steer the projects and other actions to achieve the program objectives. Only the key deliverables, those directly contributing to benefits, and their milestones have to be monitored at the program level. The management of individual activities is left to the project and operational managers. The same goes for risks and contingencies as well as resources; the program team should monitor or manage only interfaces and interdependencies or program level components, or those that affect multiple projects.

9.1.1.1   Initiate components

As sponsor, it is the role of the program manager to initiate projects and authorize actions that are part of the program. It is therefore their role to issue the charter or brief. Program managers that come from a traditional project background usually have difficulty focusing on benefits rather than products when writing the charter. A benefits-based charter will take a slightly different view from a traditional product-based charter. The program manager will use the elements developed in previous stages of the program to input elements into the charter. The background, justification and drivers for the component comes from the stakeholder needs analysis (see Sections 7.2.2 and 7.2.3.2); the main objectives, major deliverables and success criteria are the stakeholder-related benefits and will be deduced from the structuring and prioritizing of the benefits, which comes from the benefits breakdown structure (see Section 7.2.3.3) and weighted CSFs (see Section 7.2.4.1); benefits measurement criteria will come from the KPIs and benefits register (see Sections 7.2.4.2 and 8.3.7). Key milestones and deliverables, those linked to benefits, will be based on the roadmap (see Sections 7.2.5.3 and 8.3.3). Finally, the parameters, constraints, assumptions and risks that will be part of the charter will have been identified during the achievability analysis (see Figure 8.3 and Section 8.2.2).

Component Charter

PROGRAM LEVEL

The objective of the first two sections is to describe how the component fits within the program and how it will contribute to it.

1. Background and justification (Business Case) – WHY?

The purpose of this section is to explain how the component has come into being. Use the stated strategic objectives and stakeholder analysis to clarify why this component was initiated; identify critical issues and drivers. This is also a good place to identify the key stakeholders of the component.

2. Component purpose (objectives, "intent" of component) – WHAT?

This is a series of simple statements that define the expected contribution of the component to the overall program and strategy. Use the benefits breakdown structure and CSFs to clarify what is expected. It will normally include a description of the benefits to which this component is expected to contribute.

COMPONENT LEVEL

The objective of the next sections of the charter is to define the intended scope of the component and identify its deliverables and success criteria in regards of the above two sections.

3. Expected key deliverables (component results)

This section is a brief description of the component's expected results as understood by the stakeholders. Usually the program manager will prepare a high-level WBS, based on the program's KPIs, to orient the component and make sure that the deliverables that are significant for the delivery of benefits are included.

The component key deliverables are those results that must be delivered in order to consider the component completed and secure acceptance from key stakeholders. These key deliverables will become the milestones of the component and those that will be reported at program level. They will drive the component's schedule and be based on the program's benefits pacing.

4. Parameters (discretionary limits to capabilities)

Parameters are management-imposed limits. They include, among other elements, the time frame, milestone dates, allocated budget, processes, contractual formats, resource availability and other factors that define the limits of the component manager's authority. Typically parameters are negotiated and agreed between the sponsor and the component manager. In a program, they are extracted from the component's achievability analysis.

5.   *External and internal constraints (mandatory limits to capabilities)*

Constraints are generally imposed and non-negotiable. They are typically imposed by context, circumstances or regulatory authorities. They are normally identified during the program risk analysis process.

6.   *Current high-level risks and basic assumptions*

During the elaboration and decision process leading to the approval of the current cycle of the program, the program team has performed a risk analysis and made assumptions on a number of issues. Those that affect specific components should be clearly outlined in the charter because they will directly affect the planning process.

In addition to these, a standard Charter could also include the following.

7.   *Organizational elements*

Who will be involved in the component and how; roles and responsibilities; communication and reporting systems, etc.

8.   *Tactical elements*

The manner in which the component is to be conducted.

9.   *Management approval*

Management approval of the above.

The program manager, in collaboration with the component sponsor, if they are not the sponsor, will then issue the charter/brief and ensure that the key roles and responsibilities, authority and lines of communication for the component are clearly defined. Some of the important elements that component managers should be made aware of are the priority of actions that concern them, any supporting actions that are related to their components and all interactions and interfaces with other components or programs.

The program manager will allocate or reallocate funds and other resources according to priorities (see Section 9.1.2.2), including contingencies (see Section 9.1.2.8). Ultimately, they will authorize the actions and the implementation of the planning process and, in order to gain mutual agreement and commitment, organize a start-up or component launch meeting where all the key stakeholders of the component will be invited. Typically, the scope statement of the component will be agreed by all the stakeholders at the end of this meeting.

9.1.1.2   Plan Components

The role of the program manager during the component planning phase is to monitor the elements of planning that affect the program, in particular other components within the program. More specifically, the program manager will want to be involved in decisions concerning resource usage (see Section 9.1.2.2), interdependencies (see Section 9.1.2.3) and aggregated risks (see Section 9.1.2.4).

The scope will align with the program BBS, the schedule will be based on the program milestones and the component's acceptance criteria will be linked to program KPIs. Any resources shared with other components or with the business will be identified to enable the program manager to ensure a better coordination between components or with resource owners. Project risks are classified as single project risks or aggregated risks.

Two key elements of the project plan are time and cost; at program level the component planning of the schedule and budget should address the following elements:

For the schedule:
- resource-based task or activities criticality;
- identification of significant component outputs;
- setting of key deliverables, and stage gates.

Once each component for the current cycle has submitted their schedule, they are incorporated in the program master schedule (see Section 8.3.1).

For the budget:
- verification of cash flow needs to avoid negative cash flow;
- consolidation of cash flow needs between components;
- securing necessary funding, prioritizing component requirements.

The program manager will also make sure expected benefits are well understood and any change is communicated quickly to the concerned component managers. The program manager will approve the component's resourcing plan, communication plan, risk management plan, including contingency plan, and procurement plan. If the component's scope includes transition elements or actions, the business integrator should be involved in its development and approval. It is also the program manager's role, in collaboration with the PMO if applicable, to make sure that component managers are aware and follow organizational processes and policies concerning these elements of the overall project management plan.

9.1.1.3   Integrate all program activities

The program manager reviews all components to verify any conflicts in terms of schedule, resources, scope and transition. Including a risk analysis and response and adjusts the program plan if required. Particular points to verify are aggregated risks, shared resources, interfaces, client commitments, transition activities and funding.

The program manager is responsible for this integration, which is verified in collaboration with the sponsor and the business integrator.

9.1.2   OVERSEE AND INTEGRATE COMPONENTS

This step involves the monitoring and coordination of program components in order to produce expected benefits, which may require integration and transition activities at program level. This activity requires a value chain approach (see Figure 3.2), rather than a traditional top-down approach.

9.1.2.1   Coordinate actions

The main role of the program manager during overseeing and integration of program components is to manage interfaces and shared resources between the different components, so benefits can be achieved. It includes the management of program and aggregated risks as well as contingencies. The program manager has to make sure that projects and other components deliver usable capabilities in alignment with the program roadmap. The program team seeks to manage value, which means that the use of resources is optimized for the benefits realization and resource owners have to be engaged and committed to the program objectives.

9.1.2.2   Manage and prioritize resources

The purpose of this process is to develop a flexible resource loading plan that takes into account the prioritization of actions and significance of resources. This loading plan must be continually updated to reprioritize resource allocation across the program components as necessary.

Although many stakeholders, like sponsors, users and others, may be involved in the program as resources, I will only consider the resources of the program team and component projects in this section. I have already talked of the importance of resource availability in the pacing of the program (see Section 8.3.1); typically component resources should be prioritized on the basis of the contribution of the component to the expected benefits and its achievability (see Section 8.2.4). Components that score highest on these two aspects should be those that get resources first. On the other hand some actions, including projects, may be necessary for marketing, political, or communication reasons, simply as synergists, because they are a necessary input to a prioritized project, or because they will ease transition into the business. This is a secondary analysis that has to be made by the program team, in particular by the program manager and the business integrator within the context of the Program Board.

The first aspect of resource prioritization is to have a good picture of the resource workload; this involves a good understanding and assessment of resource availability, comparing the prioritized and paced resource requirements (demand) with resource availability (supply). I have already explained how to measure resource requirements through the prioritization of projects and other actions. Once prioritization and pacing are agreed, actual numbers will be supplied by estimation techniques, which are not part of the scope of this book.

There are many ways to measure resource availability and a number of factors will enter the equation. The most common way to measure resource availability is to consult the project management information system, better known as PMIS, and estimate use of resources for projects that have already been initiated, but this gives only a partial image of the availability and does not enable the program team to precisely assess resource needs in the medium term. In most organizations I have worked with, we have successfully established a resource assessment system that includes not only authorized projects, but also those that the Program Board or executive sponsor have committed to.

Different organizations understand commitment in different ways, but my experience shows that all actions that have passed the outline business case step should be considered. This means that the program team will have a clear picture, not only of resources required for funded actions, but also of resources that are and could be committed in the medium term.

Obviously, because a commitment at the outline business case does not mean that the action will necessarily be undertaken, a margin should be assessed for attrition between the outline business case and authorization to deploy. This margin will depend on each organization and program and should be discussed at the Program Board level.

Where the PMIS does not take committed actions into consideration, a distinct category will be created (for example: PP, for *Potential Projects*) for all potential actions and the data available at the preliminary business case will be entered in the system as if the project was being undertaken. Figure 9.2 graphically represents such a resource loading plan.

When assessing resource availability, other factors, beyond simple numbers, should also be considered when planning and assigning resources, in particular the capacity to undertake the job based on expertise, experience, competence and capabilities. For example, many project managers might be available, but none has the expertise to decommission a nuclear plant or to apply agile management techniques to an IT program development. For any gap in resource availability, procurement is to be considered either

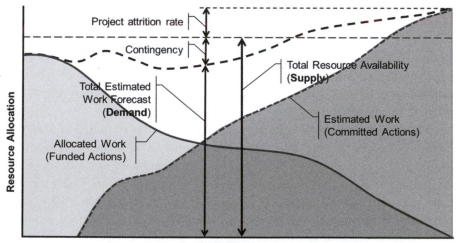

FIGURE 9.2   RESOURCE LOADING PLAN

through hiring, secondment or contracting, otherwise the action needs to be reconsidered.

As explained in the outline business case section (see Section 7.2.6.2) the team defines key resources required and available for each action as soon as possible and assesses their availability. This includes shared resources, resources that have particular competencies or specificity and resources that are booked to maximum availability. In this case it means human as well as technical or equipment resources. In terms of human resources, the best people are assigned to the most significant assignments. Although this seems like common sense, it is often not practised in organizations; the first available "good enough" person is usually assigned to a new task rather than "the best suited", which often requires a reshuffling of resources among projects.

The resource workload (for human resources) and usage (for systems, equipment and facilities) is continually updated and reprioritized, if necessary. These are some of the questions that need to be answered on an ongoing basis:

- What percentage of the available resources is allocated to each action?
- How many resources can be freed to work on an emergent action?
- Given the program's pace, what mix of actions can be undertaken?
- Which are the key resources that have unique skills and/or are shared?

The program team needs to be able to generate consolidated data about availability of, and demand on, resources, so that they can make the best possible decisions about how best to allocate resources to realize the benefits. They should have a flexible resource loading plan, which comprises the prioritization of all actions that are part of the program; the significance of resources for each action and for the program; a continually updated and reprioritized state of resource allocation; secured commitment of resources at scheduled time and a capability to rework activities around key resources, as well as a quick response plan in case of unavailability or change in schedule.

The program team must keep their attention on the broad final goals, but have clear short-term objectives and focus on the elements required to produce next outcome. They should not invest resources in the planning or executing of work that does not support the program objectives.

The program manager is responsible for producing the resource loading plan and gaining commitment from the resource owners. The program sponsor's role is to support the program manager.

9.1.2.3   Manage interdependencies

Interdependencies between actions are the main difference between program management and multi-project management or portfolio management. The program team is expected to concentrate on project interdependencies, rather than on individual project activities. The detailed program cycle roadmap, set during the preparation stage, is the key tool to manage interdependencies (see Section 8.3.3). In terms of the component product, program level intervention should only consist of assessing benefits of major deliverables and output–input relationships between components, not solving the technical or operational level problems. A common mistake among program managers that have a strong project background is to delve too deeply into the tasks; the role of the program manager has to remain at a high level.

Often organizations link the program with the delivery of individual project deliverables; the responsibility of the program manager is to deliver business benefits, which can only be measured after the projects are finished and "operationalized" in the organization or delivered to the marketplace. In particular, in terms of schedule and costs, the program manager must maintain a high level of oversight and support component managers to help them transition capabilities to the stakeholders, therefore the importance of managing the interfaces. The program team always keeps their eye on the program stage gates, which are based on major component deliverables and expected benefits delivery. The way in which every action in the program will contribute to the collective achievement of these benefits should be clearly outlined. The program team develops a review and approval system with clearly established roles and responsibilities for each deliverable, more specifically those that constitute inputs to other actions, or are directly linked to CSFs and KPIs.

This will require controlling only key and interfacing activities and rework of activities around key and shared resources (see Section 8.3.3). The program manager's role requires balance and good conflict resolution skills as contention over limited resources appears when interfacing activities are at risk; this is when the collaboration between the business integrator and program manager becomes essential. The roadmap, showing interfaces and how individual activities are consolidated at program level (see Figure 8.8, p. 197), can be the basis for a solid communications plan destined to keep an open channel with and between the various component managers of the program. Project managers are often focused on their individual projects and it takes a continuous commitment from the program manager to make them work as a team.

9.1.2.4 Manage aggregated risks

During the planning of projects, the program manager will make sure to coordinate risks across the projects and to identify any risks that can be aggregated. Usually I like to hold a risk workshop where all the project managers of the program participate in the aggregated risk qualitative analysis. As for the program risks, aggregated risks are prioritized using the CSFs (see Figure 8.9, p. 199). I have found that many times project managers do not systematically include risk responses in their project scope; to balance this, I often identify specific actions resulting from risk response as *risk packages* that need to be included in the project scope and WBS (work breakdown structure) as any other work package. Figure 9.3 below shows a generic example of this approach.

Some of the risks identified in Figure 9.3 have a negative impact, it is important to also identify risks that have a positive impact as shown in the third

Type	Proj #	Risk #	Risk Description	Risk Response	Risk Packages
AGGR	Pg	1	**Loss of key resources**	**Mitigate**: Detailed resource justification in BCA **Avoid**: Delay planned targets according to resource availability **Accept**: Re prioritise/negotiate scope/deliverables to match resource availability **Transfer**: Seek alternative (internal/external) funding	Prepare resourcing plan Review resource requirements against workload Use internal appraisal procedures to justify/secure resources Market Program in internal publications and stakeholder material Use matrix to secure support and resources (internally) and seek potential funding sources (externally),
AGGR	Pg	2	**Insufficient budget and resources**	**Mitigate**: Involve stakeholders from the onset to ensure commitment and confidence Early lobbying of key partners Secure support early and on ongoing basis Demonstrate benefits **Transfer**: Sign contracts with partners	Define scope of required stakeholders support Identify key partners Communicate and market program to secure support (workshops, meetings, publications) Commit key stakeholders through written agreements Demonstrate achievements as projects progress
AGGR	3.4	4	**Increased coherence with client**	**Enhance**: Market benefits of early uptake Ensure consistency of data in replication **Share**: Build trust relationship **Accept**: Negotiate commitments early Raise issues immediately	Demonstrate potential for success Harmonise & agree measurement methodology Offer practical support to integration of outputs (plan effort) Perform and share risk analysis & response development Clarify replication procedures

FIGURE 9.3   RISK RESPONSES AND RISK PACKAGES

risk or, for example, the availability of a new government grant for this type of program. Notice though that all the risk packages, even those concerning threats, are a positive way to enhance the management of the components and easily integrated into the execution process, therefore making them cost and time effective.

Once the risk packages have been identified, they should be included in the project scope and monitored in the same fashion as other work packages, focusing on those that directly deliver benefits or improve the probability of delivering a benefit.

9.1.2.5   Execute components

The execution of components consists of implementing all the activities and processes required to complete the work outlined in the component plan. The program manager will ensure that the right resources are available for the component at the time they are needed. This responsibility clearly belongs to the program manager because of the level of authority required to perform this task.

If internal resources are required from other company departments, it is the role of the program manager to negotiate commitments and ensure that these commitments are upheld. It is also the responsibility of the program manager to ensure that component managers keep the concerned resource owners updated on any change in resource needs, whether these concern the timing or the specificity of the resources requirement. In terms of external resources, the program manager has typically more authority than component managers to negotiate or renegotiate contractual commitments with contractors, vendors or consultants and collaborate with the procurement department to finalize or review contracts. The program manager will also be responsible for implementing any contingency plan or use any reserve that is in excess of the project schedule or budget and for reallocating resources to, or between projects, if required.

In terms of the product or service design and development, it is the program manager's role to ensure that the component manager gets all the support required from users and sponsors, including details of functional, technical and operational requirements, timely transitional product design and development reviews and approvals, final design and development approval. The same applies to the development of the production process and the product or service realization. If any value analysis or value engineering process is required, the program manager will supervise it because it involves the key stakeholders and often a questioning of the component's objectives.

9.1.2.6 Monitor components

At program level the monitoring should not only be based on the comparison of the work against the baseline component plan, but also take into account and approve any changes to the plan. The program manager will make sure that the component review and approval processes are in place and agreed with the key stakeholders to monitor and approve the key component deliverables at approved milestones. They will also monitor and control component interfaces, using team meetings to make sure there are no issues regarding interdependencies between components or new aggregated risks.

In terms of the component schedule, the program manager will focus on milestones of key deliverables rather than monitoring each activity in the component (see Figure 8.7). In terms of resource usage, the program manager will focus on buffer penetration rather than on time spent. This means that the focus is on how much of the component's overall contingency and management reserves are used as a component progresses, rather than measuring the accurate execution of each individual task or contingency reserve. A graphical example of this process is shown in Figure 9.4 below.

The use of component buffer is inspired from Goldratt's Critical Chain concept (Goldratt, 1997) and requires a culture change from traditional project management approaches because planning will be based around significant deliverables and key resources' availability rather than individual activities that are on the critical path and total float. Although critical path and float remain a

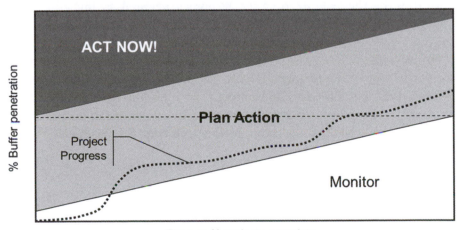

Time or % projects complete

FIGURE 9.4   GRAPHICAL REPRESENTATION OF BUFFER PENETRATION

point of control at the component level, the program team should concentrate on milestones and key resources. Component priority also comes into play and component managers have to commit to the success of the program rather than focus solely on their individual components. The program manager will not care if individual activities are late or over budget as long as the usage of the overall contingency reserve, or buffer, for the component is not affected beyond the limits shown in Figure 9.4. If the program team decides to use this method, there is a need for continuous iteration of the buffer penetration data.

The program team will also assess component performance against benefits delivery. In order to do this, component key deliverables that lead directly to an identified benefit will be linked to CSFs and their KPIs for assessment through the benefits register and, as explained in other sections, these key deliverables are really significant and therefore, should be part of the highest levels of the WBS. Component reporting to the program manager and sponsors should be focused around these key deliverables. Regular progress reports and formal project reviews at pre-set gateways and milestones. Sections 9.2.1 and 10.2.3 discuss stakeholder engagement and reporting requirements.

It is the role of the program manager to manage stakeholders' expectations against results and to identify and act upon any emergent changes. Once approved, component level changes will be managed by the component manager, but any changes that affect the program or other components will be closely monitored by the program manager. The need for change is assessed against the expected capability delivery of the component and CSFs of the program and final decision on the change will be authorized at the level of authority that has control over the resources required to implement the change or will be affected by the change (see Figure 8.10). The change decision process should imply an assessment of the change against the CSFs to validate their need, as well as an assessment of their feasibility. It should be a process similar to that of the Strategic Decision Management process described in Section 4.2.2 and illustrated in Figure 4.1. In brief, the team should clarify the need for change (sensemaking), generate alternatives (ideation) and define viable options (elaboration), before making the actual change decision and committing resources to it.

9.1.2.7 Manage component change

Before implementing a change in one of the program components, the need for change has to be evaluated and, in order to make the decision, alternatives must be sought and appraised, impact should be understood and estimated so that the change can be authorized. These aspects are discussed in detail in Section 10.1.2.

In a program, change can happen at different levels: component, program or business. Each level of change is managed in a different way. Figure 8.10 shows a flow diagram of the change process in a project-based organization. It identifies four decision loops, depending on the impact of the change. Traditionally, project level change is aimed at realigning the project to the baseline plan; in a program, opportunities are examined and the value of the change be assessed in regards of its contribution to benefits or to the ultimate value to the business. Any change that requires a reassessment of the component parameters or objectives should address the impact of the change on the following elements: scope, human resources, cost target and budget, timing (milestones) and risks.

Depending on the impact of the change, different stakeholders will be involved in the decision and in the implementation of the change (see Figure 8.10, p. 201). Each program change will be managed like a small project. The change authorization contains elements similar to the project initiation documents (charter or brief); the change is planned during the estimation leading to its authorization. Its execution will be handled like a project, if the change impacts the program or business loop, or like a work package, if it is within a component loop. In the case of a change that impacts the sponsor loop, transition and preparation of the business for the change should be a concern for the Program Board.

9.1.2.8   Manage contingency and management reserves

To begin with, I would like to clarify the definitions of contingency and management reserve. A reserve is a provision in the estimate to mitigate possible overruns to a level acceptable to the sponsors. A *contingency reserve* is a planned amount of money or time which is added to an estimate to address a specific risk (also referred to as "known-unknown") whereas the *management reserve* is a planned amount of money or time which is added to an estimate to address unforeseeable situations (often called "unknown-unknowns"). Whereas contingencies are typically included in the baseline, reserves are not and require a sponsor decision to be used. Management reserves are estimated, based on the overall uncertainty of the component or program; based on experience and historical data, they constitute a fund that will be used only in case of emergency. Management reserves are usually kept until the end of the component or program, but as uncertainty and ambiguity are reduced, they can also be used for other activities. In this section, I will focus on the management of contingency reserves.

Contingency reserves are determined, based on the risk response decision. Like risks, there are three types of contingencies for the program: component contingencies, program contingencies and aggregated contingencies. Since contingencies are estimated as part of the risk management process, it is important to associate contingencies with specific risks so, when a risk is passed, the contingency reserve can be used for other means. For example, if non-availability of a specialist resource at a certain time has been identified as a risk for a component within the program, the risk response will identify either the hiring of an external resource if time is critical or the postponement of the task if cost is critical. The estimated additional cost to hire the external resource and the estimated additional time to accomplish the task are both contingencies. Typically, if the risk occurs, the component manager will decide to use one or the other alternative depending on the circumstances. At program level, the program manager will monitor risks and use of contingencies to be able to reallocate time or monies to more urgent tasks within the program if the risk has passed and the contingency has not been, or been only partially, needed.

When the program team has an updated list of prioritized actions and an up-to-date workload, available resources can be reallocated quite effectively at short notice. Whereas it may be too tedious to follow every risk, I typically ask component managers to identify contingencies per phase of the component and when the phase is completed, we examine together the contingencies used and agree on what is still required for the next phases. Component managers have a tendency to want to keep contingencies for as long as possible in case something goes wrong, therefore this system will only work if they have confidence that the program manager will authorize the use of management reserves when needed. All contingencies coming from aggregated risks are managed directly at the program level.

The key to reserve management is to keep only what is necessary, so that all actions can be implemented as soon as resources become available and minimal resources are being kept in reserve. Good reserve management is directly dependent on good resource management and risk management.

9.2   Capabilities Transition

Because programs are first and foremost about delivering benefits, it is essential that the outputs produced through components are operationalized and that new capabilities are transitioned into business-as-usual. This section will address the stakeholder engagement as an ongoing means to prepare for transition and actual transition of component inputs into the customer organization. Whether the new capabilities are destined for internal or external customers, the same care should be taken in preparing the organization to absorb the change.

9.2.1   ENGAGE STAKEHOLDERS

The activities required for this ongoing process are those that enable the team to continually engage the stakeholders, particularly the key stakeholders. I have already pointed out the need to identify the contribution of the stakeholders to each component and the setting of milestones for each key deliverable. These are the two main elements of successful stakeholder management. The first will ensure ongoing commitment of the key stakeholders, the second will foster their motivation through marketing and proof of benefits being realized through the key deliverables.

The Power/Interest Grid (see Figure 7.2, p. 151) is an essential element in the management of stakeholders. In order to remain engaged, key stakeholders, usually those with both high power and interest, must be kept involved at all times, especially in the decision-making process. My own experience is that programs that don't address this are either challenged or, worse, stopped because they lose their stakeholders' support. Despite studies, like the PMI's *Executive Sponsor Engagement* executive report (PMI, 2014), many organizations still resist involving some key stakeholders, clients for example, in program decisions. This is a mistake; clients and other stakeholders that are actively involved may be perceived at times as being too demanding, but by not involving them the team run the risk of making them feel depreciated and losing their support, and worse, they may reject the final deliverables because they do not represent their needs or expectations at the time of delivery.

The stakeholders that have power but limited interest can quickly develop a negative interest if they feel their needs are not taken into account. Stakeholder management will therefore consist of making sure they are, as much as possible, satisfied: if they are negative, try to keep their interest limited by not challenging them; if they are positive, try to gain their support by satisfying their interests.

Users and beneficiaries are usually in the category that has high interest and low power. The key here is communication, communication, communication!

Consult these stakeholders at the beginning to understand their needs and concerns, explaining that all their expectations may not be satisfied for achievability and prioritization reasons, but that this will be an objective and open process. Keep them informed regularly of the progress of the program and of the realization of benefits that concern them. Try to plan for information sessions, meetings to share concerns and address issues as soon as possible. Some of their concerns may not seem important to you, but if they take the time to share them, they are important to them. This group has to be constantly monitored in terms of power.

Suppliers, including consultants, are also part of this group. The key with suppliers is to work on a long-term trust-based relationship. Whereas it is easy to focus on short-term cost-based relationships in a project context, the program team will work for a much longer period with the same suppliers. It is also a fact that programs are more complex and will be subjected to many changes along the way. A relationship based on contract terms only is likely to sour quickly in a turbulent environment, whereas a relationship based on trust will be much more fruitful for both parties.

As for the last group of stakeholders, which I call marginal, they need to be regularly monitored for changes, otherwise take into consideration any expectation you are aware of, but do not consume too many resources in that area.

Additionally, the team would be expected to continually monitor changes in the stakeholder status or the appearance of new stakeholders and realign its stakeholder management activities accordingly.

9.2.1.1   Engage program team

One of the difficult aspects of managing the program team is to manage the project managers. Whereas project managers are usually quite happy performing in a well-defined environment, they are generally averse to change when they need to focus on their deliverables. It is the role of the program manager and of the program management core team to engage component managers. There are a few issues that need to be addressed. In our experience, and as advocated by guides and standards, program managers should enforce a standardized project methodology for the components of the program. Whereas reporting needs to be consistent and there should be an agreement on the methods used to manage components, it is our experience that, mostly when working with senior project managers, it is best to let them "choose their own path". Experienced managers are usually good at what they do and, over the years, have developed or chosen methods they are familiar with. A good program manager will empower these project managers, but create a responsibility to respect the agreed reporting process, so that the right decisions can be made, based on consistent data.

Project managers are generally "change averse", and, to be effective, project management has to have a well-defined scope from the beginning. The program manager and program management core team's role is to make sure that before a component is launched, the scope is reasonably well defined and that any changes are approved and consistent with resource availability.

Because they are asked to perform at a high level, component managers are generally not team players. They are accountable for their deliverables and are in charge of their team. A few studies have demonstrated that under stress, project managers will use a more transactional and authoritative leadership style. Because they are results-oriented, it is often difficult to convince them to share resources for the good of the program, or even to collaborate with one another. One of the main and most difficult tasks of the program manager and program management core team is to create a collaborative system between the component managers of the program. In a few large programs, we have experienced success with targeted team events that focused on collaboration in a stress free context.

9.2.1.2   Engage executive stakeholders

During the deployment stage, the program team needs to maintain engagement of the executive stakeholders who will continue to support and fund the program. The stakeholder analysis should be updated at least at the beginning of each cycle to ensure continued mastery of stakeholder impact.

Goal-based, or Telic, motivation theories are useful for long-term stakeholder engagement. They rely on three main principles:

1. Stakeholders should actively participate in the setting of the goals so that they are meaningful to them.
2. The achievability of the goals must be established so that they do not seem unattainable or trivial.
3. The regular progress towards the final objective should be made obvious to maintain motivation in the long term.

Point (1) is covered by the whole value proposition and objectives definition, leading to the BBS and assessment of alignment and point (2) is covered by the achievability analysis. It is during deployment that the program team addresses point (3) and ensures continuous motivation of the stakeholders through marketing of the program and meaningful reporting (see Section 10.2.3).

9.2.1.3   Engage partner stakeholders

In the same fashion, the program manager and program team should engage partner stakeholders: change agents, line managers, contractors, consultants and others by involving them in decisions that regard their area of influence and inviting them to participate in team meetings. I have always had a lot of success by making attendance to program meetings open for partners, even if they are not directly concerned. In the beginning, the attendance is high and the first meetings are difficult to manage, but participants quickly learn to come only if they are concerned. The difference is that they do it on a voluntary basis and don't feel excluded from decisions.

9.2.2   TRANSITION AND CLOSE COMPONENTS

The transition phase is often neglected in programs. It usually overlaps the delivery of capabilities because many of the activities required to transition and integrate capabilities into the business start as soon as the component is initiated.

Component transition includes all the activities to successfully transfer component results into the business. Closure follows the satisfactory final review and verification of results, including transition activities.

9.2.2.1   Deliver component outputs

Component outputs are measured in four core dimensions: scope, quality, time and cost; all other areas of component management are enablers to achieve these. These four elements are intimately linked; scope and quality are defined by the users' needs, and time and cost by the sponsors' means. In the formulation stage, the program team has helped define the program's objectives by balancing needs with means to create value. The team has defined the program's success criteria through critical success factors and key performance indicators. The components have been defined, based on the achievement of these CSFs and KPIs. If the program team has kept track of stakeholders' needs throughout the program and updated the requirements accordingly, component outputs should be in line with those capability requirements. Outputs should also be coordinated between the different components that contribute to an operational capability, process improvement or added competitiveness so that the change is paced in an acceptable way and the organization is ready to implement the new capability.

Together, the sponsor, business integrator and program manager will ensure that the component outputs will create expected outcomes and deliver intended benefits. The main responsibility of the program manager is to make sure the component deliverables are in line with the stated requirements; the sponsor confirms alignment with the evolving strategy; and the business integrator regularly monitors changes in the users' needs and validates the fit of the component deliverables with those needs. Together they will ensure that the organization is ready to absorb the new capabilities delivered by each component. They should work as a team and coordinate their roles through the Program Board (see Figure 4.4).

The outputs delivery will always be assessed against stated requirements, but sometimes undefined requirements may appear that could not have been predicted. If the Program Board has worked as a coordinated unit, if users and customers are involved in component reviews and if component changes have reflected any additional feature required or adaptation to new requirements, then the delivery should only be a formality; if this is not the case, changes may be necessary at delivery to match current updated requirements. Any such case requires a learning loop process (see Section 4.2.2) to make the decision on whether a change is necessary or not.

9.2.2.2   Transfer capabilities

The transfer of capabilities to business-as-usual often requires more than a simple handover, the transference of possession and authority; technical and operational testing and balancing of systems, training, coaching, mentoring and support are other elements of a successful transfer process. Developers and designers, technical and operational experts, as well as component managers, are often involved in the process. They work under the joint authority of the program manager and the business integrator. When a contract exists between the program team and a customer, the transfer process should be detailed and levels and scope of responsibility and authority clearly outlined. The integration activities must be included in the component's WBS. Many of these activities start at the planning stage and must be recognized at the risk of missing on benefits. Whereas it is important to establish boundaries between the delivery team and the users' responsibilities to avoid scope creep, it is also important to plan for overlaps where knowledge and skills are transferred at the right level and support is available if needed.

Training, in particular is an important part of the transfer process and often a distinct component in the program. Training should be designed to ensure a thorough knowledge transfer, but also a hands-on skills transfer. Whether the training is technical, operational or procedural, coaching and support should be included to ensure full capability.

The program manager and business integrator are jointly responsible for the identification of integration activities. The program manager will monitor then at program level, whereas the business integrator will monitor the organization's readiness.

9.2.2.3   Market component outputs

The key principle of marketing is that the customer does not want a product, but a benefit. As people start using component outputs (products, services and capabilities) results are starting to show. The delivery of these outputs should be used to secure further funding and support from the stakeholders, and particularly the sponsors. This is why it is essential to prepare a preliminary marketing plan that clearly links key deliverables with expected benefits (see Sections 3.2.1.7 and 8.1.3).

Do not forget that, as in any market, different programs and projects are competing for limited resources and stakeholders are looking for competitive advantage. You have to demonstrate unequivocally that your program is the best investment. You have already determined its CSFs, based on stakeholders' objectives, you must now show that you are achieving the objectives they have bought into. Marketing an output means advertising its realization and making the most of it. The blueprint and the roadmap are essential elements of the marketing plan since all the key deliverables and expected benefits are listed in them and deliverables are linked to each benefit.

When a key deliverable is achieved all the stakeholders that are concerned either with the added operational capability, marketing and sale of the product, or impact of the change should be contacted. The program team will emphasize that the deliverable has been delivered as agreed and on time; if this is not the case, the team will start communicating with the stakeholders as soon as a slip is observed and will keep them informed as corrective actions are taken. At the end, the key point is to be able to say: we did what we said we would do! When stakeholders start to realize that they can trust the program team, they will be more than willing to invest more resources and energy in the program.

This aspect of program management is especially important because the ultimate results cannot be accurately predicted and will evolve. This is the main reason customers are actively involved in agile management.

9.2.2.4   Close components

Components are typically closed when their scope has been achieved and the product or service delivered. Program managers will supervise the scope verification and final review to make sure the component outputs satisfy the requirements. Their role will then be to ensure that the business integrator or customer is ready to use the new capabilities and integrate them into the operational side of the business.

The program manager will also conduct component reviews and command audits if required. A review is an internal assessment of component processes and results by the program team and sponsor. They will assess the component's expected benefits to business, the efficiency of the component process, the effectiveness of the deliverable and make sure lessons learned are developed and the results recycled into the program and the organization. This last step is often carried in collaboration with the PMO if there is one. An audit is an external, independent assessment of the component processes and results. It can be carried on by other departments like quality, legal, procurement, the PMO or by external regulatory bodies. It generally involves verification of the compliance to a standardized quality process or policy, compliance to external or internal safety requirements, compliance to regulatory procedures or other regulatory requirements.

In terms of transition, also called commissioning or transfer, the program manager's role is to evaluate operational performance in close collaboration with the business integrator, make sure warranties are enforced and training is finalized. The program manager must ensure that the transition strategy is implemented and that there are no major issues that need to be addressed.

The program manager will also make sure that all information and data concerning the component is collected and that all documents are updated and completed and component files archived for future use. The component or phase closure should then be documented, all outstanding issues closed, formal acceptance secured, and this acceptance communicated to all concerned stakeholders. The component closeout report is issued by the component manager and approved by the program manager and customer, if appropriate.

Program Deployment (Capabilities Integration and Benefits Appraisal)

In Chapter 9, we have seen how to manage projects and other actions from a program point of view, in Chapter 10 I will describe in detail how to integrate the new capabilities in the organization. I will also discuss the program evaluation process and how it differs from traditional evaluation. We will see how to manage program changes to create opportunities, as well as the management of program knowledge so that it can be used for the next cycles. I have also decided to add a short section on transition to the next cycle because one of the roles of the program team will be to manage cycle transition, including reformulation and realignment of the program, if necessary.

This Chapter is divided in three sections:

- 10.1   Capabilities Integration
- 10.2   Benefits Appraisal
- 10.3   Transition to Next Cycle

10.1   Capabilities Integration

Because programs are first and foremost about delivering benefits for the organization, it is essential that the outputs produced through components are operationalized and that new capabilities are integrated in the organization. This section will address the program's support for the sustained integration of new capabilities into business-as-usual (BAU), including changes to the program resulting from this integration or changes in the context of the customer organization. Whether the new capabilities are destined for internal or external clients, the same care should be taken in preparing the organization to absorb the change.

10.1.1   SUPPORT BUSINESS INTEGRATION

The support of business integration is a key aspect of the success of a program. Many of the tasks required to support business integration are program tasks related to the management of change and will be under the direct responsibility of the program manager.

In coordination with business integrator, the program manager identifies any additional operational support activities required to ensure full sustainability of the benefits. The program team offers support to the operations team to verify and integrate all systems as well as to ensure their full understanding by users. They conduct change management activities if required in order to ensure that the change can be sustained. The relationship between program management and change management is well detailed in the recent *Managing Change in Organizations: A Practice Guide* (PMI, 2013c).

In addition to the component transition and change management activities, the program may need to include some operational activities like: service management, user engagement, customer support, or others. These activities must be clearly identified in the preparation phase of the program or be included in component's scope. The risk of not identifying these activities is to have extensive scope creep.

The purpose of this set of activities is to ensure full integration and sustainability of the program benefits into the business.

10.1.1.1   *Prepare organization*

The analysis of the organization's readiness and the pacing of the program have a direct impact on the successful implementation of change See Section 8.3.1. These activities are undertaken during the preparation phase of the program and lead to the planning of change management activities to support the change process. During deployment the program team implements the planned change management activities (information and decision meetings, interviews, and workshops in addition to communication, training, coaching and consultation). They monitor the transition and integration process to identify any resistance to change, change of pace in delivery of benefits, perception of benefits value, level of performance, or change in priority of CSFs.

It is the role of both the program manager and the business integrator to prepare the organization for change. The role of the program manager consists of making sure project outcomes are delivered as agreed and coordinated together to enable easy operationalization; the role of the business integrator is to make sure all the elements required for a successful integration of the outputs are in place at the operational level and that business continuity is ensured during the transfer and transition processes. Jointly, they will prepare the people, the recipients of the change or users, to accept and embrace the change and engage in its implementation.

10.1.1.2   Sensemaking activities

I have already discussed the concepts of sensemaking and pacing in Section 8.3.1; in this section, I will develop these concepts further.

Sensemaking is an essential element of successful change. It can be described as the process and time necessary for people to come to terms with the impact and consequences of a change and to become aware of its value in regards of one's own value expectations. Sensemaking activities are essentially facilitated activities directed at a better understanding of the impact of the change for both individuals and groups and their engagement towards the change. It implies that change recipients are given the time to "make sense" of the change and embrace it.

Sensemaking efforts in programs will be directed at two levels: first, at the key stakeholders, when identifying their needs and expectations and defining the expected benefits of the program during the formulation stage; secondly at the users (customers) which will use component outputs to realize the program outcomes through enhanced capabilities. The first level has already been discussed in the Formulation Section, in particular in Sections 7.2.3 and 7.2.4. In this section, I will essentially address the second group of stakeholders.

10.1.1.3   Change agents

In most organizations I have worked with, I have used the concept of change agents to facilitate change. This concept has been extensively discussed in the organizational management literature. The predominant perspective is that change agents are the representatives of the sponsors and implementers of the change; it is presumed that change agents are positive to the change and doing the right things while "change recipients" will generally be negative and put obstacles or barriers in the way of the change. Change agents and change recipients have to engage in sensemaking together to determine the best way to accomplish the change and determine how its value can best be recognized and achieved. Change agents are both the implementers and recipients of the change, and often the same people playing dual roles.

In most situations, I will collaborate with the business integrator to identify the individuals that are most receptive to change at all levels of the organization. Once these people have been identified, I will conduct regular information workshops to explain what the change will be and discuss how it will affect them, both on a personal and work level. This will enable the program team to identify any issues that could obstruct the change implementation process. The program team ought to be very open to receive ideas from these change agents, which means it is not just a matter of delivering information, but also of getting feedback and making sense together to facilitate the change. The change agents are then expected to go back to their job and spread the new ideas to their colleagues as well as gather potential implementation issues from them to report back to the program team.

10.1.1.4   Resistance to change

Managers, whether they are program managers, business integrators or executives, must understand that recipients' resistance to change is not necessarily an obstacle to successful change. On the contrary, dissidence can add value to a change, both through the engagement of the resistors and the generation of new ideas to address a situation. Obviously the sooner resistance is addressed, the better; hence the stakeholder analysis and needs identification processes at the formulation stage, but it should also be addressed on a continuous basis and especially during the transition process as new issues will arise and users, who saw the change as a theoretical process, can now appreciate its full extent and its consequences for them.

Another point is that there is often no consideration of the possibility that change agents contribute to resistant behaviours through their own actions (Ford, Ford and d'Amelio, 2008). But change disrupts normal organizational patterns and requires participants to enact new patterns. This creates a mix of deliberate and emergent processes that increase ambiguity (Mintzberg and Waters, 1985), including for the change agents. Change agents must be capable of assessing their own contribution to resistance.

Resistance can be seen as conflict, and conflict, when handled openly, has been found to strengthen and improve not only the quality of decisions but also participants' commitments to the implementation of those decisions (Amason, 1996). If the program team is open to resistance and deals with it openly, it can become an asset and a resource in change implementation.

10.1.2   MANAGE PROGRAM ADAPTIVE CHANGES

Change is an integral part of the program management process. Programs need to respond adaptively to changes in context, new stakeholder expectations and integration issues on a continual basis. Whereas in operations and single project management, change is seen as a deviation from the baseline that needs to be corrected, in programs changes should be seen as opportunities to improve value. In operations and projects, outputs should be predictable, maintenance and controlled management are expected; efficiency and reliability are the true measure of value. In programs, where transformation and emergent unpredictable outcomes are the norm, agility and flexibility are expected to achieve evolving strategic objectives; responsiveness is the real measure of value. Change can be expected or unexpected, the purpose of adaptive change management activities is to reduce the amount and impact of unexpected change.

Adaptive change is linked to the governance process and in particular, decision-making. Researchers (Simon, 1955; Heller et al., 1988; and Kleindorfer et al., 1993) have classified organizational decisions in three categories. I will use Heller's wording: strategic, tactical and operational. Strategic decisions are usually longer-term and have an organizational impact; tactical decisions are medium-term and have a contained impact, but may have a cumulative organizational impact; finally, operational decisions are repetitive and have a limited impact in the firm. Low-ambiguity decisions are typically of operational nature, including component decisions. High-ambiguity and low-uncertainty situations can be dealt with at the tactical level, but high-uncertainty, high-ambiguity situations need to be considered as strategic. This is the nature of program adaptive change.

10.1.2.1   Evaluate need for change

The first element in any change process is to evaluate the "real" need for change. Change is often brought upon organizations as a knee-jerk reaction to unfamiliar situations; it typically falls in the high-ambiguity zone and can carry either low or high uncertainty, but typically the response will be based on administrative, power or performance (rational) decision-making (see Figure 1.2) and dealt with as an operational or at the most a tactical decision. Decision-makers often choose the first acceptable solution, rather than look further to find an optimal solution which would require more resources. In the case of a situation where both uncertainty and ambiguity are high, this is not acceptable.

Adaptive change is an ongoing process, but typically follows benefits appraisal (see Section 10.2), when realized benefits are compared to expected benefits. Following this appraisal gaps or opportunities may be identified that require a decision. As stated above, other triggers may be changes in context or changes in stakeholders' expectations. The decision to implement a program change requires a learning cycle (see Figure 4.1 and Section 4.2), where decision-makers try to make sense of the situation, look for feasible alternatives and examine options before making a decision. The evaluation of the need for change is part of the sensemaking effort; it requires decision-makers to examine why the change is necessary and what it is aiming to achieve, followed by an evaluation of its alignment with the defined CSFs of the program or strategy. It also requires the decision-makers to seek alternative solutions so as to have a greater choice of options available.

10.1.2.2   Estimate impact of change

The impact of a program change is estimated at different levels (see Figure 8.10); different impact levels require different decision-making levels. Typically, operational and component changes can be dealt with at the local level; changes that affect the program should be handled by the program manager if they are tactical, and by the Program Board if they are of strategic nature. Changes that affect the strategic objectives are dealt with at the appropriate executive sponsor level.

The program team will review the program plan according to the change recommendations and seek feedback from its key stakeholders, including sponsor and business integrator, to assess support for the change. Once support is secured the change will be presented for authorization.

10.1.2.3   Authorize change

Program changes are authorized by the appropriate hierarchical level, as stated above. The program management team should have in place a formal change request and authorization process stating the need for change, nature and impact of the change, the different steps of the change process and estimated impact on the program process and the organization, and, at each level, the required authorizations to proceed. In the case of significant changes, the change process can be tiered in a similar way as in the business case process (see Figure 4.6).

Once the changes are authorized, the activities they entail become part of the cycle's deployment process.

10.2   Benefits Appraisal

A program typically extends over a period of many months (IT supported change programs, Business Process Re-engineering, etc.) or many years (drug development, transportation infrastructure refurbishment, etc.); some programs (crime prevention, water management, etc.) can even be ongoing. Even in ongoing programs, appraisal is carried out on a regular basis and, each time the program team asks itself: should the program continue, be realigned or even stopped?

Benefits can only be assessed once the component outputs have been fully transferred and put into use. The program therefore extends beyond the component closing phase. Many organizations claim that a program ends when the last component output is delivered. This can be true in highly technical programs with a low uncertainty and ambiguity factor, for example a production facility upgrading or product improvement in a known market. This can also be true for programs where there is a long lead period between the delivery of outputs and the possibility to measure benefits; government programs like crime prevention, alphabetization or large infrastructure construction often fall into this category, benefits then become part of a portfolio or even operational process.

In most other cases, the program scope should extend until all the business benefits have been realized (see Figure 2.2), or at least until there is no doubt that they will be realized. Obviously, as stated in the program definitions (see Section 1.2), programs should be assessed against the benefits they deliver and these must be greater than those of managing components independently. So, although the program may continue, the program team may not be involved full time and authority may be transferred to the business integrator in order to finalize program tasks. A long-term component that is part of a program, training for example, could be managed by the business integrator or another operational manager without involvement of the original program team, but measures of success should still be set and achievement of benefits evaluated. It is then that manager's responsibility to feedback to the sponsor if any other actions are required to achieve the program objectives.

Benefits appraisal is an ongoing process which addresses both the delivery of capabilities and the achievement of the benefits that stem from them.

One important aspect of program success is to market benefits to the key stakeholders to keep them engaged and gain their continuous support.

10.2.1   TWO TYPES OF EVALUATION

In any stable relatively predictable environment, where ambiguity is low, evaluation is typically made against a baseline. Evaluation is based on an assessment of the variance with the baseline, and control aims to correct any deviations. Traditional baseline evaluation is well covered by project and operational management literature, for example the PMI® *Guide to the Project Management Body of Knowledge*. Programs will be assessed on the baseline, but also on opportunities, at the organizational and project levels.

When the environment is turbulent and unpredictable, typically in high-ambiguity situations, evaluation consists of evaluating results and readjusting the means to realize value improvements; I have called this type of evaluation "opportunity evaluation". In programs, like in agile management, control does not only consist of a simple comparison with a baseline, on the basis of pre-set performance criteria, and then a readjustment to align to this baseline; it consists of a continuous re-evaluation of the program objectives, in relation to the achievement of organizational benefits and realization of opportunities. In a program, parameters and scope are determined through an interactive negotiated process and will therefore evolve, not only in terms of who evaluates, but also in terms of when the evaluation is made. Satisfaction with the intervention will be measured in regards of the perception of the difference between the desired outcome and the actual outcome and these will both evolve as the program progresses, hence the importance of maintaining the blueprint and benefits register updated during the program. Program benefits appraisal requires a constant re-evaluation of results and objectives based on emergent inputs. The program manager has to assess deliverables against milestones and performance against benefits delivery, but also manage stakeholders' expectations against results as well as identify and act swiftly and effectively upon emergent changes.

10.2.1.1   *Program Level Assessment*

When assessing the delivery of benefits from a program point of view, the team takes a broad perspective and looks at three different levels.

1.   The first level is organizational: the team will generate feedback about the effective delivery of expected benefits and satisfaction of critical success factors. Beyond the actual measure of benefits, the team assesses the continuous and effective management of changing corporate or client objectives, which could lead to re-evaluation of needs and expectations; reprioritization of CSFs. This could lead to a re-evaluation of the program's circumstances.

2.   The second level is the management of the program's value chain, particularly the effective use of shared or limited resources, the interface between function and component managers, the clear definition of roles and responsibilities and mutual support of all actors to achieve corporate goals, the effectiveness of the component review and approval process, and finally, the individual component managers' focus on key business issues.

3.   The third level of assessment is the measure of the benefits delivery as defined in the blueprint (see Figure 8.4, p. 190). In particular, the program level assessment against the benefits realization plan and the benefits register updates both during transition and post-transition.

The program manager should ensure that appraisal data is recycled into a feedback loop, for the next stage or future programs.

10.2.1.2   Component level assessment

Component results are evaluated as part of the deployment stage, the detail of which was discussed in Section 9.1.2.6. Based on those results, the program manager or program team assess the component's performance against the program objectives. Below are the main points that must be assessed from a program point of view:

- Overall performance of components against business benefits. In particular:
  - quality and timeliness of deliverables in regards of changing needs;
  - resource usage and budget in regards of achievability factors;
  - use of contingencies to address identified risks and emergent events;
  - management of interfaces and interdependencies.
- Response to new threats and opportunities; implementation of changes, as required.

- Re-plan of work and relative priorities, when required.
- Loop back to component charter and scope and capability to readjust, if required.

Following this appraisal, the program team will review the priority of different components against each other, resource allocation, compared pace of components, and eventually the need to replace component managers.

10.2.2   ASSESS BENEFITS REALIZATION

Benefits are measured on a regular basis against the detailed benefits register and blueprint during the program cycles to verify their alignment with the agreed objectives and benefits realization. These are typically evaluated by the sponsor and program board on the basis of program status report and updated benefits register stating alignment with objectives. It is essential to set intermediate benefits to show progress towards the ultimate benefits and engage the stakeholders.

Following approval or feedback, the program manager will issue change requests and program plan reviews if necessary. The team will market benefits achievement to other concerned stakeholders. The program board will then confirm the decision to undertake the transition to next cycle or go to program closure.

The *benefits register* is the means by which the program team can measure the delivery of benefits along the program. Typically the team will use three elements to establish the measure of a benefit. Starting with the KPIs they will define one or more criteria of measure, a target level to be achieved for each and an acceptable level flexibility, or tolerance (see Section 7.2.4.2). These elements are usually established during the definition stage of the program, but can be detailed during the deployment stage. Figure 10.1 is a partial example of a deployment level benefits register. Starting with outputs (Level 3 of the BBS), it shows the KPIs and, for each KPI, one or more criteria. Each criterion is given a level and flexibility measure, a deadline and the party accountable for its delivery. In the example, benefits 1.1.1, 1.1.2 and 1.2.2 are given only one criterion and will therefore be assessed at a higher level; benefit 1.2.1 is given three and will therefore be followed more closely. The level of detail of the benefits register can depend on resources available for the appraisal, criticality of the benefit for the program or importance for key stakeholders.

Outputs (Level 3)		Capability (KPI)	Criterion	Level	Flexibility	Deadline	Accountable Dep't	Actual	Variance	Delivery Date
2.1.1	Define selection criteria based on strategic objectives	Implement Pj/Pg selection process (Based on SOs)	% of projects selected using SO process	80%	-5%	6 months	Business Development	75%	-5%	6 months
2.2.1	Define achievability criteria	All Pg/Pj selected based on achievability criteria	Achievability criteria approved by sponsors	100%	0%	2 months	Finance / Portfolio Direction	100%	0%	1 month
2.3.1	Put in place governance forums (Decision-making)	Governance System in place and agreed	Governance system fully operational	6 months	+ 2 weeks	6 months	CEO Office	24 weeks	-1 week	24 weeks
2.3.2	Select pilot projects & test achievability criteria	Project selection criteria tested and validated	Achievability criteria tested on completed projects	50 projects	-1%	10 months	Project Management	50	0% -2 mths	8 months
2.4.1	Use achievability criteria on all projects	All projects selected using achievability criteria	% of projects selected using achievability criteria	100%	0%	12 months	Finance / Portfolio Direction	85%	-15%	12 months
2.4.2	Monitor strategy alignment	Governance decision forums regularly attended	% of managers attending mandated forums	80%	-5%	9 months	Business Development	90%	+10%	7 months

FIGURE 10.1   DEPLOYMENT LEVEL BENEFITS REGISTER

As the program progresses, the team will use the benefits register to measure the realization of benefits. If the program is based on the use of a BBS or similar method, the realization of benefits, measured through KPIs, will warrant the realization of strategic objectives and overall strategic value. As the benefits delivery data is generated, the team will analyse it. In the example, you will notice that although the program team seems to have progressed well on putting in place the systems, the uptake is deficient as the number of components selected using criteria based on strategic objectives and achievability factors is not up to expectations. This could mean two things: either the expectations were too high and need to be adjusted (see Section 7.2.3), or the organization has not been prepared well enough (see Sections 8.3.1 and 10.1.1). The team must then decide how to tackle this issue and which changes to introduce to achieve the objectives (see Sections 9.1.2.7 and 10.1.2).

10.2.3   COMMUNICATE PROGRESS

My experience is that program deployment reports should be available on demand for all key stakeholders, even if they are typically destined to the program sponsor or client representative. This encourages active participation and engagement.

10.2.3.1   Executive level report

The executive report presented to the Program Board should be based on the measure of generic program expectations, typically:

1. Continued alignment of objectives.
2. Predictability of outcomes for cycle.
3. Effectiveness of cross organization relations.
4. Efficiency of transition process.
5. Benefits realization.

Additionally, for each program, the program team should report on the achievement of program-specific CSFs. These are identified as part of the formulation stage and constitute the high level of the program Benefits Breakdown Structure (BBS) and Outline Blueprint. Milestones are set in the roadmap, which includes high-level program deliverables (intermediate benefits) and work-streams (component projects and program level activities).

10.2.3.2   Program deployment report

The program deployment report is based on the approved detailed BBS-Blueprint-Benefits Register developed during the preparation stage and updated for each program cycle. It contains:

Validated or updated benefits breakdown structure (BBS), including CSFs
The initial BBS is developed during the Formulation stage and completed during the Preparation stage. It is revised at the end of each cycle for the next cycle. The BBS identifies the program's specific Critical Success Factors as well as the KPIs that will be measured for each CSF. Since the CSFs are weighted, their successful achievement will form the basis for the measure of success of the program.

Validated or updated blueprint
The blueprint serves as a basis for reporting progress towards the expected future state. The program team will identify specific capabilities and outcomes

to be delivered at each cycle. For each cycle, the program team will identify intermediate benefits and their measures. These will be part of the detailed benefits register.

As capabilities are delivered and outcomes achieved, the program team will record them and report progress and status in the report. Any variation with the cycle planned schedule and scope will be highlighted.

Validated or updated benefits register, including KPIs

The benefits register is the basis for the progress and status report. It is developed during the preparation stage and updated for each program cycle. The benefits register contains all the program-specific KPIs, linked to the CSFs; for each KPI it states criterion of measure, target and flexibility as well as expected milestone and accountable party.

Each accountable party reports data on the progress of the KPIs they are responsible for to the program manager who compiles this data into the benefits register. The report will record progress and status of the progress towards the final KPIs and achieved intermediate benefits in alignment with the benefits register.

The final report consolidates this data at CSF level and is the basis for the executive report.

10.3   Transition to Next Cycle

At the end of each cycle, the team must prepare for the next cycle and review all steps and documents in regards of the results of the current cycle.

End of cycle benefits are measured against the detailed benefits register and blueprint to verify their alignment with the agreed objectives and benefits realization. At each cycle, the program objectives (CSFs) are re-evaluated and validated in order to ensure adaptability to changing circumstances. If necessary, the team evaluates the need for change or for re-prioritizing CSFs. If necessary, the program value proposition, definition and strategy are reviewed and updated; if this is the case, the business case can be reviewed.

End of cycle benefits measurement provides the basis for the next cycle's plan adjustments. It has been demonstrated that communication targeted at specific stakeholders and marketing of results achieved can improve the engagement of key stakeholders. So, it is the opportunity to make adjustments to the strategy and re-engage the stakeholders.

10.3.1   REVIEW RESULTS AND REALIGN OBJECTIVES

The program team, in collaboration with the Program Board should ask themselves several questions such as:

- Have the expected benefits for this cycle been achieved?
- Have the program or business circumstances changed?
- Have stakeholders' needs or expectations changed?
- Does the rationale for the program still exist?

Because program appraisal does not simply consist of an evaluation against a baseline, the appraisal process itself requires the measure of benefits at organizational level, including the integration of capabilities. The program team will loop back to the formulation and strategic plan of the program (see Figure 6.1), in order to reassess the validity of the original needs as regards external or internal developments since the program began.

At every end of cycle, the Program Board evaluates the opportunity to continue the program and reassesses the strategic objectives of the program. One of the reasons for the program to exist is to generate benefits over and above those that would be generated by activities managed individually. A key difference between project and program management is that, whereas in projects control involves taking action to correct deviations, in programs appraisal is a way to help decision-making. The actual decisions concerning corrective action are taken through reformulation at the strategic level, typically by the Executive Sponsor and Program Board. Obviously different levels of corrective action will require different levels of authority (see Figure 8.10).

As the program cycle nears completion, performance and prioritization of individual components within the program require closer scrutiny. Program size and time span make for a more complex environment, but each component is appraised in terms of quality and timeliness of deliverables, resource usage and budget, use of contingencies to counter risk events, and especially the interface and interdependencies in relation to the other components in the program.

Following the analysis of each component, a reallocation of priorities may be in order for the next cycle of the program. At the component level, the program team needs to review relevance of components that are spanning a number of cycles and the aggregated benefits of all the components that are part of the cycle. The compared pace of each component will be examined since resource allocation should be based on benefits realization. In particular, the program team needs to assess overall performance of components against business benefits, including emergent factors.

The team will also identify new threats and opportunities and re-plan work and relative priorities, at business level, for the next phases or components. This involves reviewing component definitions and readjusting, if required, ensuring data is recycled, for the next cycle or future programs. It may also involve considering changes to the program. And of course, there may also be the need to replace component managers whose performance does not add benefit to the overall completion of the program cycle.

Figure 10.2 shows how the program team and board typically would respond to different situations requiring change.

Situation Assessment	Change Decision
Change in priority of CSFs Internal requirements change External pressures require adjustment.	Reprioritize objectives and resources as required.
Integration of change Changes integrated slower/faster. Resistance to change identified	Adjust pace as necessary; hold information workshops, training sessions, etc.
Delivery of benefits Benefits not delivered as expected. Benefits impact not perceived as well as planned	Reassess distribution of period of stability and end of cycles as required.
Level of performance General performance drops Specific areas are in difficulty	Review priorities and reallocate funds to urgent matters accordingly.

If considering a change:
- **Estimate the need for change**
- **Evaluate the impact of change**
- **Authorize change**

FIGURE 10.2 TYPICAL RESPONSES TO DEVIATION

10.3.2 MANAGE PROGRAM KNOWLEDGE

There have been many good books written on knowledge management, so I do not plan to spend too much time on this subject. Let me just say that there are two important knowledge concepts in program management: first, the program is cyclic, so the knowledge produced in one cycle can and should be used in the next cycle; second, program management has a strong learning aspect, therefore concepts relating to the utilization of knowledge to support organizational learning can and should be considered as part of the program management process. Knowledge management is an integral part of the ongoing appraisal process.

10.3.2.1   Use program data for next cycles

One of the key aspects of the definition stage is to describe the needs, expectations and objectives in measurable terms; during the deployment stage measures of success are taken to ensure achievement of benefits and realization of value. The program and component reporting processes, monitoring of benefits realization and program change control are some of the key aspects of knowledge management in programs. As key deliverables and benefits defined in the business case and scope are delivered the program team will report on any discrepancy and analyse it to find corrective actions for the next stages or cycles of the program. This aspect of knowledge management is closely linked to change management.

10.3.2.2   Knowledge and learning

Researchers in Organizations as Learning Systems, Nevis, Di Bella and Gould (1997), have defined a three-stage model for the organizational learning process:

> *Knowledge acquisition – The development or creation of skills, insights, relationships.*
>
> *Knowledge sharing – The dissemination of what has been learned.*
>
> *Knowledge utilization – The integration of learning so it is broadly available and can be generalized to new situations. (Nevis et al., 1997, p. 3)*

Knowledge acquisition is part of the formulation, organization and deployment stages of the program and this knowledge is then collated and analysed in the appraisal stage. It is at the appraisal stage that knowledge is shared; it is utilized through reformulation and reorganization of the next cycle. Because each organization is different, researchers stress the importance of integrating the learning framework with the organization's culture, using the right learning methods for the right culture. In a program culture, knowledge interpretation and sharing must be agreed. Only shared values and learning framework will lead to accepting acquired and shared knowledge being utilized. If the learning framework is in conflict with the dominant organizational paradigm, data will be interpreted differently by different actors and knowledge will not be used to learn.

Some of the contributing factors to knowledge utilization are:

- agreed information gathering practices;
- shared perception of actual and desired state;
- capacity for self-assessment and commitment to measurement;
- commitment to learning and openness to change;
- variety of control methods, procedures and systems;
- systems perspective.

10.3.3   AUTHORIZE PROGRAM DEPLOYMENT OF NEXT CYCLE

The Executive Sponsor or Program Board will authorize the program to proceed to the next cycle, based on achievement of objectives and the PMO, if applicable, will review the process for compliance. If approved, the program goes to the next deployment cycle, if rejected, the program is either stopped or alternatives are identified.

In this chapter, we have found out that programs have to be evaluated at different levels. This evaluation enables us to decide if the program should continue, be reformulated or maybe stopped. If it is realigned we have looked at the way the value of a change is evaluated and how its impact is measured. In Chapter 11, I will examine what happens when the decision is made to stop the program and how program dissolution should occur.

CHAPTER 11
Program Closure

Program closure consists of measuring ultimate success against objectives and to finalize or transfer any residual work before drawing lessons learned. In Chapter 10 we have examined how program success is evaluated and how the

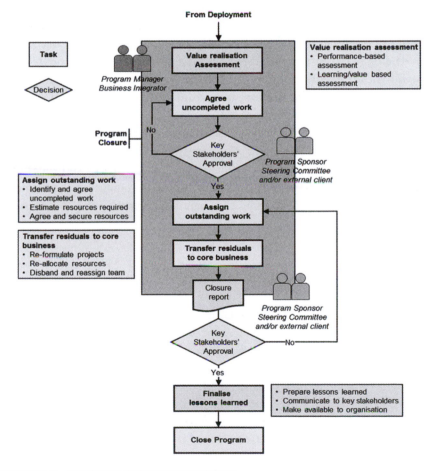

FIGURE 11.1   PROGRAM CLOSURE FLOWCHART

decision to continue or stop the program should be based on measured results. In Chapter 11, I will examine motives to make the decision to stop the program and how to implement the decision. I will then explain how to create valuable knowledge for the organization from the program process. Figure 11.1 on the previous page represents the outline flowchart of the program's definition stage.

11.1   Value Realization Assessment

The measure of benefits realization has been discussed in the deployment stage (see Section 10.2). At the closure stage the objective is to assess the realization of value for the business and to agree on any outstanding work to be completed. Value stems from the sum of "all" the benefits that constitute the scope of the program and some benefits can only be measured in the long term. The final assessment will therefore take into account the probability of achieving these benefits, not necessarily their actual realization. The objective is that the program should not extend beyond what is reasonable in terms of resource commitment versus return.

There are essentially two dimensions to the assessment of value realization: a performance-based assessment that considers the conformity with the business case (realization of CSFs within achievability factors), and a learning, or value-based assessment that considers the achievement of the strategic objectives in the context of changes that may have arisen in the course of the program.

11.1.1   PERFORMANCE-BASED ASSESSMENT

Performance-based assessment is essentially centred on the baseline. Program results are measured against each element of the operational blueprint. These elements typically correspond to the KPIs of the program and/or component deliverables. Most elements of the blueprint can only be measured after component results have been transitioned into the business. Therefore it may be necessary to transfer some work to the business (operations).

The first and most obvious reason to stop a program is that all the initially agreed benefits have been realized within the achievability factors agreed at the business case. The second reason, for which a program needs to be stopped, or at least questioned, is that the investment in the program (cost, resources, time, etc.) becomes greater than the benefits it delivers. In this case, the Program Board should reconsider the continued existence of the program on the basis of the new available data, based on contribution to benefits and achievability (see Section 7.2.6, p. 165).

11.1.2   LEARNING/VALUE-BASED ASSESSMENT

Value-based assessment is generally based on opportunities; it can be measured against elements of the strategic blueprint which are typically CSFs. The program can be closed on the basis of the value it brings to the organization. Even if all the specific benefits have not been realized, the program could have achieved its expected business value. If the environment or context has changed to a point where the sought benefits are no longer required, the continuation of the program should be questioned; maybe it needs to be reformulated in depth or stopped. It could also be estimated that the implementation of ending cycle(s) demonstrates that ultimate purpose cannot be achieved; this may be caused by changes in the context or environment, unanticipated unavailability of resources, erroneous assessment of expected benefits or incorrect estimation of achievability. The two latter cases require the Program Board to be involved, but also the key stakeholders, sponsors and maybe the customers (see Figure 8.10). The decision will then either require a reformulation of the program or the implementation of the closure process.

The program manager is responsible for managing the closure process. The program sponsor, program board and, if applicable, the external client approve the closure proposal and transfer of residuals. The business integrator may take responsibility for delivering outstanding benefits.

11.2   Manage Program Completion

Even in the best managed programs, it is likely that at closure some uncompleted work will need to be finalized. All the program documentation must be updated, a post-program review will be conducted and closure report completed. Acquired knowledge will then be compiled in a lessons learned report and shared to be utilized. Once all this has been achieved, the program closure team is disbanded and reassigned.

Program closure is a phasing-down process, much more extensive than project closing. Whereas closing of projects is a rather short administrative and legal process that concludes a fairly linear process, a program does not have a defined end and will go through a phased process rather than a quick close. When the decision has been made to stop a program, a number of people and funds will be reallocated to other ventures; it is likely that the team will be reluctant to "let go'". For reasons of efficiency, some organizations even choose to involve a team external to the program and a different program manager to manage the closure.

The program manager is responsible for preparing a completion proposal. The business integrator participates in the elaboration of the proposal. The Program sponsor and, if applicable, the external client approve the completion proposal.

11.2.1   AGREE AND ASSIGN OUTSTANDING WORK

In order to make a measurable assessment of work to be completed, the team will use the KPIs (see Section 7.2.4.2). Following this assessment, the team, with the approval of the program board, will recommend work that can be completed within the closure stage and also determine projects or activities that will be completed outside the program. Typically, a list of outstanding activities and of parties responsible for their completion will be issued. The main objective of the program is to ensure that benefits are coordinated to achieve strategic objectives; when it is agreed that this is not at risk, some outstanding projects or activities may be completed on their own. In other cases, it will be necessary to reassign outstanding work to other programs and reformulate these.

The program team will produce a list of outstanding issues, a completion schedule and estimate of the resources required. These will be approved by the program sponsor. This process must be coordinated with the business integrator who will be involved in any transition and residual work.

11.2.1.1   Identify and agree uncompleted work

Outstanding work that can be completed within a reasonable period of time needs to be agreed and assigned; residuals that cannot be reasonably completed will be reallocated to operations or other programs, which are then reformulated as required. Work to be completed within the closure stage is dependent on benefits delivery. The program team will compare results with the blueprint and identify benefits partially, or not, delivered.

11.2.1.2   Estimate resources required to complete the work

Once uncompleted work has been identified and the management approach has been agreed, the team will estimate the resources required to deliver the outstanding benefits and the value to do so (expected benefits versus resources necessary). This will enable decision-makers, typically the program board and sponsor(s), to agree on what needs to be done to complete the program work.

11.2.1.3   Agree and secure necessary resources

Resources will be committed either to the dissolution, individual activities or projects or other programs.

Once commitment has been made, agreed work will be completed and verified using KPIs and achievability factors. As part of the closure activities, the program team should plan for a post-program feedback and knowledge transfer. Many organizations do not include program feedback or knowledge transfer in the program budget and schedule. This is an essential activity of the learning process and is necessary for the organization to improve its practices.

11.2.2   TRANSFER RESIDUALS TO CORE BUSINESS

Any residual work that has been allocated to other programs involves a reformulation of these programs. Depending on the significance and scope of the work, it can consist of a simple change request, a reorganization, or a full reformulation. Program resources will be reallocated as required to the other program.

As part of this process, the program team will issue updated component plans and a final completion report. Agreement to the plan must be secured from all key stakeholders, more specifically external clients and resource owners.

11.2.2.1   Reformulate components

Residual work can be assigned to existing program components, new discrete projects undertaken outside the program, other programs or operations, under the supervision of the business integrator. Program components or other programs are reformulated to include any residual program work that was not part of their initial scope. New projects are chartered and operational work is clearly scoped to allow formal launch and resource assignment.

11.2.2.2   Reallocate resources

Resource allocation is negotiated with resource owners and resources are allocated accordingly to agreed activities.

11.2.2.3   Disband and reassign program team

Once the program is completed to the satisfaction of the executive sponsor, the program team is disbanded. Some team members may be reallocated to reformulated components as required.

11.2.3   PROGRAM CLOSURE REPORT

The program closure report is built on the same basis as deployment reports (see Section 10.2.3.2). In addition it will identify any outstanding work to be completed before the program is closed. This list of outstanding work must be agreed by the sponsor or client. Once it is agreed, the report will outline a plan for two main tasks:

1. Work to be completed within the program:
    - Identify what can be completed within reasonable period.
    - Present execution plan (scope, cost, time).
    - Agree and secure resources for completing work.
    - Plan disbanding and reassignment of program team.

2. Work to be transferred to core business or other programs:
    - Agree allocation of outstanding work to operations or discrete projects.
    - Confirm resource allocation with resource owners.
    - Reformulate discrete projects and submit completion plan.
    - Identify targets and identify roles and responsibilities for completion.

The closure report officially closes the program. All contractual or financial completion documents are finalized following the approval of the report.

The closure report is prepared by the program manager and approved by the program sponsor, program board and, if required, by the external client.

11.3   Lessons Learned Finalization

As stated in the appraisal section (see Section 11.1) knowledge management is an integral part of the management of a program and should be included in the program budget and schedule. At the closure stage, the team will prepare a full lessons learned report for distribution. Ideally the organization will agree a standardized format for this report to easy knowledge transfer and utilization.

11.3.1   PREPARE LESSONS LEARNED

Typically the report will comprise two sections, which have been discussed in the Section 8.3:

- a program process analysis; and
- a benefits delivery analysis.

Aside from the points identified in the appraisal section, the team needs to draw lessons learned for future reference: what they have done right and what they could have done differently or improved? By asking the question in this fashion the program team will not feel threatened to identify mistakes as they will be given an opportunity to analyse them and suggest improvements that will avoid them next time. Often there are delicate areas in this analysis, as individuals, some with power, may be identified as having contributed to mistakes or inefficient or ineffective work. Although it is necessary to identify potential improvements for the future, it is also important to do it in a way that is non-threatening if the organization wants to implement a no-blame, learning culture.

11.3.2   COMMUNICATE TO KEY STAKEHOLDERS

The lessons learned will be consolidated in a report that will focus on the same elements as the executive report (see Section 10.2.3.1):

- alignment of objectives;
- predictability of outcomes;
- effectiveness of cross organization relations;
- efficiency of transition process;
- benefits realization.

Additionally, for each program, the program team will report on the achievement of program-specific CSFs and of the blueprint. Other elements of the report should include:

- continuing measure and delivery of benefits, using Milestones, CSFs, and KPIs in Benefits Register;
- demonstration that changing corporate or client objectives have been taken into account and addressed;
- evidence that evolving circumstances and context developments have been evaluated and addressed;
- confirmation that use of shared, limited resources has been optimized;
- verification that both function and project managers have focused on corporate and/or client goals;
- assessment of how well project review and approval process has been focused on benefits realization;
- any other element related to specific organizational or client context.

11.3.3   MAKE AVAILABLE TO ORGANIZATION

I have been successful in implementing project and program knowledge transfer in a few organizations through the set-up of lunch presentations by project and program managers that had completed their work. Project and program managers were asked to present lessons learned to their peers in the form of a summary presentation. This initiative was accompanied by an intranet-based program and project database which contained an outline charter or brief, budget, schedule, type of program/project, name of project/program manager and lessons learned which enabled any project or program manager to quickly find references concerning projects or programs similar to theirs. This system has many advantages: it forces the program manager to summarize their work and make the report available; with little energy, other program managers can learn about other programs in the organization and know whom to ask information from if they have similar problems.

This method works well if it has enough support from management to be sustained in the long-term.

11.4   Closing the Loop and Preparing the Next Challenge

The program has now come to an end, either because all its expected benefits have been fulfilled or because a decision has been made to stop it before its expected end. Program management teams should continually evaluate the value of the program for the organization and sponsors should not fear to stop a program if its value cannot be justified. The program team has to make sure they can continually demonstrate the value of their program and its capability to deliver its expected benefits.

Conclusion

Whether you are an executive, a sponsor, manager of a PMO, a program or project manager this book will help you understand what your role in a program is and how program management can help you achieve your objectives.

Program management is the link between the business strategy and the value it will generate when implemented. It is the process through which *executives* will be able to express their needs and make sure they are fulfilled; *sponsors* will be able to define the improvements they are expecting and clearly link them to the strategy to make sure they are realized and aligned with the business objectives; *managers of PMO* will have a clear view of what is expected form a program and how its processes can be monitored; *program managers* will understand how to support both executives and sponsors in a tangible way and how to deliver measurable results to the business; *project managers* will understand how their role is essential to the program's success; and finally, *operational and technical actors* will be able to make sure the expected improvements are well integrated and produce the expected results.

This book will also help any organization that makes the decision to implement a program management framework and the structures and systems necessary to support it. By looking at the organizational context as well as cultural and maturity issues, change managers and change agents will understand how to implement a sustainable program management culture by making sure they create a strong foundation that includes the support of senior management and a clear distinction between the project and program paradigms; they also need to put in place the structures that support knowledge management and a systemic view of resource management (contingencies, personnel, funding, priorities); finally, and this is what will take the most time, they change people's attitudes so they are aligned on vision and strategy rather than technical or operational results; they aim their effort at stakeholders' benefits; and develop an openness to change and ambiguity.

Today, there are five essential components that sustain the program:

1. *Benefits management* is recognized as the main thrust of the program. It is the program's purpose to deliver benefits to the organization and its stakeholders.

2. *Stakeholders' engagement* is the second key element of the program, to motivate the stakeholders, understand their needs and negotiate expected benefits.
3. *Governance* is essential not only to control the achievement of the vision, but to create that vision and commit to put in place the necessary structures to achieve it.
4. *Change management* has become an essential part of the management of programs and understanding change and the effect it has on people's commitment to a future state is essential in today's world.
5. Finally, *decision management* is really at the heart of the management of programs which is fundamentally a decision-making process, followed by a decision implementation methodology.

Whereas benefits management, stakeholder engagement, change management and decision implementation are mainly the domain of the program team, governance, and particularly, creating the vision, committing the resources necessary to success and decision-making are highly dependent on the executives and sponsors performance and commitment to the program.

At all levels, the program actors must commit to generate benefits over and above those which projects generate on their own, to move away from using a project (performance only) management mind-set and methodology and to articulate why program management might be implemented in their organization and understand how it can be sustained.

References

Amason, A.C. (1996). Distinguishing the effects of functional and dysfunctional conflict on strategic decision making: Resolving a paradox for top management teams. *Academy of Management Journal*, 39, pp. 123–48.

APM (2000). *The APM Body of Knowledge*. High Wycombe: The Association for Project Management.

APM (2004). *Directing Change: A Guide to Governance of Project Management*. High Wycombe: The Association for Project Management.

APM (2006). *APM Body of Knowledge*, 5th Edition. High Wycombe: The Association for Project Management.

APM (2012). *APM Body of Knowledge*, 6th Edition. High Wycombe: The Association for Project Management.

BSI (1997). Value management, value analysis, functional analysis vocabulary. Standard BS EN 1325–1:1997. European Committee for Standardization (CEN) Technical Committee CEN/TC 279-British Standards Institute (BSI) Technical Committee DS/1, Chelsea, UK.

BSI (2000). Value management. Standard BS EN 12973:2000. European Committee for Standardization (CEN) Technical Committee CEN/TC 279-British Standards Institute Technical Committee DS/1, Chelsea, UK.

Burns, T. and Stalker, G.M. (1961). *The Management of Innovation*. London: Tavistock Publications.

CCTA (1999). *Managing Successful Programmes*. London: Central Computer and Telecommunications Agency (now called OGC-Office of Government Communications).

CEN VM Vocabulary Standard EN 1325–1, 1997.

Chapman, C. and Ward, S. (2000). Project risk management: The required transformations to become project uncertainty management, in *The Frontiers of Project Management Research*, edited by D. Slevin, D. Cleland and J. Pinto. Newtown Square, PA: Project Management Institute.

CIO Executive Council (2008). The State of the CIO '08: Overview, Findings and Editorial Analysis. Extracted from: http://a1448.g.akamai.net/7/1448/25138/v0001/compworld.download.akamai.com/25137/cio/pdf/state_of_cio_08.pdf on 3 March 2009.

CMAA (2002). *Construction Management Standards of Practice*. McLean, VA: Construction Management Association of America.

CMI (2013). *The Effective Change Manager: Change Management Body of Knowledge*. Sydney: Change Management Institute.

Cooke-Davies, T. (2002). Establishing the link between project management practices and project success. *Proceedings of the 2nd PMI Research Conference, July 2002, Seattle*. Newtown Square, PA: Project Management Institute.

Dallago, B. (2002). Corporate governance, governance paradigms, and economic transformation. *Proceedings of the Institutional and Organisational Dynamics in the Post-socialist Transformation Conference*, Amiens, 25–26 January 2002.

Dann, C., Le Merle, M. and Pencavel, C. (2012). The lesson of lost value. *Strategy+Business*, 69. Booz&Co online publication. Extracted from: http://www.strategy-business.com/article/00146?pg=all on 20 February 2013.

De Wit, B. and Meyer, R. (2004). *Strategy: Process Context, Content: An International Perspective*, 3rd Edition. London: Thomson Learning.

Drucker, P. (1989). *Managing for Results*. London: Heinemann Professional.

DSMC (1999). *Program Management 2000: Know the Way: How Knowledge Management Can Improve DoD Acquisition (1998–1999)*. Washington, DC: Defense Systems Management College Press Publications.

Duggal, J.S. (2001). Building a next generation PMO. *Project Management Institute 32nd Annual Seminars and Symposium Proceedings*. Drexel Hill, PA: PMI Communications.

Dye, L.D. and Pennypacker, J.S. (1999). An introduction to project portfolio management, in *Project Portfolio Management: Selecting and Prioritizing Projects for Competitive Advantage*, edited by L.D. Dye and J.S. Pennypacker. West Chester, PA: Center for Business Practices.

Earl, M.J. and Hopwood, A.G. (1980). From management information to information management, in *The Information Systems Environment*, edited by H.C. Lucas, F.F. Land, T.J. Lincoln and K. Supper. Amsterdam: North Holland Publishing.

Elonen, S. and Artto, K. (2002). Project portfolio management: Managerial problems in business development portfolios. *Proceedings of the IRNOP V Research Conference*, Renesse, Netherlands.

European Foundation for Quality Management (EFQM). (2000). The EFQM excellence model. Extracted from: http://www.efqm.org/model_awards/model/excellence_model.htm on 8 February 2004.

Ford, J.D., Ford, L.W. and d'Amelio, A. (2008). Resistance to change: The rest of the story. *Academy of Management Review*, 33(2), 362–77.

Freeman, R.E. and Reed, D.L. (1983). Stockholders and stakeholders: A new perspective on corporate governance. *California Management Review*, 25(3), pp. 88–106.

Goldratt, E.M. (1997). *Critical Chain: A Business Novel*. Great Barrington, MA: North River Press.

Hambrick, D.C. and Fredrickson, J.W. (2005). Are you sure you have a strategy? *Academy of Management Executive*, 19(4), pp. 51–62.

Hamel, G. (2011). "Reinventing Management for the 21st Century." University of Phoenix's Distinguished Guest Video Lecture Series, May 20, 2011. Extracted from: http://www.managementexchange.com/video/

gary-hamel-reinventing-technology-human-accomplishment on 23 June 2013.

Hatch, M.J. and Cunliffe, A.L. (2006). *Organization Theory*, 2nd Edition. Oxford: Oxford University Press.

Heller, F.A., Drenth, P., Koopman, P. and Rus, V. (1988). *Decisions in Organizations: A Three Country Comparative Study*. London: Sage Publications.

ICCPM (2012). Complex Project Manager Competency Standards, Version 4.1. The International Centre for Complex Project Management. Canberra, Australia.

IPMA (2006). ICB – IPMA Competence Baseline, Version 3.0. International Project Management Association. Zurich, Switzerland.

Kaplan, R.S. and Norton, D.P. (2004). *Strategy Maps: Converting Intangible Assets into Tangible Outcomes*. Boston, MA: Harvard Business School Press.

Kleindorfer, P.R., Kunreuther, H.C., and Shoemaker, P.J.H. (1993). *Decision Sciences: An integrating Perspective*. New York: Cambridge University Press.

KPMG (1997). What went wrong? Unsuccessful information technology projects. Extracted from: http://audit.kpmg.ca/vl/surveys/it_wrong.htm on 10 August 2002.

Larman, C. (2004). *Agile and Iterative Development: A Manager's Guide*. Boston, MA: Addison-Wesley.

McGregor, D. (1960). *The Human Side of the Enterprise*. New York: McGraw-Hill.

McNamara, C. (1999). Program planning and management. Extracted from: http://www.mapnp.org/library/prog_mng/prog_mng.htm on 15 June 2005.

Mendelow, A. (1991). Stakeholder mapping. *Proceedings of the 2nd International Conference on Information Systems, Cambridge, MA* (cited in Johnson, G. and Scholes, K. (1998), *Exploring Corporate Strategy*. Harlow: Financial Times/ Prentice Hall).

Mintzberg, H. (1990). The design school: Reconsidering the basic premises of strategic management. *Strategic Management Journal*, 11, pp. 171–95.

Mintzberg, H. and Waters, J.A. (1985). Of strategies, deliberate and emergent. *Strategic Management Journal*, 6(3), pp. 257–72.

Moss-Kanter, R. (2006). Innovation: The classic traps. *Harvard Business Review*, 84(1), pp. 72–83.

Murray-Webster, R. and Thiry, M. (2000). Managing Programmes of Projects, in *Gower Handbook of Project Management*, edited by R. Turner and S. Simister, 3rd edition. Aldershot: Gower, pp. 47–64.

NASA (1998). NPG 7120.5A: Program and Project Management Processes and Requirements. Extracted from: http://nodis3.gsfc.nasa.gov/library/displayDir.cfm?Internal_ID=N_PG_7120_005A_&page_name=main on 3 February 2002.

Nevis, E.C., Di Bella, A.J. and Gould, J.M. (1997). Understanding organizations as learning systems. The Society for Organizational Learning Website [Online repository]. Extracted from: http://www.solonline.org on 17 May 2004.

OGC (2005). *PRINCE2*. Norwich: Office of Government Commerce.

OGC (2007). *Managing Successful Programmes*, 3rd Edition. Norwich: Office of Government Commerce.

OGC (2011). *Managing Successful Programmes*, 4th Edition. Norwich, UK: Office of Government Commerce.

Olson, E.E. and Eoyang, G.H. (2001). *Facilitating Organization Change: Lessons from Complexity Science*. San Francisco, CA: Josey-Bass/Pfeiffer.

Organisation for Economic Co-operation and Development (2004). *OECD Principles of Corporate Governance*. Paris: OECD Publications.

Partington, D. (2000). Implementing strategy through programmes of projects, in *Gower Handbook of Project Management*, edited by J. Turner and S. Simister, 3rd Edition. Aldershot: Gower.

Pellegrinelli, S. (1997). Programme management: Organising project-based change. *International Journal of Project Management*, 15(3), pp. 141–9.

Pellegrinelli, S., and Bowman, C. (1994). Implementing strategy through projects. *Long Range Planning*, 27(4), pp. 125–32.

Project Management Professionals Certification Center (PMCC) (2004). *P2M: A Guidebook of Project and Program Management for Enterprise Innovation*. Tokyo: PMCC.

PMAJ (Project Management Association of Japan) (2010). *Project and Program Management: Guidebook*. Volume 1 (English translation). P2M, 2nd Edition. Tokyo: Project and Program Management for Enterprise Innovation.

PMAJ (2015). *A Guidebook of Program and Project Management for Enterprise Innovation* (Review version of English translation). P2M, 3rd Edition. Tokyo: Project Management Association of Japan.

PMI (1996). *A Guide to the Project Management Body of Knowledge*. Sylva, NC: Project Management Institute Standards Committee-PMI Communications.

PMI (2000). *A Guide to the Project Management Body of Knowledge*. Sylva, NC: PMI Publishing Division.

PMI (2004). *A Guide to the Project Management Body of Knowledge* (PMBOK® Guide), 3rd Edition. Newtown Square, PA: Project Management Institute.

PMI (2006). *The Standard for Program Management*. Newtown Square, PA: Project Management Institute.

PMI (2008). *The Standard for Program Management*, 2nd Edition. Newtown Square, PA: Project Management Institute.

PMI (2013a). *A Guide to the Project Management Body of Knowledge* (PMBOK® Guide), 5th Edition. Newtown Square, PA: Project Management Institute.

PMI (2013b). *The Standard for Program Management*, 3rd Edition. Newtown Square, PA: Project Management Institute.

PMI (2013c). *Managing Change in Organizations: A Practice Guide*. Newtown Square, PA: Project Management Institute.

PMI (2014). *Pulse of the Profession® In-Depth Report: Executive Sponsor Engagement – Top Driver of Project and Programme Success*. Newtown Square, PA: Project Management Institute.

PMI (2015). Talent Management Resources. http://www.pmi.org/learning/talent-management-resources.aspx.

Porter, M. ([1985] 2004). *Competitive Advantage*. New York: Free Press (Simon & Schuster).

PWC – Price Waterhouse Coopers (2009). PricewaterhouseCoopers 12th Annual Global CEO Survey 2009. Extracted from: http://www.pwc.com/ceosurvey/download.html on 26 June 2010.

Rappaport, A. (1986). *Creating Shareholder Value*. New York: The Free Press.

Rappaport, A. (2006). Ten ways to create shareholder value. *Harvard Business Review*, 84(9), pp. 66–77.

Reiss, G. and Rayner, P. (2002). The programme management maturity model: An update on findings. *Proceedings of the 5th PMI-Europe Conference*. Cannes, France.

Rockart, J.F. (1979). Chief executives define their own data needs. *Harvard Business Review*, 57(2), pp. 81–93.

Schmetterer, B. (2003). *Leap: A Revolution in Creative Business Strategy.* Hoboken, NJ: John Wiley & Sons.

Shimizu, M. (2012) *Fundamentals of Program Management: Strategic Program Bootstrapping for Business Innovation and Change.* Newtown Square, PA: Project Management Institute.

Simon, H.A. (1955). A behavioral model of rational choice. *Quarterly Journal of Economics*, 69, pp. 99–118.

Standish Group International (1996). *A Standish Group Research on Failure of it Projects.* Yarmouth, MA: The Standish Group.

Thiry, M. (2000). A learning loop for successful program management. *Proceedings of the 31st PMI Seminars and Symposium.* Newton Square, PA: The Project Management Institute.

Thiry, M. (2007). Program management: A strategic decision management process, in *The Wiley Guide to Project, Program and Portfolio Management,* edited by P.W.G. Morris and J.K. Pinto. New York: John Wiley and Sons.

Thiry, M. (2008). Managing programmes of projects, in *Gower Handbook of Project Management,* edited by R.J. Turner. Aldershot: Gower.

Thiry, M. (2010). Program and agile management. *Proceedings of the PMI North American Global Congress, Washington, DC.* Newtown Square, PA: Project Management Institute.

Thiry, M. (2013). *A Framework for Value Management Practice,* 2nd Edition. Newtown Square, PA: Project Management Institute.

Thiry, M. and Deguire, M. (2004). Program management as an emergent order phenomenon, in *Innovations: Project Management Research 2004. Proceedings of the 3rd PMI Research Conference,* July 2004, London. Project Management Institute.

Thiry, M and Morris, P.W. (2006). Structuring project-based organisations to create value. *Proceedings of the Third International Conference on Project Management (ProMAC),* September 2006, Sydney, Australia.

TRB (2015). *Guide to Project Management Strategies for Complex Projects*. Washington, DC: Transportation Research Board.

Van de Ven, A.H. and Poole, M.S. (1995) Explaining development and change in organizations. *Academy of Management Review*, 20, pp. 510–40.

Vereecke, A., Pandelaere, E. and Deschoolmeester, D. (2003). A Classification of Programmes and their Managerial Impact. Vlerick Leuven Gent Working Paper Series 2003/07.

Weick, K.E. (1995). *Sensemaking in Organizations*. London: Sage Publications.

Winch G., Usmani, A. and Edkins, A. (1998). Towards total project quality: A gap analysis approach. *Construction Management and Economics*, 16, pp. 193–207.

Index

Note: page numbers in *italics* refer to image and table material.

Fundamentals of Project Management

Series Editor

Professor Darren Dalcher is founder and Director of the National Centre for Project Management, Professor of Project Management, University of Hertfordshire and Visiting Professor of Computer Science, University of Iceland.

This companion series to the Advances in Project Management Series provides short guides to a set of key aspects of project management: Benefits Management; Business Case; Change Management:

Cost Management; Financing; Governance; Leadership; Organization; Programme Management; Progress Management/Earned Value; Planning; Quality Management; Risk Management; Scope; Scheduling; Sponsorship; Stakeholder Management; Value Management.

Each guide, as the series title suggests, aims to provide the fundamentals of the subject from a rigorous perspective and from a (if not the) leading proponent of the subject. Practising professionals and project students will find in the fundamentals a definitive, shorthand guide to each of the main competencies associated with project management; a book that is authoritative, based on current research but immediately relevant and applicable.

...an excellent bridge between PM theory and practical ways to reach organizational goals using program management. This is truly brilliant!
Deniz A. Johnson, PMP, Vice President, Program Management, Acadian Asset Management LLC, Boston

For more detail, see: www.gowerpublishing.com/pmfundamentals

Currently published titles

Project Stakeholder Management
Pernille Eskerod and Anna Lund Jepsen
9781409404378 (paperback)
9781409404385 (e-book – PDF)
9781409484462 (e-book – ePUB)

Managing Risk in Projects
David Hillson
9780566088674 (paperback)
9780566091551 (e-book – PDF)
9781409458531 (e-book – ePUB)

Project Governance
Ralf Müller
9780566088667 (paperback)
9780566091568 (e-book – PDF)
9781409458456 (e-book – ePUB)

Forthcoming titles

Project Portfolio Management
Alfonso Bucero
9781472423184 (paperback)
9781472423191 (e-book – PDF)
9781472423207 (e-book – ePUB)

Agile Project Management
Tristan Boutros and Jennifer Cardella
9781472462800 (paperback)
9781472462817 (e-book – PDF)
9781472462824 (e-book – ePUB)

Managing Knowledge in Project Environments
Judy Payne and Steve Simister
9781472480279 (paperback)
9781472480286 (e-book – PDF)
9781472480293 (e-book – ePUB)

GOWER